american
university
studies

Series XXVI
Theatre Arts

Vol. 31

PETER LANG
New York • Washington, D.C./Baltimore • Bern
Frankfurt am Main • Berlin • Brussels • Vienna • Oxford

ADVANCE PRAISE FOR

Breaking the Bounds

"Dr. Godiwala has the rare gift of combining contemporary feminist and performance theories with an acute grasp of the effect of her chosen plays in performance. Thus she offers the reader an applied theoretical framework that is always tested by the reality of the theatrical experience. Her reading of the plays takes full account of the varying aesthetic intentions of the playwrights and constitutes a significant contribution to the discourses of female writing for the theatre."

Tim Prentki, Professor, King Alfred's College, Winchester, England
Author of Popular Theatre in Political Culture

"As we rush into the twenty-first century head-on, it remains frustrating for scholars of even the recent past to uncover detailed analyses of women's traditions and texts. Dr. Godiwala's book asks us to refocus our attention and to take another look at women's contemporary (or late twentieth century) drama. She focuses primarily on texts read in political and social context, and shines some illuminating spotlights on performance as well...."

Lizbeth Goodman, Director, The SMARTlab Centre, England
Author of Contemporary Feminist Theatres

Breaking the Bou

Dimple Godiwala

Breaking the Bounds

British Feminist Dramatists Writing in the Mainstream since c.1980

PETER LANG
New York • Washington, D.C./Baltimore • Bern
Frankfurt am Main • Berlin • Brussels • Vienna • Oxford

Library of Congress Cataloging-in-Publication Data

Godiwala, Dimple.
Breaking the bounds: British feminist dramatists writing
in the mainstream since c.1980/ Dimple Godiwala.
p. cm. — (American university studies. XXVI, Theatre arts; Vol. 31)
Includes bibliographical references.
1. Feminist drama, English—History and criticism. 2. Feminist and litera-
ture—Great Britain—History—20th century. 3. Women and literature—Great
Britain—History—20th century. 4. English drama—Women authors—History
and criticism. 5. English drama—20th century—History and criticism.
I. Title. II. American university studies.
Series XXVI, Theatre arts; v. 31.
PR739.F45 G63   822'.914099287—dc21   2002016257
ISBN 0-8204-6135-0
ISSN 0899-9880

Die Deutsche Bibliothek-CIP-Einheitsaufnahme

Godiwala, Dimple.
Breaking the bounds: British feminist dramatists writing
in the mainstream since c.1980/ Dimple Godiwala.
-New York; Washington, D.C./Baltimore; Bern;
Frankfurt am Main; Berlin; Brussels; Vienna; Oxford: Lang.
(American university studies: Ser. 26, Theatre arts; Vol. 31)
ISBN 0-8204-6135-0

Excerpts from *Three Plays: Piaf, Camille, Loving Women* by Pam Gems
(Penguin Books, 1985) copyright © Pam Gems, 1979, 1985,
reproduced by permission of Penguin Books Ltd.

The paper in this book meets the guidelines for permanence and durability
of the Committee on Production Guidelines for Book Longevity
of the Council of Library Resources.

© 2003 Peter Lang Publishing, Inc., New York
275 Seventh Avenue, 28th Floor, New York, NY 10001
www.peterlangusa.com

Printed in the United States of America

For Mummy and Daddy;
Falguni, David and Rohan;
Leena, Peter and Taira,

—— ✳ ——

with love

It is not possible for us to describe our own archive. Constituted and formed within it, it delimits us as we speak from within its very rules. It is that which gives to what we can say its modes of appearance, its forms of existence and co-existence, its system of accumulation, historicity, and disappearance.

Who then can hold the mirror up to us? Who can describe us as we are, in the mode of our becoming, even as we transform ourselves? Is it not one who is interstitial—inside enough to understand fully our boundaries and delimitation, at once close to us, and yet different from our present existence, someone on the border of our time and our presence, someone who can indicate yet its otherness and our possibilities, one who is a presence in the gap between our own discursive practices?
                    —Michel Foucault, *The Archaeology of Knowledge*,
                              p.130–1; translation modified.

CONTENTS

—— ⚜ ——

ACKNOWLEDGMENTS

MY THANKS TO Prof. Tim Prentki (King Alfred's College, Winchester), Dr. Vincent Gillespie (St. Anne's College, Oxford) and Nizwar Karanj for their support and encouragement; Prof. Robert J.C. Young (Wadham College, Oxford), Dr. David Rudd (Bolton Institute), Prof. Bill Luckin (Bolton Institute), Dr. Susan Jones (St. Hilda's College, Oxford) and Dr. Alison Forsyth (University of Wales, Aberystywyth), who gave generously of their time to read large parts of the manuscript, for which I am grateful; Pam Gems, Anne Devlin and Caryl Churchill for sending me copies of the often out-of-print texts. I am also immensely grateful to Terry Fairbank-Wilson who helped proof read the final document.

Lastly, thanks also to York St. John College for the use of resources, and to all who helped produce the book at Peter Lang.

For permission to print from plays I thank Faber & Faber (*Ourselves Alone*); Methuen (*Churchill: Plays One & Churchill: Plays Two*); Oberon Books (*Queen Christina*); Penguin (*Three Plays: Piaf, Camille, Loving Women*)

—— ✣ ——

INTRODUCTION

(...) to be a feminist scholar is to practice political resistance to tradition, to dominance, to patriarchy.

—Janelle Reinelt[1]

FEMINISM IS A practice with a theoretico-critical agenda—a force with a ruptural tendency which has made possible power within institutional frameworks such as the theatre. Theatre is a public space, and, in the course of the century's history of feminist intervention, has been (in terms of literary work) the last site of negotiation. Although women severally enter published discourse (the novel, poetry) around the nineteenth-century, the public space of British *dramatic* discourse is the last remaining site of intervention and rupture. The *fin de siècle* suffragette dramatists, although supported by various authority figures such as George Bernard Shaw, had support as women fighting for suffrage and *not as dramatists* of any stature. They did not in fact enter dramatic discourse in that period at all, but rather, make their way in predicated on critical feminist discourse only in the 80s, 'discovered' in archives by feminist herstorians.

'Feminism begins with a keen awareness of exclusion from male cultural, social, sexual, political and intellectual discourse', notes Jill Dolan, as Janelle Reinelt's words usefully provide an extension: 'and ends with a resolve to radically change these circumstances'. The act of feminist scholarship 'is itself a form of action and struggle'.[2]

The five dramatists considered in the critical body of the thesis have been engaged with what might be considered a form of feminist scholarship. Since male discourse is mainstream (thus deserving of the epithet 'malestream'), the struggle—to be interventionist or ruptural—must needs be conducted on this territory. Mainstream of course means majoritarian—which in England means white, male, heterosexual and middle-class; in theatre it often means left-wing rather than conservative. And, of course, mainstream usually means English. It's no use talking of a 'British mainstream'. The mainstream stages have always been in London, although they do extend to large cities such as Manchester in the North, with, of course, the Edinburgh Festival which has, however, been more notable for what happens on its fringe (hence the term). Anything theatrically significant happening anywhere in Britain seems to be a national tour of a play which has opened in one of these three cities.

Post-war it was class which broke the bounds of the mainstream stages, with gender following in around the 80s. It remains for stages of race to take their stand, and it can be seen to be happening around the time of the century's end. However, the most challenging plays of the 50s were Samuel Beckett's *Waiting for Godot* (Arts Theatre, 1955) and Harold Pinter's *The Birthday Party* (The Royal Court, 1958). Both writers are now considered establishment. Possibly the worst play was the one most lauded—John Osborne will not, I think, go down as one of the century's better dramatists for *Look Back in Anger* (1956) nor for the sequel *Déjà Vu* (1992). In the 50s context of talented new writers of class, it is possibly Shelagh Delaney and later, Arnold Wesker and perhaps most importantly, Edward Bond who make their mark.

The tradition of post-war *feminist* drama can be said to begin in 1958 with Joan Littlewood's production of Shelagh Delaney's *A Taste of Honey*. The play dramatizes the milieu of the working classes, with subversive role reversals and, for this early piece, has representations of not just class, but gender, sexuality and race, making it a classic of the British stage. Most importantly, for the women writing for the theatre subsequently, it is written from the viewpoint of women. Although there were a few other women dramatists writing at this time, notably Anne Jellicoe whose *The Sport of my Mad Mother* was also staged in the same year, it was not until 1974 when the Working Women's Charter was drawn up and, contemporaneously the first Women's Theatre Conference took place that British feminist drama can be said to have actively begun. Dramatists voicing feminist agendas who were notable in the 60s were Maureen Duffy and Anne Jellicoe. Others such as Margaretta D'Arcy, Pam Gems, Caryl Churchill, Bryony Lavery and Mary O'Malley wrote steadily through the 70s and into the 80s.[3]

British drama begins to be marked by gender increasingly over the last hundred years. This is mainly a result of women's *public* (as different from earlier individual or private) social, economic, political and intellectual struggles. As Michelene Wandor argues in *Understudies*, not only is dramaturgy a public art as compared with the private acts of novel or poetry writing, in that it involves interaction with often prejudiced and predominantly male artistic personae within the public sphere of the theatre, but also that the cultural roots of women's experience have not traditionally involved public social or political struggles. It is only the twentieth-century that has seen women in the public spaces of culture and society, beginning with the movement for women's suffrage.[4] The twentieth-century saw social, theatrical and intellectual women's groups which were organized and occupied a place in the public sphere. This was in direct contrast to the relative gender isolation of the milieu in which past female dramaturgs had penned their work (such as Aphra Behn in the seventeenth-century). Consciousness-raising in public and collective venues led to a conducive environment for women dramatists. It has been variously noted that women dramatists often find a voice at strategic moments of 'social change which involves morality and sexual ideology', such as the period following the Restoration, suffrage playwriting at the turn of the century, and contemporaneously with the advent of (1960s second wave) feminism.[5] In the first two decades of the twentieth-century, the suffrage movement produced strongly political plays. Feminist theatre in Britain has since been linked to the socialist movement, with a strong socio-political agenda.[6] Feminist theatre resurfaced during the so-called Women's Liberation movement in the post-war second half of the twentieth-century.[7] It was feminist—as distinct from woman—dramatists of second-wave feminism who attempted to break the bounds of masculinist hegemonic theatre writing by actively de-constructing the different and often quickly changing role of women in modern society. Conterminous with women writers, the institution of British theatre, which jealously guarded its doors, slowly allowed the occasional woman director and lighting designer in, but even at the start of the twenty-first-century the representation of women in positions of authority in the theatre is not equal to men. It was in the 70s and 80s, notably with Gems and Churchill, that we see feminist dramatists consciously breaking the bounds in a consistent manner by an onslaught on regulated awareness. This is not—as radical American feminists have it—an agenda of 'overthrowing the patriarchy' as much as it is a means of finding a niche within it by destabilizing it. As Jane Gallop notes, 'patriarchal culture is that within which the self originally constitutes itself; it is always already there in each subject as subject. Thus how can it be overthrown if it has been necessarily internalized in everybody who could possibly act to overthrow it?'[8] The contemporary feminist writers represented in this text all work at pulling down and getting behind what I call 'patriarchal perceptual screens' from which conventional theatre audiences view society and wo/man's place within it. Zimmerman, quoting Julia Penelope Stanley, speaks of heterosexism as '*the* perceptual screen provided by our cultural conditioning'.[9] However, what is effected is a systematic normalization of the individual as well as the group (society) within the bounds of patriarchy which results in the normative order. '*Ni roi, ni loi*' escapes the centuries old discipline of normative rationality. This regulatory mechanism would then function as a screen—what I call a Patriarchal Perceptual Screen—through which all subjects view the world. The Foucauldian injunction is 'not to discover what we are, but to refuse what we are', thus promoting 'new forms of subjectivity through refusal'. Thus *the* perceptual screen is that of a pervasive patriarchy rather than mere heterosexism, the latter being one aspect of regulatory imposition of subjectivity.[10]

Instead of 'toppling' the patriarchal structures of society and culture, the oppressed (women, gays, blacks) can only succeed by destabilizing the structures of society from within the existing framework by creating an onslaught on regulated and normalized consciousness—exercises in Foucauldian refusal—and thereby create changes in the structure from within. If feminist drama is didactic then it is with the aim of creating such awareness amongst mainstream audiences and not just the ghettoized fringe where some such arguments are already accepted. For example, 'coming out' themes have steadily formed the subject of much gay and lesbian theatre on the fringe. To address this and concomitant issues on the mainstream stages, where the average theatregoer occupies what Judith Butler calls 'the heterosexual matrix', and views from behind he/r patriarchal perceptual screen, requires an openness of mind down the hierarchy of those who formulate these stages; but mostly it is in the dramatist's ability subtly to address these issues and subversively overturn the dominant paradigms without upsetting the entire apple-cart that mainstream success lies. These dramatists manage to transform their material—the play itself—by broadening its scope and making it palatable and appealing to the average white middle-class heterosexual theatregoer which enables the play to be 'acceptable'. These feminist dramatists are writing the new or neo-avantgarde in that they are experimental, subversive and innovative in their theatre practices, refusing the traditional male forms and styles. They make possible a space for rethinking convention and illuminate the pervasive patriarchal practices of culture and society. For the writers in this critical study, accepted ways of seeing in terms of spectatorship no longer work. Not all women dramatists transgress accepted or patriarchal constructions; I have included the work of those who, for the most part, refuse conventional forms of representation and create spaces for women's bodies and ideas in the malestream.

'Performance Theory': What is it?

Stanislavski and Strasberg offered a 'performance theory' to the director and the actor: a system of rehearsal useful for performance. These 'systems' were a 'method' useful in 'dir-acting' naturalism and realism and continue to be useful for film's new 'minimalism' though debunked by feminists for the linearity of character development seen as male, and by postmodern critics as disregarding of the contemporary notions of discontinuity and destabilization of the subject. Moreover, underlying natu-realism is liberal humanism, the Eurocentric Enlightenment belief in the universal and neutral subject.[11]

Richard Schechner's inter-textualization of anthropology, ritual, rites of passage and shamanism with theatre though useful, pretends at being the definitive contemporary version of 'performance theory' as implicit in the title.[12]

Structuralist semiotics—'sign-systems and the signifier', is something which Michel Foucault speaks of as the 'correct [...] style of political discourse [for] the [European] intellectual [during the years 1945 and 1965]'.[13] Although presaged by Barthes,[14] semiotics enters theatrical critical discourse in a sustained way only in 1980 with Keir Elam's seminal text *The Semiotics of Theatre and Drama*. This is semiology posing as the definitive theory of performance criticism: more 'performance theory'.[15] Most other readers and anthologies focus on the writings of seminal European practitioners in the area of 'performance' as the focus on theatre gets diffused, etiolated even, as 'drama' gives way to 'theatre' gives way to 'performance theories' on music, dance and, even the 'art' of the strip tease[16] in a moment when every act in daily living is performance which yields itself up to analysis. This last surely is cultural theory or anthropology, but all these burgeoning texts labelled 'performance theory' take us very far away from notions of drama or theatre.

Here, I would like briefly to consider a kind of 'performance theory' useful to the critic of performance: not the broadsheet reviewer of the institutional apparatus of the media, but those of us whose job it is to look at the deep structures of drama—the director, the thinking actor, the critical theorist who contribute to making 'new' acts of performance.

Using the philosophical concept of 'performativity', I extend upon it to establish a 'performance theory of the text' or what I call the *performativity of the dramatic text*. Whilst Stanislavski is useful in conservatoires and in rehearsal, the director or performer as a critical reader uses the the theory of performativity which is *an analysis of speech acts from the page*.

The 'performativity of the dramatic text'

As Eve Kosofsky Sedgwick points out,[17] speech as act is coeval with language itself. It was, however, the publication of J. L. Austin's *How To Do Things With Words* in 1962 that gave us a definition of 'performativity'. Although Austin excludes from his definition of 'performative utterance' any theatrical or poetic utterance,[18] Derrida's subsequent reading argues that it is '*cita-*

tion (on the stage, in a poem, or in a soliloquy), the determined modification of a general citationality—or rather, a general iterability—without which there would not even be a "successful" performative'.[19] Thus, with Derrida, the citationality of theatrical 'speech' becomes an exemplary ('successful') speech 'act'. With Butler, citation becomes performance itself; all gender is citation, imitation, drag.[20] Both theorist-philosophers bring the notion of performativity to bear directly upon theatrical performance, thus linking the concept with performance theory.

It was originally Shakespeare who said that all the world was a stage upon which we are all performers. Thus life itself is a kind of citationality, where—in Austinian extremist terms—'all' speech *is* 'act'. However, the 'act' of writing-for-performance is an expectation that the text will be read-for-performance, *i.e.*, the dramatic text is, in itself, an 'act'. That Haupttexte consists of speech (monologue, soliloquy, dialogue) makes the text-on-the-page a speech *act*, where dramatic text *is* performance itself, an 'act' (indeed, infinite acts) of performativity on the page. Encoded in the speech acts on the page and predicated on and betwixt the lines of the verbal text is a *limitless text* of performativity, limitless because it is the reader (director, actor, set or lighting designer) whose imagination and interpretation of, both, Haupttexte and Nebentexte, will produce a wholly original and new performance of the text-on-the-page, which is always referred to as a *dramatic text*.

Patrice Pavis separates, in theory, the dramatic text and the performance text.[21] The dramatic text, for Pavis, is the verbal script which is heard or read in performance; the performance text is all that is made visible or audible on stage; and the *mise en scène* is the confrontation of all these various signifying systems. Thus, the Pavisian notion of the birthing of a play is not the traditional conception of 'translating' a text into performance; the relationship between text and performance is not one of conversion, translation or reduction, but one of the *confrontation* of two *oppositional* semiotic systems. The systems of page (dramatic text) and stage (performance text) are opposed because of the difference: verbal and non-verbal, symbolic and iconic. The text entire is the *mise en scène*.[22]

I would argue, however, that the dramatic text itself *elicits* the performance text; not because it is translated or indicated by the Nebentexte (which Pavis would have us ignore) but because the speech acts together with the gaps and the silences and the pauses elicit a multiplicity of meanings within the dramatic texts and *are a performativity in themselves*. What I call a *performativity of the text* overlaps with the Pavisian concept of 'metatext'. The 'metatext' is not a text parallel to the dramatic text, but inside it. It is the result of what Pavis calls the *concretization circuit*: a 'circuit' involving signi-fier, social context and signified of the text, where 'text' is 'a discourse of the *mise en scene*'. Although it is in this totality of the confrontation of the dra-matic and performance texts that a critic must make her or his reading, the very reference to *a* performance text calls for the analysis of a particular pro-duction, a particular performance. Given that it is the dramatic text that contains a limitless performativity, reading the 'metatext' of a particular *mise en scène* would then limit one's critical reading. As Terry Eagleton puts it: 'The character of [the director's reading of] a text will determine the nature of the production but conversely *the production will determine the character of a text*'.[23] It is the nature of the production, which is one (and perhaps the first) of a limitless number of infinite possibilities of performativities which would then—in turn—strongly influence the critical reception text. When a semi-nal and successful production (performance) text accrues onto the the criti-cal meaning of a new dramatic text, it influences the proximal performance text. This is by no means a bad thing, but can—in time—prove stultifying, even 'deadly'.[24] Thus, *e.g.*, every Shakespearean text is palimpsestic, as it is a confluence of the multiple dramatic/performance/critical and reception texts of generations of performances. The corpus of dramatic texts considered in this critical text is fairly new, and many texts have been produced just the once, which leaves the field wide open for a multiple reading of dramatic text enabling comment on the *performative possibilities* of each text. Addi-tionally, reading the performativity of the text from the page, allows me to alternate as both, director-as-critical-reader (performance text/non-verbal/iconic possibilities) and as a critical-reader-of-drama (dramatic text/verbal/symbolic possibilities). As the theatrical spaces of the imagination open up, elicited by and yet confronting the speech acts on the page, I am enabled, as a critic, to 'read', say, *Queen Christina* in three different ways. This might point to at least three different *productions* of the play, a kind of multiple critical-reading made well nigh impossible if one was merely critiquing a par-ticular production of a play, in the style of the broadsheet reviewer.

Thirdly, as a theorist reading the deep structures of speech 'acts', this text aims to offer complex readings of performativities off the page, so future productions are enabled to transfer these deep readings onto the stage. Thus, my reading of, for example, *Top Girls* is able to see the possibility of the si-lenced other (the waitress) as black: this critical reading, then, though 'off the page' becomes a performative possibility, and is *a performance theory lo-cated in the dramatic text*.

All critical readings are contextual, in social and historical ways. The other texts and discourses about reality produced by a society determine the

Pavisian 'Social Context'. Each level of the text, whether dramatic or performance or the *mise en scène*, relate not just with each other, but intertextually with the discursive and ideological structures of a period of time; the corpus of texts of a given historical moment. Even within a particular historical moment, the same dramatic text produces an infinite number of readings.

To Pavis' 'Social Context' I would add the subject position of the critic. Constituted within the difference of the discourses of east and west, black and white, self and other, my interstitial position determines my reading of texts such as *Cloud Nine* or *Chiaroscuro*, and oft-times enables me to offer indications—such as a performative possibility of *Top Girls*—which are not 'obvious' to the subjectivity of the white western director/writer/critic. Furthermore, it would be almost impossible for me, as a theorist or critic, to offer alternative performative possibilities if my readings were based on my role as a spectator of a particular performance. To quote Terry Eagleton's brief but perspicacious remark yet again, the production makes or breaks the character of the dramatic text; the production values that accrue onto the dramatic text are always contextual and would thus *take away from* the dramatic text over a period of time. This is a loss of the original context within which the performative has been uttered, thus it would in time make for what Peter Brook would call a 'deadly' *mise-en-scène*. It would be equally unholy if the original productions of a new dramatic text are mis-directed: a good example is Pam Gems' *Piaf* (see reading below) where Elaine Paige's excellent singing overshadowed a perfectly good piece of subversive feminist de-mythologizing.

A critical analysis of a particular performance/production is of crucial importance, of course—especially for the purposes of the documentation of the transience inherent in the very nature of theatre. The transience of the theatrical moment lies in the particular contextual interpretation, yes, but also the reputations and biographies of important actors, directors and other participants of that particular production. The critical document of a particular production is a rich text which will yield up its several social, institutional and ultimately historical texts to us now, but most importantly, to the future as it will function as the archive of a certain moment. This moment may be as brief as a year (Salman Rushdie's *Haroun and the Sea of Stories* was staged at London's National Theatre at the precise moment of the lifting of the *fatwa*; the play is a comment on art, the freedom of expression and censorship); it may be the record of the ideology of centuries as well as the events of a decade (70s sexual liberation; imperialism and *Cloud Nine*, as discussed in the chapter on Caryl Churchill, later in the book). The recording of production texts (Pavis' *mise en scène*) is an important counterpart to the work of the philosopher-critic who may also function as director or advisor to a particular production. The multi-layering of meanings upon an ancient classic may be compared to a canvas which has been painted over several times, with the original artwork underneath. Restoration would require time and patience but above all an educated, cultivated expertise comparable to a philosophical understanding of a particular subject. The production of an ancient text will never be wholly new just as the restored artwork will always display the signs of its restoration, but these are the signs of acculturation of meaning. The stripping of layers carefully like an archaeologist excavating an historical site for signs of a living theatre of a past civilization will be a necessary task for future theatre scholars and therefore it is the duty of theatres to keep detailed records and for the televisual media to document the current transience.

In contrast, the critical readings in this text are based on the performative possibilities of dramatic texts which is *the performance theory of the page*.

Often the plays critiqued are bawdy and funny; 'the [performance] often leads one to believe it is all fun and games, when something essential is taking place, something of extreme seriousness'.[25] If my analysis does not always comment fully on the aspect of entertainment provided by the plays, it is not to ignore what ought to obvious; plays entertain as well as educate, and my job as a critic is to point to the buried structures of the texts, the hard work which underlies the imagination of the dramatist, instead of the surface of things. That these plays have been successfully performed on the stages speaks for their saleability, perhaps. That the deeper structures need analysis is what is addressed by this thesis.

The Thesis

The general thesis is a critique of western patriarchy, and considers feminism as a rupture in an unbroken episteme substrated by the patriarchal impulse. Proceeding from this general Foucauldian thesis, I analyse it with regard to British dramatic discourse in some specificity. The theoretical framework is a genealogy of patriarchy, deploying and developing Foucault's ideas on discourse especially in *The Archaeology of Knowledge* amongst other texts. Having defined and explicated western patriarchies and how they work, the argument, laid out fully in Section I, moves to the celebrated mainstream feminist text of *Top Girls*. A detailed analysis of the text is used to support the argument that western patriarchy consists of one unbroken episteme as *the patriarchal impulse* substrates the epistemic breaks indicated by Foucault.

— ❧ —

The theoretical text goes on to speak of the twentieth-century feminist rupture to patriarchy, the moment of rupture defined as an historical moment.
Pausing to analyse the dramatic feminist *adieu* to the twentieth-century, the
brilliantly wrought *Blue Heart* which celebrates a century of European and
British dramatic discourse even as it awaits the feminist epistemic break, the
main body of the thesis moves on to examine in detail the texts of five
mainstream feminist dramatists who have successfully effected an intervention in the British *grand récit* of undeniably male dramatic discourse.

The analysis is of dramatic discourse and its constitutive texts. Since the
texts are dramatic, references will be made to performance when relevant,
but there is no primary intention to deal with the theories of performance,
except in so far as the dramatic text may be read as a series of imagined performance readings (see above).

The dramatic texts chosen are from those written in the last twenty
years by feminist (rather than women) dramatists which were produced in
the mainstream and its adjacent and supplementary stages. The focus on the
mainstream is because of the idea that a successful transgression in and a reformulation of discourse can only be achieved when addressing the con-
vertible rather than preaching to those who already accept the alternative
practices. One can transgress patriarchal discourse when one's own discourse
carves out a space within it and affects it rather than locating one's text on
(patriarchally) ignored margins, where one would no doubt be heard by
one's specific and minority audience, but where one is not effecting a transgression *even if one's practice is more radical than anything performed within the
mainstream.*[26]

The dramatists are: Caryl Churchill, Pam Gems, Sarah Daniels, Clare
McIntyre, and Anne Devlin. The thesis analyses how they have broken the
bounds of male discourse in terms of style, form and content.

*Caryl Churchill breaks the bounds of traditional dramatic forms by cre-
ating experimental, non-patriarchal, neo-avantgardist forms (*The Skriker*;
Traps; *Cloud Nine*; *Blue Heart*); by stepping into what was previously male
territory by examining politics and war (*Mad Forest*) and money and power
(*Serious Money*; *Owners*); by consciously working with a feminist group
(*Vinegar Tom* with Monstrous Regiment) and putting feminist concerns with
form and style on the dramaturgical agenda (*Top Girls*).

*Pam Gems re-works and revisions famous icons who have achieved the
status of myth, both fictitious (*Camille*) and real (Marlene Dietrich, Edith
Piaf, Queen Christina of Sweden) in non-linear narratives which appropriate much of cinematic techniques. In the process of rupturing the narrative
by using almost cinematic time shifts, dislocating time, place and event she

de-constructs the legends by making them metaphors for contemporary women in terms of gender identity and the freedom of sexual orientation, but also achieves an interrogation of women's various freedoms won so late and at great cost. Gems intervenes in male representation by *herstoricizing* and making women central characters where previously we have had only men. She gives us women from all classes who attempt to negotiate with the new freedoms (*Dusa, Fish, Stas and Vi; Loving Women;* the women in *Stanley*).

Sarah Daniels, seen as assimilationist from radical margins but in the context of the British mainstream a force radical by its difference, boldly goes where only dramatists such as Bond have dared to go in seriously indicting the evils of contemporary society. Daniels' intervention is a 'coming out' within the spaces and on the stages of the mainstream, bringing the elided issues of incest, gay lives, abuse, pornography, male control over women's bodies to the fore in her drama. She reinvents a traditional genre—melodrama—in order to bring her always serious, undoubtedly hilarious, plays to speak for the radical-lesbian in the mainstream.

Clare McIntyre and *Anne Devlin* explore women's private and intimate space on stage in terms of the social construction of their desire (McIntyre) and how the political controls their personal lives (Devlin) by the use of the female soliloquy which positions women at the centre of plays in which they are gripped within and controlled by the power of societal structures.

These women dramatists use their craft to intervene severally and individually to rupture and reformulate the patriarchal, male tradition of English drama so that by the century's end the mainstream incorporates and reflects the difference of gender which has never made its presence felt quite so strongly and plurally in the malestream.

PART ONE

— ✤ —

WESTERN PATRIARCHY AND THE FEMINIST EPISTEMIC TRANSGRESSION

Maybe the target nowadays is not to discover what we are, but to refuse what we are. We have to imagine and to build up what we could be to get rid of [a] political 'double bind', which is the simultaneous individualization and totalization of modern power structures. The conclusion would be that the political, ethical, social, philosophical problem of our days is not to try and liberate the individual from the state, and from the state's institutions, but to liberate us both from the state and from the type of individualization which is linked to the state. We have to promote new forms of subjectivity through refusal of this kind of individuality which has been imposed upon us for several centuries.

—Michel Foucault, 'The Subject and Power'

CHAPTER ONE

— ✠ —

PATRIARCHY AND THE (WESTERN) PATRIARCHAL IMPULSE

'[W]hom Does Discourse Serve?'
Alessandro Fontana & Pasquale Pasquino to Michel Foucault
in 'Truth and Power'

WESTERN FEMINISTS OFTEN speak of what they call 'Patriarchy'. Although spoken of in monolithic terms, 'the Patriarchy' is not necessarily a huge, impenetrable and/or intractable monolith. To understand its nature, one can, via Michel Foucault, regard it as a complex, interactive web of intermingling or disparate and discrete discursive and post-discursive[1] cultural practices, acts, techniques and methods. Ideals of masculinist (and cultural) superiority achieved immanence in the articulation, documentation and institutional setting up of these methods. Notions of masculinist and racial superiority inhered in the very production, accumulation, circulation and functioning of discourses and were instrumental in establishing, consolidating and implementing these ideas which permeated the social body as non-discursivity is, in turn, characterized and constituted by these very relations.[2] As an example of this let us consider the Freudian and Lacanian schools of psychoanalysis. These can be regarded as statements which contribute to the construction of one (theoretically discrete) discursive field (psychoanalysis) which is generally supportive of notions of a phallocracy; these statements also contribute as events in the formation of, e.g., twentieth-century literary criticism, thus intermingling with critical literary discourse amongst other fields.[3] Thus régimes[4] of thought produce 'truths' which are maintained over time. This 'double-conditioning' allows for certain notions to achieve an immanence within the social field, and through the continual temporal variations in the matrices of transformations such ideals get concretized (reified) and are perceived as 'natural law'.[5] Patriarchy's repressive and regulatory structure becomes immanent as self-reifying masculinist power.

If patriarchy is regarded monolithically as a discourse (a system of formation), Foucault's discourses would then become statements in the formation
of the master discourse of the patriarchy. These statements would be related
within the discursive field of the patriarchy, arising in conditions in and under which it is possible for these particular enunciations (discursive events)
to take place. Foucault emphasizes that there is no temporal point of origin,
but rather, the system of formation be regarded as a system of rules. These
rules come into operation, *i.e.*, underlie, every instance of transformation,
enumeration and at every new development or modification of a strategy to
ensure that even with every change in and to the discourse, and in spite of
intersection with and influence of other discourses and practices, it is still
ever this same discourse with a regularity which is maintained over time. 'It
is not an atemporal form, but a schema of correspondence between several
temporal series.' Thus does patriarchy maintain and sustain itself as its rules
are always and forever transcribed within it and come into operation at
every temporal point of its existence.[6] These 'rules' are not necessarily written or articulated, but exist as a *condition* at the prediscursive level: a condition which aids in the formation of the particular system of thought. It is a
'silent murmuring, the inexhaustible speech that animates from within the
voice that one hears [...] the tiny, invisible text' which enables the appearance of one statement rather than another.[7] This prediscursive condition,
this silent invisible text is what I call '*the (western) patriarchal impulse*', an
impulse which unifies and sustains statements within disparate discourses
(statements of the master discourse), forming the seemingly atemporal con-
tinuities and unities which support the truth régimes *of male as well as cultural* superiority, domination and control, and through which social
cohesion is achieved. Thus the statements are legitimated by the unifying
and regularizing nature of the patriarchal impulse which is not necessarily
male, but differentiated, doubly-conditioned and located in subject positions
and discourses. The *patriarchal impulse* and the concomitant *colonial impulse*
are enmeshed in social structures—these are interlaced through a whole
range of institutions, economic requirements and political issues of social
regulation.[8] The patriarchal impulse is imbricated in the very fabric of what
we call society.

Fredric Jameson speaks of a 'master code'—an ideology which underlies
what Jameson identifies as literature.[9] The patriarchal impulse would also be
a master code which functions as a 'strategy of containment' which is but
another way of articulating what Foucault describes as a system of delimiting
rules which have a schema of correspondence through time (see above).

Foucault describes power as neither an institution nor a structure but 'the name that one attributes to a complex strategical situation in a given society.'[10] It is those techniques and procedures which are *necessary* and *important* to the social body. If a technique is politically useful, if it lends itself to economic profit it becomes colonized and maintained by global mechanisms and the entire state system (hence, the third in the triad of impulses: the capitalist impulse). The patriarchal impulse, then, is *also* the name of that 'multiplicity of force relations' which has been immanent in the sphere of western discourse(s) through the centuries; it is that process which has strengthened and supported the regimes of patriarchal domination and control as constituted within discourses; it is that strategy whose general design or institutional crystallization is embodied in the state apparatus, in the formulation of the law, in the various social hegemonies; it is that strategy which has enabled its own maintenance by being useful and of economic importance and profit.[11]

This *patriarchal impulse* has been the moving substratum of force relations inherent within western discourse(s). These knowledges produce and are produced by social practices, forms of subjectivity, and power relations which constitute the unconscious and conscious and emotional life of the subjects of, and those subjected by, these discourses. Thus, over centuries of western history, minds and bodies have been infiltrated by this shifting substratum of patriarchal power—the patriarchal impulse—as it has been 'permanent, repetitious, inert and self-reproducing'.[12] It is within *the general system of formation* of what one terms the patriarchy, that the discourses which constitute it are formed and transformed.[13] Like 'war' and 'politics' which Foucault explains as two discrete yet overlapping strategies for the deployment of force relations which are 'unbalanced, heterogeneous, unstable, and tense'[14], the patriarchal impulse has been pervasive as a strategy throughout the western social, political, economic and intellectual body.[15]

Sustained within dominant western discourses through centuries, the patriarchal impulse is continually reinforced, reinvented and thereby reified as a timeless truth statement. Cf. Althusser's Ideological State Apparatuses[16] which would be *the apparatuses of containment of* the web of discourses. These ISAs maintain and sustain the discourse of patriarchy regardless of the class holding State Power. In the Althusserian sense then, the patriarchal impulse could be referred to, albeit monolithically, as the ideology of gender. It is through Foucault that this notion can be apprehended most fully. His hypothesis on the nature of power dismantles the monolithic nature of Althusser's theories as Foucault is lateral in his strategy of studying the techniques and tactics of domination, forms of subjection and subjugation, the inflections and utilisations of localised systems, and his readings of strategic apparatuses is complex and differentiated. Cf. also, Deleuze: like Reich (*The Mass Psychology of Fascism*) who established that fascism was a collective fantasy of the masses, and via Ronald D. Laing, who analysed psychological disorder as a cultural system where the individual (schizophrenic) took on the dysfunction of the entire society (capitalism), Deleuze and Guattari's *Anti-Oedipus: Capitalism and Schizophrenia* offers a reading of the functioning of patriarchy.[17] Patriarchy can, via Deleuze, be read as a desiring machine born and maintained by the perverse and collective desire of the socius. To synthesize Deleuze briefly, desiring-production, which is the same (sic) as social-production, is a group fantasy. However, two types of group fantasy are possible because 'two different readings of this identity are possible, depending upon whether the desiring machines are regarded from the point of view of the [...] masses[18] (the Foucauldian network of intermingling discourses; knowledge) or [...] from the point of view of the elementary forces of desire' (Foucault's force field of power; the patriarchal/colonial impulse). Thus, they continue, 'revolutionary desire' can be *'plugged into the existing social field as a source of energy'* (thus effecting the epistemic rupture). This is the point where the horizontality of Foucault's genealogy and the simplistic basis of Deluzean hypothesis is most clear. To describe change and transformation as effected by a *sudden* surge of electrical-like energy into the machine of the social body is surely facile. The nature of what constitutes individuals and subjects is surely too complex to be likened to a machine which couples in linear fashion with sources of energy and, in itself, sounds inert and lifeless.[19] By contrast, Foucault explains rapid transformations in discourse as a sign of *modification in the rules of formation* of statements. It is not, he continues, a change in content, nor a change in theoretical form, but a question of what *governs* statements and the way they *govern* each other so as to constitute a set of propositions which are scientifically acceptable, verifiable or indeed, falsifiable by scientific procedures. The internal *régime* of power which circulates within discourses at certain moments undergoes a global modification.[20]

Shifts and Transformations

In contrast to the totalizing and homogenizing theories of Althusser and Deleuze, Michel Foucault's genealogy is trans-discursive and truly horizontal in its applications. The laterality and subtlety of Foucauldian analysis is apparent as he explicates shifts in discourse, lending himself easily to feminist interpretation.

The network of discursive fields (substrated by the patriarchal impulse) has always contained points of resistance, but, prior to the movement seeking the enfranchisement of women, these have been isolated: 'the points, knots, or focuses of resistance are spread over time and space at varying densities, at times mobilizing groups or individuals in a definitive way (…)'[21] It is in the twentieth-century that the 'great radical rupture' within the patriarchal system of formation gathers momentum. As an analogy to this greater rupture, this splicing within patriarchal systems, I offer the example of Kristevan psychoanalytic methods which are a resistance to the phallocentricity of the Freudian and Lacanian schools whilst conterminous with the discourse of psychoanalysis which can be named a patriarchal discourse.[22] The rules for resistance or refusal are inscribed within discourse itself, and come from within it. Thus, the Kristevan resistance is *to the patriarchal impulse within the discourse* and not to the discourse of psychoanalysis itself, within which her work is constituted.[23] Feminists who speak of 'overthrowing the patriarchy' are speaking of overthrowing the very system of formation that they, as subjects, are constituted in. Instead, feminist strategies, whether radical or materialist or any other, can only *resist the patriarchal impulse within* the social, economic, political and intellectual bodies and discourses they are part of, and not Patriarchy itself.[24]

At various historical moments there have been resistances to this pre-discursive condition, the silent invisible text which underlies all the workings of the system/s of formation. These shifts have not, until the nineteenth-century, shifted the underlying notions of male and cultural superiority and domination to female and/or racial others. These notions neither receded nor diminished with what may be seen as distinct historical shifts. The break in the notions of equality produced by The French Revolution and The American Declaration of Independence—*liberté, egalité* and *fraternité* for all—were conterminous with the statements which led to the formulation of the ideas of Nation, Nationalism and Other-Worlding.[25] Although the popular slogans called for an end to aristocratic systems, the nation-state was viewed as ideal and ethnic homogeneity and racial purity was advocated by thinkers such as Immanuel Kant[26], Louis Agassiz and Arthur Gobineau.[27] Thus, the underlying condition inscribed within the system of formation of western discourses kept the rules of gender *as well as cultural superiority* a constant through the significant variations, even breaks, within the western social, political, economic and intellectual body. Thus the patriarchal impulse (conjoined with the colonial as well as the capitalist impulse/imperative) remained as a constant, and, within the web of discursive fields is multifariously reinforced and continually reinvented thereby maintaining its ability to present itself as a timeless and natural category.[28] The primary agency of the reinforcement of the patriarchal impulse is Language.[29]

Thus unmasked, patriarchy is revealed as an invention which continually reinvents itself as it is concretized and solidified over centuries of reinforcement and reification.

Top Girls as a Document of a Foucauldian Episteme (c. Ninth-Century C.E. to 1980) Characterized by *The Patriarchal Impulse*

In this section I use my reading of Caryl Churchill's *Top Girls* to continue exploring Foucauldian thought and to help explicate my thesis 'statement' further. The playtext is used as an example of a document which supports my reading of the patriarchal episteme as uninterrupted through feminist eyes. In contrast to the content of the feminist debates of the text, the *writing* of *Top Girls* was the single most conscious intervention that British feminist dramaturgy was to make on the patriarchal mode of dramatic discourse: Churchill's whole concept of what drama was like, what drama was about, was formed by the lineage she was then part of—the patriarchal male-ordered discourse of the mainstream stages. It was during the writing of her first all-female play which continues to transgress linearity in form and narrative structure, merges the phantasmatic with sur-realism and detailed naturalism that Churchill made the conscious link between the way she used to write (having internalized male rules about drama) and the way she now, as a woman, *ought* to write.[30]

Thus the opening act, the now famous 'Dinner Scene', juxtaposes a kaleidoscope of women. Each is divided from the next by race, nationality, class, education and historical moment. However, each is linked to each by virtue of being an occupant of the same episteme: the unbroken episteme of patriarchy which dictates their oppression.

With its all-female cast *Top Girls* is about women and the choices allowed and denied them from the present of the 1980s to a past which stretches as far back as the ninth-century. The first scene with Churchill's original and well-honed skill of overlapping dialogue (see section on Churchill, below) is surreal and fantasy-like in the presentation of seven women—historical and contemporary, fictitious and allegorical—who embody specific time periods, societies and cultures, allowing Churchill to map differing identities within the gender. Dining together at a restaurant we find Pope Joan, thought to have been Pope in the ninth-century; Lady Nijo from thirteenth-century Japan where she was concubine to the Emperor before she became a Buddhist nun; the patient wife Griselde whose story has been told in turn by Petrarch, Boccaccio and Chaucer; Dulle Griet, the subject of a Pieter Brueghel painting of the sixteenth-century, and mentioned in Brecht's notes on the Elder Brueghel;[31] the more contemporary nineteenth-century traveller and writer, Isabella Bird; and 1980s Marlene, a woman who has recently displaced a man to take her place at the top of the capitalist ladder as director of a prominent employment agency. Their evening together projects a surreal kaleidoscope of women from the ninth to the twentieth centuries whose lives are circumscribed by a male world order. They represent the choices they had available to live their varied lives within the bounds of these patriarchal systems of formation. The juxtapositioning of the six women opens up a plethora of feminist concerns and issues. Underlying the intimate social discourse and the emergent cultures and ways of life is a vast realm of male dominance and female repression, and each woman surfaces as a response to and a victim of a patriarchal society, where, as in the case of Pope Joan, the mask falling off could even mean death. Even the twentieth-century Marlene, seemingly having shrugged off male dominance, is revealed in the second act as still living within the oppressive nature of a patriarchal system which denies her the societal framework necessary for a single working woman to care for her child. This leads the tough top girl to opt to live by male norms similar to those espoused by the oppressors of Lady Nijo and Griselde: having abandoned her young daughter to her sister's care in search of career prospects in a city which allows only the goal- and achievement-orientated to succeed, Marlene functions by the values of the patriarchal oppressors of the famous but battered women of yesterday.

And they are all battered: Griselda, the obedient wife who is subjected to years of mental torture and agony, even if she does accept it dutifully and with complete resignation, as her children are apparently put to death by her wealthy saviour-paterfamilias, the Marquis Walter; Pope Joan who, having attained a position traditionally denied to women, in a moment when she is at the height of her glory—in 'splendorem purpureai'—is mercilessly beaten, denounced as a devil and stoned to death as she, unaware of her biological processes, gives birth to her baby in the streets of Rome. Lady Nijo, having fallen out of favour with her Emperor is discarded like a suit of old clothes while her children are taken away by their fathers to be given a legality denied to her. She is also a victim of the ancient Japanese custom which, in a bid to ensure that male heirs be produced, subjects the woman to a severe beating across the loins, while the hapless Dulle Griet sees her baby daughter pierced through with a soldier's sword.

Documented faithfully by three males, Petrarch, Boccaccio and Chaucer, Griselda is the male construct of an idealized gender identity. Repressed utterly and constantly, and, because she is subservient as well as socially situated as far beneath her patriarch as possible, unable to reveal an iota of non-compliance or discontent, Griselda displays a devotion that is constant as it is remarkable by the rules of her society whilst living in total subjugation. She becomes, in effect, a Top Girl by traditional patriarchal norms—the rules of the system of formation within which she is constituted.[32]

Being the Top Girl within the bounds of her patriarchal system comes almost naturally to the young Joan, who, disguised in male clothing, leaves home to live as a lifelong male, devoted to long hours of learning and study which lead the erudite woman down a path of achievement the ambitious would envy: she becomes Pope, still disguised as a man, as the discursive field which constitutes popedom, constitutes it also as a distinctively male-sexed space. Thus it is impossible, through the long *episteme* of this particular patriarchal structure, to occupy the position whilst the person simultaneously occupies the sexed category of woman. Joan loses this position because she lapses in the celibacy imposed upon her, and possessing a woman's body, her lapse has consequences. It is not the only instance of a Pope being unable to honour the chastity vow—Leo VIII is supposed to have died in the act—but Joan is unsure of her female body, as she has long been constituted within the bounds of the knowledge of the discourse of the male gender. Failing to recognize the signs of pregnancy or the onset of labour, she is forced to give birth during a procession in the street, whereby she is branded a devil and stoned to death.[33]

At the dinner, however, Joan is almost a token man, in that her point of view is more detached from the intimate female confessions surrounding her. Linguistically, she occupies a traditionally male discursive space especially at the end of the scene, when, at the point of Nijo recounting what is perceived by Joan as a pathetic triumph over a patriarch, she quotes in Latin from Book II of *De Rerum Natura* (*The Nature of Things*) by Lucretius. The lines echo by way of language and symbolism her stance of being apart and removed from the oppressions and confessions of female victimization which she scarcely identifies with:

> It is pleasant (…) to watch the great struggles of another from the safety of dry land; not because anyone's afflictions are a source of delight, but because it is nice to witness the ills which one has escaped oneself (…) but nothing is sweeter than to sit in a quiet stronghold, fortified by the teaching of wise men, and to be able to look down on others in their aimless wandering in search of a way of life.[34]

Joan is the male in the gathering as she speaks in 'a language pervasively masculinist, a phallocentric language [within which] women constitute the unrepresentable […] a linguistic absence and opacity. Within a language that rests on univocal signification, the female sex constitutes the unconstrainable and undesignatable'.[35] The overlapping speeches of the women thereby break the bounds of the female's position in discourse, even as Joan's Latin is all but drowned out.

Even as s/he 'looks down on the rest', Pope Joan's last word at the close of the act is '*terrorem*', just as Marlene's daughter Angie closes the play on the echo 'frightening'. This is an emotion which is constituted by a particularly female space within the public domain of patriarchies past and present and this links *Top Girls* chronologically backwards with *Vinegar Tom*'s women, and forwards to the contemporary rural women of *Fen*. (See Churchill, below).

Churchill's mimicry of the classic realist well-made play which relied on closure has been commented on. 'That closure lay in disclosure'; whereas Churchill's disclosure [that Marlene is Angie's mother] leads to more questions [in an ending—'frightening'—which leads back to the first act and Pope Joan's cry '*terrorem*'.] It is a disclosure which destabilizes Marlene's position of emancipated woman to that of the victims of patriarchal systems in the dinner scene.[36] This is achieved by untying the traditional linearity of the narrative, and leaving the play as one which poses questions rather than one which offers answers or posits paradigms for change.

To be in a world dominated by men, whether one has lived as a man (Joan) or is in awe of an aunt who possesses the driving force and ambition to displace a man in top management, it is still 'frightening' that the twentieth-century woman seems to have to sacrifice marriage or motherhood or both to keep up with careers as demanding as a new born babe.[37] It seems to be at the cost of an integrated womanhood—one which privileges as well as supports her biological and social role as mother—that the twentieth-century woman is able to get ahead and keep ahead. Thus, to most critics, Marlene's self-advancement seems to be a direct result of her rejection of 'human feelings and moral values'.[38] However, in societies which have only recently opened the doors of economic freedom to women without providing for their very different (basic, biological as well as cultural, social) needs as mothers, the choices open to career women are as limiting as their sisters of yesterday. Like the other women at the table, Marlene's choices for autonomy (in the sense of being a working single mother in society) are limiting and limited. Constituted within the framework of contemporary patriarchy seems no different to the positions occupied by yesterday's Nijo or Griselda, as Marlene can only move between the choices the women from different time periods and cultures have had *or move on over to the other side*—the side of the oppressors, represented in the play by the men in Griselda and Nijo's lives. Thus Marlene's position can be read as not one of personal choice, but as perhaps *the only choice open to her within the system of formation in which she is constituted.* The lineage of this choice can be traced back to the woman from the earliest time period: Pope Joan from the ninth-century—revealing one long episteme of patriarchy.

Within this single and centuries long episteme of patriarchy, women have been exploited in various ways and this is revealed in the dinner scene as each signifies a repression, a frustration, a handicap, that has impeded womankind from progress toward a healthy autonomy or integrity of self. This opportunity to shed the limitations thrust upon women by their patriarchal societies has been a state which the twentieth-century woman hoped for and aspired to. In this respect, Isabella Bird is an achiever of sorts, having written and travelled extensively, attaining a kind of freedom rare in her time period. However, this freedom comes late, only after the death of her husband. Dulle Griet, who leads a horde of women through hell to kill the devils who torment women (signifiers of the masculinist oppressor), displays a very early feminism. Freedom, however, is achieved using masculinist tools: warfare, swords, violence, murder. Interestingly all the women in the group who have achieved anything of *worldly* measure have done so by adopting the male norms of success (Pope Joan, Dulle Griet, Marlene), whilst the others have succeeded as ideal women in their specific time and culture by fulfilling roles which are male gendered constructs (Griselda, Lady Nijo). Even Isabella Bird has fulfilled traditional responsibilities before being able to fulfil her personal interests.

Act Two opens up Marlene's private life and the price she has had to pay for her material success, as well as bringing into focus the Top Girls Employment Agency, the social discourse of which (in the form of conversational exchanges and interviews) reveal the criteria for top women achievers in the patriarchal system of 1980s Britain.

None of the women in the agency is married: while Win is in a semi-precarious relationship with a married man ('the minute it's not a secret I'm out on my ear') and enjoys her situation which she describes as 'a bit of fun', Nell revels in a solitary independence—having been out with two different men over the weekend and kept Sunday to watch 'the telly', she confides, 'Sunday was best, I liked the Ovaltine'. While ostensibly sexually active, marriage is frankly seen (and cited to female clients) as an impediment to their careers, a long term job not being consonant with a time-consuming institution.

Jane Thomas argues that because all the woman characters in *Top Girls* 'deny and conceal their maternal function in order to participate fully in patriarchal society', the play is therefore revealing of 'the single-minded abandonment of the future generation by 'Top Girls' throughout history.' To support this reading Thomas quotes Churchill: 'I meant the thing that is absent to have a presence in the play (…) I thought, what the hell; if people can't see the values, I don't want to spell them out.'[39]

Most feminist critics have assumed, rightly, that what Churchill meant by 'them as different from me' was 'Look! Women are like men and take on male values to get ahead in the world.' By making these assumptions and locating herself as *external to* this ideology, Churchill (and the Anglo-critics) can be deconstructed as constructed by a contemporary patriarchal system which assumes that childcare and child-rearing are activities belonging solely to the mother. What happens to Marlene if the "truth" (read, rules underlying the current systems) change/s? If, *e.g.*, childcare is provided free of charge by the state thereby acknowledging that women possess a biological and social maternal function; and that creating a space for them in non-domestic sites—from education to employment—necessitates that supplementary or adjacent sites be created in order that they might be able to successfully fulfil their biological role?

Thomas and Churchill are right. The 'absent values' of patriarchal systems do speak loudly and clearly. The successful women of the past and present are depicted as almost always single and childless unless they are idealized constructs who are complicit with—have internalized the ideology inscribed within the discourse(s) of—the patriarchy. This is because they are pushed into being so by the economic and political structures of their societies which make no allowances for *the public* as opposed to domestic, and *the single*, as opposed to married woman's child-bearing and -rearing potential, leaving the single-minded achiever no societal framework within which to develop her potential, forcing her thus to choose between alternative and contradictory lifepaths. *This is the trans-historical 'truth' which unites all the women in the play in a single Foucauldian episteme from the ninth-century to the present day* making *Top Girls* a document of an unbroken Foucauldian episteme characterized by the patriarchal impulse.[40]

The subversion of traditional (male) figures of power and the changing roles of women occupying positions of authority are new and singular to the twentieth-century workplace. Mrs. Kidd's attempt to plead her superseded husband's case before his successor, the achievement-orientated Marlene, brings into confrontation two opposing types of women, but both, ironically, living by the same (masculinist and patriarchal) norms. Both are occupants of the same patriarchal system within which each has made a choice: Marlene in an internalization of masculinist rules and the other in compliance to her position as a married woman in a patriarchal society:

Marlene: What has happened?
Mrs. Kidd: You should know if anyone. I'm referring to you being appointed manag-

ing director instead of Howard (…) if you could see him you'd know what I'm talking about. What's it going to do to him working for a woman? I think if it were a man he would get over it as something normal (…)
Marlene: Are you suggesting that I give up the job to him?
Mrs. Kidd: It had crossed my mind if you were unavailable for some reason, he would be the natural second choice I think, don't you? (TG, Act II, Sc.ii)

After centuries of male authority, the twentieth-century seems amenable to women who deservedly work their way to the top of fields newly (and, albeit reservedly) opened to them. Marlene's frank approval of Margaret Thatcher at a time when the latter had just gained power ought, perhaps, to be seen in a slightly different context than Innes' '[explicit] Thatcherite competitive ethos.'[41] It is, rather, a celebration of *representation* at the top—a toast to the fact that women are not only able to be occupants of, but succeed in the realms which have traditionally been the domain of men.[42]

However, Marlene has created an alternative, resistant role for herself within the confines of the rules of her patriarchal system, and she remains, at best, a biological mother. When her abandoned daughter seeks her out at her place of work Marlene is not overly pleased. Her last word on the 'slow' Angie is that 'she's not going to make it'; when told by Win that Angie has expressed a desire to work for the agency Marlene is dismissive: 'packer in Tesco more like'. In terms of the highly competitive atmosphere the young working class country girl ('a bit thick') just doesn't fit into the fast-paced city, and, as Act III serves to point out, Marlene's occasional visits to the country are born more out of guilt than a genuine desire to see the sister and daughter she has left far behind—not merely in terms of distance, but, more importantly for Marlene, material advancement and acquisition. Marlene has slid up the corporate ladder, achieved social mobility and loathes the milieu of her childhood:

> Marlene: I hate the working class (…) it doesn't exist any more, it means lazy and stupid. I don't like the way they talk. I don't like beer guts and football vomit and saucy tits and brothers and sisters (…) (Act III)

While her sister equally despises the class that Marlene now represents:

> Joyce: I spit when I see a Rolls Royce, scratch it with my ring (…) I hate the cows I work for and their dirty dishes with blanquette of fucking veau. (Ibid.)

While Angie is caught between two Mums and two worlds:

Angie: Mum?
Marlene: Angie? What's the matter?
Angie: Mum?
Marlene: No, she's gone to bed. It's Aunty Marlene.
Angie: Frightening. (Ibid.)

Until the structures of patriarchy (especially in the public/professional space) have been re-formed to be inclusive and considerate of women's unique and therefore, different biological needs, women like Marlene will continue to make difficult choices much as women in the past were forced to do. To be in the public sphere in the late twentieth-century is still, for women, a 'frightening' place of 'frightening'ly limited personal choices. As Janet Brown remarks at the end of her essay: 'It is not the individuals, but the system itself that is being indicted'.[43]

Thus we see in *Top Girls*, patriarchal systems dictate the choices that the women have available: each has either accepted the system's construction of her identity position (*e.g.*, Griselde) or resisted subjection to create a space for herself *within the confines of power* as the subjectivity of each is also constructed by her individual resistance to repression. This repression is a function of particular economic, political and social structures (Althusser's Repressive Ideological Structures and Ideological State Apparatuses which contain the web of discourses linked by an underlying patriarchal impulse) in operation at the historical moment that each character occupies. However, these structures, although they shift and/or vary within culture(s) and across time periods, repress the women from Pope Joan (*circa* ninth-century C.E.) to the formation of Marlene's subjectivity in 1980s Britain revealing the presence of the patriarchal impulse through one long, seemingly global (consider Lady Nijo) episteme.

*What about the seventh woman? Like Marlene, the waitress is a 1980s woman. But she is silent and subservient, seen but not heard except for the sound of her shoes which echo in the pauses and between the silences of the women's conversation.[44] It is her subaltern presence which moves the position of all the other women into a site of contradiction. Whilst they (seemingly) constitute and produce the discourse of the play (whilst simultaneously being constitutive subjects of the dramatic discourse itself) the waitress occupies the dislocated position of the Kristevan hysteric as located *outside* (rational) *discourse* (see *Blue Heart*, below). This then reveals them as powerful and privileged, whilst the silenced waitress is comparable to those women of contemporary Britain who are denied occupancy of the discourse of mainstream drama *even within the resistant gendered site which is comprised of events such as Top Girls*: those silenced by their absence in the contemporary discourse of drama produced on the mainstream stages—drama formulated by English playwrights of either gender—the marginalized and minoritized black (perceived as a monolithic category) races who make up the multicultural fabric of Britain today.

The dinner scene points to the fact that white male privilege is a transhistorical truth that runs through discursive regimes—and that the women are celebrating the space they have created and negotiated within this power system. The presence of the waitress, however, points to the fact that the site the top girls occupy is *still a privileged site* within feminism. Thus, locating difference within feminism becomes important to the current feminist epistemological project. The waitress, occupant of a subaltern space constructed by occupation and, possibly, class, parallels the women of Jackie Kay's seminal play written and produced around the same time.[45] Kay's play broke the silence in (feminist) dramatic discourse on the issue of the silenced minorities of race as well as sexual orientation—black lesbian women. *Chiaroscuro* has never been produced on the mainstream stages; however, an engagement with one event which silently helped formulate a marginalized discourse is attempted within this thesis to foreground the fact that although a *gendered* space has reformulated—created a rupture, an epistemic break—in the patriarchal site of mainstream British drama (my thesis), the latter site has yet to yield to representations of race.[46]

In interviews Churchill has remarked that 'playwrights don't give answers, they ask questions. We need to find new questions, which may help us to answer the old ones.'[47]

Churchill's 'answer' is consequently to shape her subject matter differently as in the immediately written *Top Girls*. Conscious of being thus far constructed well within the ideological framework of British dramatic discourse which has long been a male tradition (as she realised with some shock) she is determined to break the bounds of patriarchal dramatic discourse and practice by subtly transforming *style and form* so it differs from any other playwright writing in the 80s. She has already experimented with *content* in her brief liaison with Monstrous Regiment (see below, *Vinegar Tom*) but now, with the all-female *Top Girls* until the master-ly (lack-ing a feminist word within patriarchally constructed language) interventionist forms of *The Skriker* and finally[48] *Blue Heart*, Churchill displays almost an excess of experiment in form and style. This (non) event begins and continues the epistemic transformation in/to patriarchal dramatic discourse, and in a span of a few years a new cluster of concerns with form, style and content is witnessed upon the stages of the mainstream.[49]

Off the Mainstream Stages: The Formation of Black Lesbian Subjectivity in 1980s British Dramatic Discourse. *Chiaroscuro* (1986)

It is important to dig up our grandmother's voices and speak for them. We are speaking for those people who didn't have a voice.
          —Hortensia and Elvira Colorado, Black-American playwrights

The silenced and invisible waitress, the minoritized Other of *Top Girls* negotiates the space between the privileged and the subaltern. In the context of
this analysis these spaces relate to the sites of the formation of English and
Black dramaturgy in British dramatic discourse.

—— ✤ ——

Privileged/Subaltern, History/Silence, 'Normal'/Other—these discrete and
contradictory sites seem always in opposition as white dramatists seldom, if
ever, represent the marginalized communities which contemporaneously
make Britain the multicultural space that it is. Black women's issues, their
identity formation, are seen as a distinct discourse which do not overlap
with 'normal' feminist dramatic space, thrusting the spaces into contradiction as they remain in a state of abeyance in English dramatic discourse.

The text of *Chiaroscuro* itself negotiates with the oppositions and contradictions of Heterosexual/Lesbian, History/Silence, Normal/Other where
heterosexuality is deemed normality within the marginal racialized space.
Typical of lesbian coming-out plays with an intrinsic difference in the ethnicity of the constitutive subjects, the text explores coming-out in the face
of prejudices within the community and also the formation of black identity
within the larger white society. This is done using the resonance of poetry,
songs and music in a text which balances naturalistic dialogue as it flirts
boldly with an experimental form resulting in a portrait of what it feels like
to be black and lesbian within a society which is overwhelmingly inscribed
with prejudice, or as Kay herself put it, 'a racist and homophobic society'.[50]

'[C]ommissioned by the Theatre of Black Women [*Chiaroscuro*] is a delicate but potentially powerful piece written in a mixture of forms [...] in
which cultural histories, friendship, 'coming out' as a lesbian and the difficulties of communication in a largely white-dominated and heterosexual
world are confronted and overcome.'[51]

'I am committed to change, personal and political, and everything I
write comes out of this commitment. Writing *Chiaroscuro* was a challenging
and terrifying experience', says Jackie Kay, the Glaswegian poet who turned
successfully to drama before writing her acclaimed first novel *Trumpet*
(1998). Influenced profoundly, as have been other black poets and dramatists, by Ntozake Shange's internationally performed play, *for colored girls
who have considered suicide/when the rainbow is enuf*, Kay blends theatre with
poetry and transgresses conventional form. Perhaps comparing the result
with Shange's, Kay felt that 'some of the dialogue was so naturalistic that
the poetry jarred with it rather than complemented it.'[52] Shange's text uses
the poetic speech rhythms of Black America which are influenced by jazz

and rap and the blues, whilst Kay attempts to draw on similar traditions which seem surpassed by her own poetic talent which informs the songs. Her imagination is a poetical one, and the experimental format allows for the interplay of naturalistic dialogue with the music and the poetry.

The four actors remain in character/s throughout as the themes of blackness and lesbian-ness are developed with some dexterity. The consciously symbolic[53] use of minimal props against the nearly bare dominantly grey set gives the play a certain depth of imagination against the surface play of the spot-lighting which throws each speaking character into relief. Dressed in all-in-one suits, the actors function as a double-sign enabling them to enact the community whilst remaining in character. The five objects which dominate the stage are the photograph album, the black doll, the mirror, the cushion and the chest. The photograph album is a symbol of black women's personal and political history and the mirror is a symbol of the identity and image-of-difference of black women in a white society. The black doll serves as a representation of the black woman, responses to which reflect the levels of prejudice toward blackness in the larger community. Thus the doll is both (Black) Self and (Black) Other. The cushion, used to signify the newly born child symbolizes the lack experienced by the four women: there is nothing that cushions them in white society. Kay intended the chest to be 'an important symbol; it functions as the past and also as the chest in the human body. In order to breathe, these four women have to get things 'off their chest'. Everything that is important to them is contained in the chest.'[54] In the production the chest also takes on the added function of being symbol of secrets and intimacy as each reveals the negative identity she has formed—thus it is the symbol of revelations as each retrieves the symbol of her fragmented identity from it.

The opening is formal and stylized as the women sit, backs to each other, rotating in turn to tell of their naming against the grey of a dreary landscape. Kay speaks of her obsession with naming: 'What do we call ourselves as lesbians and black women? how did we get our names? How do we assert our names? What are our past names?' Each of the characters tells the story of her name. She is also searching for another name. She is in flux, reassessing her identity, travelling back into memory and forward into possibility.[55]

In an attempt to erase the traces of the double-inscription of colonization and patriarchy on their patronyms, they attempt a matrilineal tracing of origins through autobiographical narration. Necessarily beginning at a time when their ancestors were located in their lands of origin, Aisha, the Indian, traces back to: 'my grandmother was born in the Himalayas at dawn'; while

'My daddy told me he called me Beth because my grandmother's African name was whipped out of her'; and the homeless orphan was named Opal, after 'a stone that was both jewel and rock (...) a rainbow, changing with the light'. And they chant in unison, 'For we have to remember it all'. The opening is the necessary baptism-through-fire: the ritual of naming the nameless ones, a ceremony which bestows upon them a past and a history which is individual and political. This is the start of their politicization which will move them into the necessary space of (re)discovery as they enter a positive threshold of definition and identity. This is of essence as their previous constructions-of-self are markedly negative. The Nigerian Yomi's doll serves as a displacement for Yomi's self-hate. White society constructs a self-hate as the blacks learn to see themselves as 'dirty' aliens, the negative remanences of white identity. Opal's mirror reflects her negative self: 'her face was a shock to itself'; and Beth's photo album reveals the negative history of her blackness. Negotiating through a constructed self-negation, they establish a history of self but display a simultaneous lack of identity because it is formed in a space posted as a negativized site by the cultural condescension of western cultures which support, consciously and unconsciously, the 'truth' regimes of white cultural superiority over races of colour.[56]

Thrust into, and formed within, the discursive space of cultural and patriarchal domination each reveals her displacement. Dark of skin and alien of culture Aisha's Asian parents 'were the invited guests who soon found out they'd be treated like gatecrashers'. Yomi holds up the quilt, symbolic of the multicultural patchwork of society that constitutes modern Britain: 'in what language are these threads?' Like the quilt the play is also a patchwork of scenes where themes interweave to work towards a whole or wholeness of being of the four women to enable the formation of an integrated identity for the doubly ostracized black lesbian women.

The songs take the women back to 'the country of origin' as they long to be accepted in society, to 'be welcomed, not a stranger/for who I am and feel at home'. The longing for 'back home' is a longing for countries they have never known or seen, an attempt to claim a lost Self in longago-lands-of-origin which are fictionalized and idealized as a result of the rejection of their present Self by the predominantly white cultures which posit themselves as culturally superior.

Complicating their variously black lineage which excludes them from the mainstream white society, Beth and Opal become lesbian partners. In their nascent relationship they demonstrate fairly 'typical' romantic behaviour, their feelings typifying those of heterosexual couples in early courtship:

Beth: maybe I should just give her a ring now. (She picks up an imaginary receiver and replaces it.) This is ridiculous! it's too soon. I could always ring her tomorrow. Oh, I just don't know what to do.

and

Opal: I can't believe I'm feeling like this. It's crazy. I've only seen her three times and seen three very good films into the bargain! Not the sort I'd usually go and see but when I'm with her it doesn't seem to matter what we do. [...] Sometimes, you just meet someone like that. (She snaps her fingers) and you feel like you've known them all your life. I feel that way with Beth. Somewhere I believe I was meant to meet her that day in that café before the sun went down and the summer slipped away. (Act I)

Kay establishes that desire is universal, that the feelings of a lesbian couple do not differ in a marked way from heterosexual romantic love.[57]

Whilst Beth and Opal engage in lesbian courtship, the other actors enact the differing attitudes of friends and community. While some put on conscious blinkers (Aisha), others are blind to the existence of lesbians amongst friends or are denunciatory of lesbianism (Yomi).

The theatricality of the play derives from the freezing technique used in *for colored girls*. The effect is cinematic and stylized as is, for example, the scene from Act I where the four women mime playing pool. Naturalistic dialogue gives way to 'freezing' three actors whilst the fourth is in a spotlight, directly addressing the audience in character:

Beth pots the black. They freeze.
Spot on Opal.

Opal: My face was a shock to itself. The brain in my head thought my skin white and my nose straight. It imagined my hair was this curly from twiddling it. Every so often, I saw me: milky coffee skin, dark searching eyes, flat nose. Some voice from that mirror would whisper: *Nobody wants you, no wonder. You think you're white till you look in me. I surprised you didn't I?* I'd stop and will the glass to change me. Where did you get that nose?

Aisha, Yomi and Beth unfreeze.
Beth goes up to Opal. Aisha stands near them.
Yomi sits on the chest, watching.

Beth: Do you still feel alone when you look in there?
Opal: No.
Beth: I don't feel alone anymore, either. When I first met you, you were so familiar, a dream I never expected to come true. Like seeing my own reflection. I used to feel that I was the only black lesbian in the world, you know. Serious. Just me on my tod. (Act I)

The dialogue intertwines negative/positive as mis-shapen black identity greets lesbian comfort: (negative-construction) like meets (positive-feeling) like. The hetero-normativity of the world outside the space the characters occupy impinges upon the play by inference of the heterosexual reader. Bound up in this interpretation is also the threat present within the play: the threat felt by the characters as the society they live in formulates their black and lesbian subject positions within/outside its Anglo-heterosexual systems of normalization.

The effect achieved by combining naturalism of dialogue with an innovatively deployed experimental, semi-Brechtian theatre technique of a multiplicity of char-actor re/presentation/s results in a character analysis of some depth whilst the cultural conditions are conterminously offered up for examination. The economy of the minimal set, the quick scene changes (effected efficiently by the use of spotlighting), the optimal use of four actors are thrown into relief by the skilful use of deeply symbolic props. The quick changes of mood allow the multifarious strands of the play to develop in short spaces of time, whilst Kay's resonant poems and songs add depths of nostalgia, and develop the real need for a past and a history by the lesbians and displaced black peoples.

Emotion is evoked sparingly, and always with the need to establish a vital thread such as the societal rejection felt by the partner: 'she is suddenly dead/I am at her funeral/and no one there knows what we meant/to each other/and all her remaining relatives wonder -/who is the sobbing woman in the dark/coat/at the back with a pew to herself?' Whilst exploring difference, the dramatist posits the tenuousness of lesbian relationships and the vulnerability of human beings (Opal) within hetero-normal feelings of emotion and attachment.

Aisha, the carpenter who builds things, is essential to the build up of the themes of difference (herself different, an Asian brown-ness in African and Caribbean blackness) and the dramatic structure as she serves as both, interlocutor and character.

The scene changes to the people of the community: they are robots, infiltrated by the dominant heterosexual ideology, they adhere to their fixed agendas representing unquestioning hetero-normativity as they are riven with negativity and prejudice. The actors wear blank masks as they mechanize their walk and gestures and become the faceless unthinking masses: 'What do they do what do they do these les-bi-ans? It is easy to imagine what men do—but women, women. The thought turns the national stomach, stomach.'

Lesbian desire is expressed through poetry—as are their hopes and fears:

> Then I see another picture
> we lie close talking tongues
> she is under my skin
> we are each other's dream
> she and her opalescent eyes
> me and my fire flies
> we are dawn and dusk together (I)

The dinner-party vignette focuses on prejudice against lesbians amongst 'friends' and the need for black women to share in a sisterhood so their minorities don't feel isolated:

> Alone in it all—the black solo
> searching for it in the rain
> we were looking for
> that meeting place
> and we needed it bad
> show us we are not the only ones (I)

Act II opens onto Opal's monologue to her self in the mirror—only now the audience serves as a mirror as Opal speaks directly to them. Her inability to come to terms with her black skin and her different facial features take away from her sense of self. While a mirror reflects an unchangingly same reflection, the monologue (ideally delivered with a breaking with the fourth wall) serves as an appeal to society to see her (a black person) differently, an eloquent expression of a need to encounter different attitudes when she next meets the Others whose responses, conscious and unconscious, serve to locate the marginalized subject within negativized sites of construction and meaning.

Opal's reverie is interrupted by Beth, who has come to terms with her blackness through an engagement with black culture/s, but, sadly, only by effecting a rejection of her host culture.

> Sometimes I feel such a sham. When I was eighteen I rushed out and bought the black records that had never sat on my shelves, the blues, funk, jazz and soul I'd been missing. It was a whole new world. James Baldwin. Toni Morrison. C.L.R. James. I was excited. I dumped Dostoevsky, Dire Straits and Simon and Garfunkel. I pretended I'd never sang Joni Mitchell's 'Blue-oo-oo-oo-oo-oo-oo' to myself in the mirror. (Act II)

It is as if subjects constructed in radical difference can never participate equally of culture/s they inhabit, but nevertheless this speech signifies a journey to an acceptance of the rejected self by finding valorized objects/subjects of same-ness (James Baldwin. Toni Morrison). Ironically, the valorization (of these writers) comes from the same dominant cultures which construct the negativity of the black subject, but the character is unaware of this as the re-construction is necessary, and identifying with a valorized same-ness enables self-validation and helps erase the feelings of self-hate.

The black characters have to journey to a place of integrity. A need for acceptance of one's Otherness in terms of a valorized culture and the appreciation of a different racial aesthetic is established, as each is now depicted at different stages of awareness and formation of identity.

Again, the prejudice of the larger normalizing community is enacted, this time to depict attitudes to persons of differing sexual orientation. A patient in a hospital falsely accuses a black lesbian nurse of touching her. As the nurse stands in a position signifying crucifixion her judges 'fire questions like bullets' thereby effecting a metaphoric execution. The vignette signifies the precarious position of the gay and the lesbian in society especially in caring jobs, such as a doctor's or a nurse's. It is easy for them to become society's scapegoats as a result of ignorance, prejudice and outright hatred. Yomi, Aisha and Beth each represent the community as Opal is crucified. They simultaneously remain in character, thereby making the partner's 'bullet' a betrayal of their personal relationship as also of their black sisterhood: As she 'fires' she says, 'Is it because you are too ugly to get a man?' as she simultaneously represents the ignorant masses.

While the blacks have a history the lesbians do not and the songs wonder at (the lack of) black lesbian roots:

> They had no one to name
> me after
> in so many different ways
> so tell me what do you call her
> a woman who loves her another like her
> what do you call her
> where are her people
> who are her ancestors
> tell me what is her name
> tell me what is her name
>
> (…) I want to find the woman
> who in Dahomey 1900
> loved another woman
> tell me what did they call her
> did they know her name
> in Ashanti, do they know it in
> Yoruba, do they know it in patois
> do they know it in Punjabi (…)

The play ends in a remembering of names, the names of their selves with which the play opened, thus giving their journey a sense of present closure, leaving the women with an identity with which to go forward. 'oppression/makes us love one another badly/makes our breathing mangled'.[58] The

women learn to accept and love one another as prejudice is curbed and attitudes relearned, and they sing of the self and their history and hope:

> If we should die in the
> wilderness
> let the child that finds us
> Know our name and story (...)
> let us never forget to remember
> all our heres and theres
> let a hot sun shine on our wishes
> let the rain fall without our tears

With *Chiaroscuro*, Jackie Kay broke the silence on black lesbian issues
and 'there is little doubt that time will prove the play to have been a turning
point in black women's theatre in Britain'.[59]

Since this seminal black play there has been much dramaturgical output
from black and Asian women dramatists; however, their voices remain separate from and on the margins of English feminist dramatic discourse. The
space between these varied and contradictory sites remains in abeyance and
ought to be negotiated.

The purpose of the analysis of this non-mainstream play is to throw into
relief, by drawing attention to the difference, the space the feminist dramatists of this thesis are writing in. Like the women of the dinner-scene of *Top
Girls*, they are formulated within a patriarchy—that of the lineage of a male
dramatic discourse—of which they break the bounds. However, conterminous with these dramatists, who has each attained recognition and success,
are many and diverse voices—of sexual orientation, race, culture, class—in
the margins and on the fringe which are not addressing—nor perhaps have
any wish to address—the typical middle-class audiences of the mainstream
dramatists. Like the waitress, invisible to the 'reader' of *Top Girls*, these
Others are 'invisible' to *the typical reader* of this critical text and almost certainly, to the theatre-audiences of the subjects of this text who are, in difference, a privileged Other. This does not mean however, that these far-from-
ideal receivers of their text (we) ought to ignore the issues of difference
which we live surrounded by and oblivious of.

The Feminist Epistemic Transgression (Transformation in Discourse)

The moment I inject discourse from my universe of discourse into your universe of
discourse, the yoursness of yours is diluted.
                    —Jane to Mr. Quistgaard in Donald Barthelme's *Snow White*

This section again takes up the strand of the thesis 'statement', which has
thus far been detailed as one long unbroken episteme of patriarchal English
drama. Here we analyse the epistemic rupture effected by feminism in the

last hundred or so years.

Although the site of English (mainstream/marginal) feminist drama has developed as discrete from that of Asian and Black feminist dramaturgy, both statements contribute to the formation of the feminist epistemic transgression which ruptures male dramatic discourse. Feminism, or, indeed, feminism/s (which draws attention to feminism as a plural site of differentiated subjectivities), has managed to disrupt, albeit gradually and over a century, the discursive regimes of patriarchy to an extent which enables one to speak of feminism as having effected an epistemological break. The status of women prior to suffrage (the movement lasting from 1860s to 1928 when full suffrage was won) is certainly starkly different from the status of women today, in terms of an inclusion in all areas of public life.[60] The transformation in western male discourse is perhaps best demonstrated by looking at the attitude of two seminal Marxists to gender: the first is Engels in *The Origin of the Family, Private Property, and The State* (1884) whose idealistic speculations on the existence of a prehistoric matriarchate are grounded only by the acknowledgement that the wife is the proletariat to the husband's bourgeoisie.[61] Engels' references to the status of women, however, exist on the margins of his primary discourse (The Marx and Engels Project, if one might call it that) and his comments are as invisible as the suffragists practising good behaviour to win the right to a full participation. In short, nobody took any notice. A century later, Britain's leading Marxist, declaring that the only valuable 'debates' postmodernism has given us are those of race and gender, proceeds to subsume these within the definition of *Marxist* practice, thus valorizing them in the only absolute way he is able to imagine.[62] The difference is that Terry Eagleton's utterance is instantly validated by the plethora of Other texts amongst which his articulation becomes one among many and settles almost immediately as a contribution to the three debates (which have already and often been subsumed in practice if not in articulation: think of an Indian postcolonial Marxist feminist) rather than a formulation of a new one. The point is that discourse—specifically that of the western male—has been ruptured by the dual practice of feminism and postcolonialism, and, in the space of a few years (or gradually over the century if one takes into account the murmurings of the Chartists and suffrage and Engels) is transformed to a very large extent.[63]

As Foucault explains transformations in discourse: Discourse has a 'permeability' and a 'mobility'. The matrix of discourses which make up the episteme 'move to the rhythm of events [at a] level of 'evential' *engagement*'. Thus it becomes possible for there to occur a transformation, a succession which follows its own rules. There are several possible (non-hierarchical) 'levels' in the density of the discourse. At a certain level of engagement, one discursive formation is substituted for another.[64] A shift is effected by transformations which take place at *different levels* in the discursive formation. These are *mutations* which are non-chronological and non-linear. This sort of transformation can be detected by noting a displacement of boundaries (as in the change in history to include *her*story); the new position and new role of the speaking subject in the discourse (woman's space; the Kristevan *hysteric*; the Deleuzean *schizo*); new functions of language with respect to objects (*Man Made Language*); new forms of localization and circulation of the discourse in the society (Gender Studies). An epistemic rupture leads to a reversal in the hierarchical order (Margaret Thatcher becomes Prime Minister in 1979).[65]

'The disappearance of one positivity and the emergence of another implies several types of transformation' and, when read as feminism's rupture to patriarchy we see this is true as the changes in society wrought by the rise in women's consciousness and their inclusion in the public space has affected several changes in the structure of the social body and its practices. Thus different elements of the system of patriarchy are transformed; the characteristic relations of the system undergo change; and the relations between different positivities also change. Old interdiscursive configurations are decomposed and modified as a place emerges for another discursive formation. The new formation is *a modification of the old* and not 'a whole world of absolutely new objects, enunciations, concepts and theoretical choices [...] fully armed and fully organized'. Not all elements of the discourse are altered. It changes gradually, so 'statements are governed by new rules of formation' and 'each transformation may have its own particular index of temporal 'viscosity'. [66]

Like Foucault's example of epistemic rupture, the French Revolution, feminism 'functions as a complex, articulated, describable group of transformations that left a number of positivities intact, fixed for a number of others rules that are still with us, and also established positivities that have recently disappeared or are still disappearing before our eyes.'[67]

It is also possible to understand how feminism succeeded in permeating the centuries old patriarchal system via Deleuze and Guattari's hypothesis.[68] Feminism's collective consciousness-raising can be seen as a collective fantasy, a desire which entered into every nook and cranny of the social body affecting a change in the fixed order of things. Although Deleuzean desire seems to be 'sudden' it is apparent that it took nearly a century of women organizing themselves in a collective way to be incorporated into previously male spaces such as the theatre. The institution of the theatre, an example of Deleuzean anti-production, was for centuries a fixed order of society, which provided a framework for possible social relations, but was itself unaffected by women writing theatre. Suffrage plays, written for and performed to the militant suffragettes, were never regarded as theatre proper and did not enter the discursive matrix which constituted theatre until the 1980s when feminists unearthed heretofore buried texts. Critical dramatic discourse of the period never mentions them. However, the group fantasy of women demanding equal rights which gathered force over a period of time changed social relations allowing the revolutionary essence of women's desire to affect and change the established order in theatre in a non-chronological, non-linear way.

Feminism's second wave has effected a rupture in intellectual discourse as, for the first time in western history, women are "allowed" to enter en masse. Through centuries of repression via the pervasive truth regimes of patriarchy, the formation of feminist discourse is a response, a construction of a new form of subjectivity *enabled by structural changes* in society (the vote, equal education, rights over our bodies, and so on). The transformation is a complex one as the patriarchal impulse is a structural rule embedded deep within the very rules of transformation—and I can offer one example which will make visible the institutional valorization of feminist discourse and its *simultaneous and instant marginalization* as a discourse of the Other—that of the academic discipline called Gender Studies. By constituting women as a separate 'subject' within the academic discipline of the Humanities the other disciplines have the freedom to continue to be male-dominated. Similarly, in literary criticism, feminist theory and post-colonial theory are separate concerns, seeming to exist apart from any other readings of literature. This lets male students off the hook as they don't need to integrate any other subject position in their reading, whilst female students continue to feel like outsiders in texts. Undeniably, however, feminism, or rather the issue of women does become assimilated into mainstream discourses which had hitherto elided the subject of gender.[69] Thus historical, social, psychological and cultural discourses have to acknowledge the presence and participation of woman. Woman now exists within discourse, having effected an epistemological break and transformed man/male/masculine orientated discourse.

Fragmenting the Western Male-Gendered Theatrical *grand récit*: *Blue Heart—Heart's Desire* and *Blue Kettle*

Will the eternal frustration of the hysteric in relation to discourse oblige the latter to reconstruct itself?

—Julia Kristeva, *Polylogue*

Caryl Churchill's *Blue Heart* which is comprised of two short pieces, *Heart's Desire* and *Blue Kettle*, was produced in the closing year of the twentieth-century. The first piece is an original and creative tribute to the (European) century's dominant and transgressive theatre forms and styles beginning with and being circumscribed by the metanarratives of naturalism and realism which were in themselves a reaction to and a radical break with nineteenth-century popular theatre. The great *natur-real-ist* narrative (or dominant western theatrical discourse), severely fragmented during the Modernist revolt, has irrupted continually, pervading all forms of theatrical practice. In the cracks of contemporary theatre one finds the remnants of both, disruptive Modernist practice/s, and the great, often circumscribing, metanarratives of naturalism and realism. Thus tradition and counter-tradition merge in original and heterogeneous ways to produce new forms and styles and new subjectivities which often go under the label of "postmodern" theatre.

The natur-real-ist metanarrative of twentieth-century European theatre is a discourse broken by discontinuities, interventions, pluralities and 'paralogy'.[70] The game rules were altered well before the turn of the century (*e.g.*, Strindberg's *Ghost Sonata* and *A Dream Play*) and the goalposts have been shifting ever since. By Lyotard's definition, 'postmodern' is 'incredulity towards metanarratives'.[71] Theatre in the twentieth-century with the onset of Modernist theatre (arguably around 1914 with Dada, but presaged by Strindberg's "expressionist" plays) is then "postmodern" since it disrupts and questions at least half a century of the Contemporary Natur-real-ist Metanarrative (which begins around the middle of the nineteenth-century with the 'well-made' formulaic plays of Eugène Scribe and Victorien Sardieu). Within the metanarrative of natur-real-alism, the primary meta-discourse of western theatre, the contemporary intervention is Feminism/s, beginning with the anti-masculinist revolt at the turn of the century (the suffrage plays[72]) but, contemporaneously, breaking—around the moment of post-*Top Girls* Churchill—with the past, fragmenting patriarchal theatrical discourse, legitimating difference and plurality and destabilizing the structures of regulatory patriarchal theatrical practices in terms of style, content, and form.

The decline of (patriarchal theatrical) narrative[73] is not here yet, at the moment of writing (1999), but the assault on the legitimized form of natur-real-ism begins with the modernist revolt in the years of the First World War and, contemporaneously, gets differentiated with the subjectivities of feminist theatre practice.

This is what *Heart's Desire* documents: the rapid shifts and irruptions in dominant western theatrical discourse which was legitimated post-war by its documentation and inclusion in canonical academic and literary discipline. The modernist revolt on natur-real-ist style, form and content was thus reified and continues to be legitimized as a valorized aesthetic becoming a metanarrative in its own time, the bounds of both to be transgressed and transformed with the onslaught of gender in the main/male stream.

Blue Kettle, the second playlet, is about language and language games. Lyotard speaks of 'language games' in the phrase borrowed from Wittgenstein, which, in the contemporary postmodern era, no longer require metanarratives to justify utterances made. The 'heterogeneity of elements (…) give rise to institutions in patches—local determinism.' We are no longer credulous: we do not expect 'salvation to rise from these inconsistencies, as did Marx'. This signals a new shift, as contemporary legitimacy resides in heterogeneity, difference, dissension and paralogy.[74] In an elucidation of Saussurean theorizing on the nature of language based on the arbitrary nature of the sign, *Blue Kettle* throws light on language as a system or structure where any individual element is meaningless outside the confines of that particular structure. As Saussure explains in *Course in General Linguistics*: '*in language [langue] there are only differences*. Even more important: a difference generally implies positive terms between which the difference is set up; but in language, there are only differences *without positive terms*.'[75] Thus signification is achieved in the relations of terms to each other within the structure of a particular language system: *blue* and *kettle* assume different meanings with the arbitrary and changing relations they are assigned within the structure of the language of the text. We see that the very terms of the system itself are the product of difference; *blue* and *kettle* are not positive terms prior to the system. Thus the text enables us to view language from the synchronic perspective emphasized by Saussure: where what counts is the situation of the terms (blue kettle) at a given moment. The changing nature of *langue* is demonstrated by reflecting on the importance of parole (which can be simplistically defined as the individual speech act) the importance of which was perhaps elided by Saussure himself. Thus Churchill demonstrates the possibility of change through individual transgressive acts just as Kristevan poetic language disrupts meaning and opens up the way to plural and new meanings, enabling new ways of understanding.[76] *Blue Kettle* charts the journey of change in discourse by promoting new forms of subjectivity. The man, signifier of patriarchal drama(tic discourse), encounters several women whom he adopts as his mother. The latter signify the several and different feminisms which have arisen to challenge tradition(al discourse). Churchill's play is a comment on the contemporary heterogeneity in discourse and the constantly changing nature of the same, where discourse becomes a *productive structure*.[77]

This heterogeneity is reflected in twentieth-century European drama which has encountered a series of irruptions resulting in breaks with tradition in the establishment of a series of counter-traditions (Dada, Surrealism, Expressionism, to name but three). Postmodernism in theatrical discourse begins with the (still patriarchal) break with nineteenth-century naturalism and realism, and continues (this time *breaking* with patriarchal theatrical traditions and significantly *transforming* them) with the feminist epistemic shift.

Blue Heart's two playlets together celebrate twentieth-century (western) theatre practice and also comment on the break with, both the naturalist as well as the male tradition (which may well be seen as overlapping discourses occupying the same field substrated by the patriarchal impulse). The opening is naturalistic as Churchill uses the metanarrative (Natur-real-ism) to circumscribe both pieces:

> Alice and Maisie. Alice setting knives and forks on table, Maisie fidgets about the room. Brian enters putting on a red sweater.
> Brian: She's taking her time.
> Alice: Not really.
> (Opening of *Heart's Desire*)

The natur-real-ism of the opening has been hinted at already in the music which introduces the play: starting with a classical piece which increasingly takes on atonal rhythms to stop and start and stop again, it presages the actions of the characters. When the play opens, they start with detailed naturalistic actions displaying a realism in dialogue, gesture and acting method, and suddenly freeze, stop and start again. The form and content transparently evoke, chameleon-like, a century of western theatre. There are almost direct references in terms of content to the early naturalists: starting with Zola's 'slice of life' (albeit interrupted to start again, differently) it moves almost immediately to a contemporary evocation of Ibsen's most cited play:

> Alice: I'm leaving.
> Brian: Oh ha ha we're all supposed to be frantic and beg you to stay and say very sorry.
> Alice: I wouldn't bother.
> Brian: I'm not going to bother don't worry.
> [...]
> Exit Alice
> Brian: was that the front door? Alice? Alice? (HD, p.7)

The next few sections of dialogue continue naturalistically with variations to freeze, and start again, but soon, naturalism gives way to parody and farce (Wilde, Shaw) evoking laughter in the stunned audience for the first time in this play which began with a coldness, a withdrawal, a breach of contract with the audience in this original (yet, enormously evocative of the modernist playwrights), disregard of the rules of drama and the expectations of the audience. The heavily laden beginning (Zola-esque in its effect and Modernist in its disruptions and breach with the audience) dissolves as the characters start similar actions and dialogue 'at double speed, all movements accurate though fast' (Stage direction, p.11). This fast forward through Zola's notion of 'a fragment of existence' (which was later paraphrased by Jean Jullien as '*tranche de vié*') transforms the stage into what, quite literally, characterized the art of the symbolist where ideas and images rush past in an accelerated spectacle. This visual symbolism gives way to the natur-real-ist metanarrative once again as the actions and dialogue slow down:

> Resume normal speed.
> Maisie: It's all this waiting. (HD, p.13)

to diverge into a formula play which has survived: the detective or crime narrative which ends in disclosure (think of nearly half a century of *The Mousetrap* at London's West End):

> Maisie: We've all got perfectly good alibis.
> Brian: But they don't believe in alibis anymore. It's all forensic, it's all genetic.
> Alice: But there can't be any forensic if none of us did anything, I don't know why you have to act like a guilty person when it's nothing to do with any of us except that the body was found in our garden (...) (HD, p. 13)

After a few more resets which seem like a playwright's false starts at writing a play (which is another level on which this piece works: the choices available to the contemporary playwright in terms of style and form and content, deep and issue based/superficial, playful; and can also be seen as a reflection on the difficulties inherent in the art of writing within an aesthetic which has a weighty lineage and a history) the play moves into a surrealist mode, as, all of a dreamlike-sudden, cutting into the naturalistic 'at home in the kitchen' setting (yes, of course there is a kitchen-sink), hordes of little children rush into the room, emerging from a kitchen cupboard which has opened often enough for the audience to notice its shallowness and emptiness. Giggling, laughing, they playfully float around the room, dozens of little children, appearing out of nowhere, instantly lifting the entire spirit, arresting the sense of dèja-vu which has settled over the series of similar/different starts and restarts. This surprising and innovative digression bestows a lightness which lasts a while, as even after the children have as suddenly left, little hands and feet peep and waggle out of kitchen drawers, to be tucked carefully away as cupboards are gently shut. Almost immediately the audience's bubble of amazed gaiety is burst as two gunmen 'burst in and kill them all' transporting the mood into a black and sombre one. Now—as the characters reset again—the dialogue (and consequently the actions), are fragmented and disjointed:

> Brian: She's taking
> Alice: Not
> Brian: We should have
> Alice: We should not
> Brian: She'll be
>
> Alice: She's a woman
>   (HD, p.17–18)

This slowly settles back into natur-real-ism:

> Brian: You've done it
> Alice: All I'm saying is
> Brian: Be nice
> Alice: Yes I'm just saying be nice to her.
> Brian: When am I not nice to her? am I not a good father is that what you're going to say? do you want to say that? say it.
>
>   (HD, p.19)

This moves into a drawing room drama and resets into a macabre black play which ends with what is stylistically a Skrikerian monologue, but one which is resonant with a (verbal) reversal of Beckett's *Not I*. Whereas in Beckett's piece a mouth dominates the stage, this section of *Heart's Desire* ends in a character being reduced to a mouth:

> Brian: Then snap snap up my legs to the knees the calves the ankles just the feet sticking out of my mouth now gollop gollop I've swallowed my feet, there's only my head and my big mouth wants it, my big mouth turns around and ahh there goes my head into my mouth I've swallowed my head I've swallowed my whole self up I'm all mouth can my mouth swallow my mouth yes yes my mouth's taking a big bite ahh. (HD. p.22)

A reset later and the piece moves into a differentiated fragmentation where only the last words of the dialogue are said (pp.22–26) as it resets to the top again to include notions of contemporary (conservative, assimilationist) gay theatre:

> Maisie: Do you know Susy very well? is she an old friend?
> Young Woman: I live with Susy. Hasn't she told you about me? I thought she wrote to tell you to expect me.

Alice: I'm terribly sorry I don't think (…)
Maisie: Is Susy not coming home?
YW: I thought that was something she didn't want to do but of course I could be
wrong. She said she was coming?

Reset to after 'those situations'. (HD, p.28)

A reset later the pace quickens and the dialogue and actions proceed
through breakneck speed to return to 'normal' (natur-real-ism) once more as
a ten foot tall bird (an ostrich, in the production) enters and the dialogue
sounds like record-scratching in rap music: 'It's not occasion occasion deliberately ruin it forty years stupid nasty'—this piece of the dialogue is familiar
to the audience as it has been repeated in several resets, for example, on
p.31:

It's not that you don't have a sense of occasion. You know exactly what an occasion
is and you've deliberately set out to ruin it. I've thought for forty years you were a
stupid woman, now I know you're simply nasty.

This takes us to the final movement when the daughter does arrive. The
entire piece has moved back and forth awaiting the arrival of the daughter
from the land of exile (Australia), symbolic of the arrival of a fully fledged
feminism in drama after centuries of women being exiled to the fringes of
the public space of theatre. The arrival of the daughter ('You are my heart's
desire') brings with it yet another version of the natur-real-ist metanarrative
as the characters take it from the top:

Brian: She's taking her time.
Alice: Not really.
Brian: We should have met the plane.
Alice: We should not.
Brian: She'll be exhausted.
Alice: She's a woman of thirty-five.
                (HD, p.33)

There is no closure, but a going back to the beginning with a new interpretation, a new reading, a new knowledge, as feminism/s bring continuing
innovations and surprises into the field of drama, where the goal posts keep
being shifted, incorporating the new and re-interpreting the old and the traditional from the new perspective of gender in the mainstream. Thus, the
metanarrative, which has circumscribed the last reset but one, finally fragments yet again, this time acknowledging as well as affirming the presence of
gender on the stage:

Susy: Here I am.
Brian: Here you are.

Alice: Yes here she is.
[...] End.

The form is from Beckett:

> As in the case of Beckett's mouth that speaks and feet that walk: "He sometimes
> halted without saying anything. Either he had finally nothing to say, or while hav-
> ing something to say he finally decided not to say it (...) Other main examples
> suggest themselves to the mind. Immediate continuous communication with imme-
> diate redeparture. Same thing with delayed redeparture. Delayed continuous com-
> munication with immediate redeparture. Same thing with delayed redeparture.
> Immediate discontinuous communication with immediate redeparture. Same thing
> with delayed redeparture. Delayed discontinuous communication with immediate
> redeparture. Same thing with delayed redeparture."[78]

The opening line of *Blue Kettle*, 'I can't speak', points to the initial location of women outside discourse, occupants of the Kristevan *hysteric*, who
had been denied a voice. However, this insurgent 'substance' (as Kristeva
problematically, and by way of slippage posits it) has irrupted into discourse
and effected disruptions causing the latter to formulate itself. This is seen
quite tangibly in the discursive field occupied by British drama which is the
specific focus of my thesis. Feminist interventions have affected the *mainstream* over at least two decades, and not merely had their impact on fringe
nor positioned itself just in alternative theatre spaces. The latter spaces have
been more amenable to feminist interventions on the whole, and, in large
part to other interventions sparked off by the consciousness raising which
feminists kicked off in the early 70s, such as lesbian and, of late, queer thea-
tre/theory. However, this thesis aims to chart the interventions of five feminist dramatists who have been produced largely in mainstream theatre,
dramatists who occupy different 'isms' within feminism, each of whom has
broken the bounds of patriarchal and male theatre practice to transgress and
formulate new forms of subjectivity on the mainstream stages of Britain.
Thus feminism can be seen to be charting a paradigmatic shift by way of intervening in plural ways over a sustained period of time, thereby effecting
changes in male discourse. In the particular case of British drama, we will see
ways in which five contemporary feminist dramatists have been instrumental
in breaking the boundaries of patriarchal drama in terms of form, style and
content.

PART TWO

— ❦ —

BREAKING THE BOUNDS
OF THE BRITISH
MAIN/MALE STREAM

*Five Contemporary Dramatists and Their
Transgressive Re-formations in the Predominantly
Male Territory of British Mainstream Drama*

[W]e are difference [...] our reason is the difference of discourses, our history the
difference of times, our selves the difference of masks. That difference [...] is this
dispersion that we are and make.
—Michel Foucault, *The Archaeology of Knowledge*, p.130–1.

THE FOLLOWING SECTION contains the specific focus of this book: an analysis of the drama created by five British women since around 1980. All the plays were performed on the mainstream stages, and each dramatist has intervened in male discourse in terms of style, form and content. My thesis has so far posited Feminism as a counter-normative, transgressive strategy to patriarchy and its constitutive discourses. However, available within Feminism is a host of different strategies of negotiating with cultural and social marginalization (whether economic, institutional, intellectual or any other) and these methods arise *from the relation of the subject position of each dramatist within feminism* and her approach to the space of male discourse—the centuries old hegemony of the *maleness* of British dramatic tradition.

Each dramatist represented has intervened in male forms of dramatic discourse, her strategy depending on her ideological position as well as the space within dramatic discourse that she regards as having been elided. Pam Gems, for example, might consider that women have not, through dramatic history, been written as the central controlling subject of drama; another, say, Caryl Churchill, might consider the *forms* of dramatic discourse need transgressing. Thus it follows that each of the following sections focus on one particular dramatist and her work, foregrounding the notion of trans-gressive (transformative) practice.

There is another reason for the dedication of a chapter to a dramatist. The death of the author debate is really about the hierarchy of the author in the process of the interpretation of the textual meaning/s. Apart from the fact that the debate smacks of endism, and of a certain lateness[1], these author-dramatists are, in the history of British theatre, a wholly new phe-nomenon. Never, in the history of British drama (apart from the *fin de siècle* suffragette playwrights), have there been so many women writing simultane-ously in the public space of theatre. This is emphatically not a(n historical) moment to suppress their authorial intentions, identities, even biographies as they impinge upon the political nature of their texts.[2] Each dramatist's work is analysed in a separate sub-section of this book. Although I do not make much reference to biographical details due to the limitations of space, there *is* a case for its inclusion. My authors are not dead, they are all very alive, both literally and in the reception of their texts. Their gender/s, their subject positions, their ideologies, determine the new forms and shapes and styles and speech patterns of their texts. These texts are *recognizably* written by women. And these women, through their texts (I make no recourse to biography) have recognizably different voices within the discourse of femi-nism. Therefore each has a chapter in this book.

CHAPTER TWO

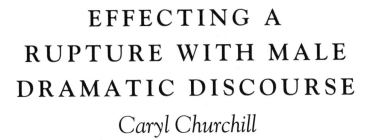

EFFECTING A RUPTURE WITH MALE DRAMATIC DISCOURSE

Caryl Churchill

[In a minor or revolutionary literature] expression must break forms, encourage ruptures and new sproutings. When a form is broken, one must reconstruct the content that will necessarily be part of a rupture in the order of things.[1]

CARYL CHURCHILL'S STAGEPLAYS can be quite clearly divided into plays written on her own and those written with theatre companies such as Joint Stock and Monstrous Regiment (both now defunct).[2] Both specialized in ensemble work and an accompanying collaboration of ideas. Some of her most political work is the result of such teamwork. Her work with Monstrous Regiment, *Vinegar Tom* (1976), betrayed the fact that Churchill is a very malleable playwright: the newly socialist writer suddenly produces a very radical-separatist-feminist piece which is not at all in keeping with her ideology.[3] Now and later, director Max Stafford-Clark is to have a profound effect on Churchill and some of her best later work is produced with and directed by the man who played an important part in the company called Joint Stock and later founded Out of Joint.[4] However, Churchill proved herself as a radio-dramatist before her stage debut, and the work and writing is undoubtedly Churchill, although she, perhaps more than any other dramatist in this critical text, betrays the influence of others in the writing process. She has however, always been a subversive dramatist who ruptures linearity and conventional narrative forms; Selmon points out that the 'clearest assault on narration [what he calls 'narrative intervention'] occurs in her first full-length play, *Having a Wonderful Time* (1958)'.[5] In fact discontinuity in linear narrative typifies Churchill: through the gamut of her plays—*Moving Clocks Go Slow* (1973), *Traps* (1977), *Cloud Nine* (1979), *Top Girls* (1982), *Fen* (1983)—'Churchill reforms through the very mechanisms she attacks'.[6]

Additionally, as Keyssar put it as early as 1983/1984, Churchill has 'permanently altered the shape and direction of theatre through [her] insistent re-
creation of the relationships between social and theatrical roles and gender'.[7]

Feminism and 'The System': The Early Reaction—*Owners*

Owners (1972) contains the germ of many of Churchill's subsequent themes:
the casualness of the conversations as they revolve around murder and suicide is a link to *Icecream*, as it lends the former play a sinister and surreal
quality. Like her early radio pieces it is concerned with the gendered mas-
ter/slave dialectic and 'the corrupting power of ownership—of human beings
[and] property'.[8] The author satirises the existing male-oriented economic
system which forbids female participation, 'because that transforms women
into surrogate men.'[9] She subverts hierarchical and/or oppositional expectations which mainstream audiences would hold about gender and class, by re-
versing and displacing the normative. *Owners* reveals Churchill's personal
rage against the sexual repression of the bourgeois woman who is in a conventional life script.[10] Her next play *Traps* explores this theme further. The
irony comes from the characters' paralysis caused by 'the anarchy of the totally communal and [...] relativistic society they have created'.[11] *Traps* entraps its characters within its own particular theatrical space of alterity
juxtaposed with the severe hierarchies of the 1972 *Owners*.

Marion, predecessor of Top Girl Marlene, embodies a bourgeois radical
feminism in which women simultaneously depend upon men and despise
them. *Owners* helps in the analysis of the writing of the later *Top Girls*: both
plays have a female protagonist who seeks advantages in an economic structure made for men by being a 'surrogate man' with the concomitant polarized 'virtues' of ruthlessness, greed and self-seeking behaviour. Neither play
interrogates social structures; constructed by men to work for men, the public space is not conducive to occupation by the female sex. Churchill puts
herself in a transcendent position *outside* the structures of society—realising
only in the mid-eighties that she, too, was constructed to kow-tow to male
ideology, male norms (see *Top Girls*, above). *Owners* was 'set in the Great
Property Boom of the early Seventies [and] the play is a harsh and comic appraisal of capitalism through the gauze of the 1972 Tory Rent Act'.[12] John
Vidal commented that when *Owners* was first staged in 1972, Marion was 'a
far more threatening figure because she represented a potential in women',
while in the late eighties she seemed 'as normal as the woman next door'.[13]

Elaine Aston claims that it was 'Thatcher's arrival in Downing Street
[which displaced] the feminist focus on women's rights in the 1970s [and
ushered in the] ideal Thatcherite woman—[the] honorary male [who inhab-

ited] a materialistic lifestyle determined by ownership and consumerism.'[14] What is defined by Aston and other Anglo-critics as 'Thatcherite' is belied by this 1972 piece as not particularly linked to Thatcher at all, but *an emerging tendency which is a reaction to centuries old patriarchy* where women reverse the power balance. Aping patriarchy, these 'superwomen' oppress women and other minorities (including weak men) and are perceived as castrating by men, unused as the latter were to women's economic, social and political power.[15] However, it is almost paramount for these 'superwomen', including Thatcher, to be 'reactionary and retrogressive'. It is in *their very ability to repress emerging feminism* that they are promoted and elected to office. The election of Margaret Thatcher in 1979 is well in keeping with the system and its rules: a woman is needed as a token representative *because* it becomes imperative for a *woman* to silence the rising cry of the feminist brigade, to repress feminism by ignoring its newly won triumphs from a position of power, a position occupied by a woman who is nothing but a surrogate man. If there wasn't a Margaret Thatcher it would have been imperative for the country to create one—as indeed Churchill does in the creation of Marion in 1972. Marion is harsher and more cruel than any man would dare. The system (a capitalist patriarchy) is in danger of being ruptured with a transformative force which has gathered power over the course of the last hundred years—feminism is now becoming a force to be reckoned with as patriarchy has to allow it 'in' yet simultaneously wants it to back out. Thus the feminist agenda gets eroded with the arrival of Thatcher (as do the Arts with major cutbacks on funding.) Marion and, later, Thatcher represent patriarchy's retrograde movement.[16] Simultaneously, women do enter the social, economic, intellectual and political sphere but slower than they might have as the power of the patriarchal impulse slows down this hysteric which longs to be a part of discourse. To label this 'Thatcherite' is a misnomer—it is *the patriarchal impulse* which rears its head, unsuppressable and unsuppressed as women everywhere take part in their 'liberation'. Impossibly indicting one woman, Thatcher, political and social analysts ignore the silent substratum which underlies political and social structures, a substratum which is awakened as the rules seem to have run amok with women's 'liberation'. *Owners* is a piece which foreshadows the future, a piece very much on the pulse of a *moment* which lasts well into the 1990s. Thatcher, remarkable as it might seem, is almost a pawn who is made queen by the social and political structures (non-discursivity or, perhaps more fittingly nominalized as post-discursivity) of a particular historical moment.[17] In terms of Deleuzean desire, the moment feminism seems to succeed as a transformative force, it turns back on itself to desire its own repression—hence feminism is best described in 'waves' as it *flows into* patriarchal discourse only to rebound back on itself and ebb, and then redouble and flow and overspill into the ruptured discursive space. Thatcher is then symbolically the fascist impulse of feminism, the Reichian who represents the collective fantasy of the historical moment.[18] To use a line of flight from the later companion volume to *Anti-Oedipus*, feminism's ruptural tendency, once established 'will start up again on one of its old lines, or on new lines. [...] Groups and individuals contain microfascisms just waiting to crystallize'.[19]

In binary essentialist terms, Marion (the fascist) defeats the very basis of womanhood by adopting the violent masculinist role epitomized by Clegg. Marion and the later Marlene are both women who 'lean too far into the other sex' as Cixous puts it in 'The Laugh of the Medusa'. They are constructed within the rigid binary male model of activity, violence and aggression (Marion) and ruthless selfishness (Marlene). The alternative in *Owners* is that of meek passivity and both, active (violent)/passive (weak), are projected as defeatist.

Domestic Colonialism: Empire, Patriarchy, Family;
Race, Gender, Sexuality—*Cloud Nine*

Whilst *Owners* (1972) is about 'the circulation of notions that can be observed between the family, sexuality and fantasy [...] and the categories of labo[u]r, money and market [the traditional realm of political and economic history]',[20] *Cloud Nine* (1979) is about 'Imperialism and the invention of race [categories, which are] fundamental aspects of western, industrial modernity.'[21] Both plays are about 'domestic colonialism'.[22]

Cloud Nine places British Imperialism in the heart of Empire (Victorian Africa) disclosing it as domestic as it is emblematically placed in the heart of the western social nucleus: the nuclear family. The family, 'history's organizing figure', is an order that is 'reinvented within the new orders of the industrial bureaucracy, nationalism and colonialism. [It took] an increasingly imperial shape as the image of the evolutionary family was projected onto the imperial nation and colonial bureaucracies as their natural, legitimizing space.'[23]

Thus we have 'sexual politics' as the basis for *Cloud Nine*, written typically after an initial period of workshops and discussions which formed the groundwork for the writing of Joint Stock plays.[24] The play explores the parallels between the colonization of races, the patriarchal subjugation of gender and the culturally determined gendering and sexuating process. Mapping out the hierarchies of gender, race and sexual orientation, they are, in the first act, placed within the family which is set in the temporal and spatial domain of the British Empire. Significantly, the temporal location is 'nineteenth-century "bourgeois" society [...] a society of blatant and fragmented perversion [one which gave rise to] a whole perverse outbreak and a long pathology of the sexual instinct', in that 'tiny, sexually saturated, familial space'.[25] A society which 'is doubtless still with us'[26] as revealed by the second act located in 'post-colonial' Britain 1979.

'The power and importance of the family was twofold. First, the family offered an indispensable figure for sanctioning social hierarchy within a putative organic unity of interests. Because the subordination of woman to man and child to adult were deemed natural facts, other forms of social hierarchy could be depicted in familial terms to guarantee social *difference* as a category of nature.'[27] Once the social subordination of women and children had been naturalized, social hierarchy could be depicted as natural, aiding in the imperial project of subjugation.

To bring the subordination of women, children and gays to the fore, the play reverses their roles. Juxtaposing black and white, women and men, children and adults, straight and gay, their presence in colonial Africa exacerbates their hierarchical pecking order even as it reflects the relationship of colonizer to colonized and to territory. The wife, Betty, is 'played by a man because she wants to be what men want her to be'[28] whilst Joshua, the black servant, is played by a white man as the latter educates and constructs black man in his own image, fostering western norms and values in the colonized.[29]

Duplicating the colonizer-colonized relationship is the child-adult formulation. The son Edward is played by an adult woman in Act I. This is Churchill's gender extension to Foucault's child sexuality and surveillance methods which it seems constituted by. It also points to gendering as a cultural process—Edward likes to play with dolls, Edward is sexually attracted to males. Edward leans far into the other sex as his adult female impersonator cries:

> She's not Victoria's doll, she's my doll. She doesn't love Victoria and Victoria doesn't love her. Victoria never even plays with her (...) She's mine and she loves me and she won't be happy if you take her away, she'll cry, she'll cry, she'll cry.
> (*Cloud Nine*, I, i)

Edward is also sexually attracted to his paedophilic Uncle Harry. How far Edward's homosexuality is culturally constructed, or indeed elicited by Harry, and how much it is 'natural' to Edward himself is unclear, although an adult Edward—played by a male actor—does appear as a gay male in Act II.[30]

Act I has the female child at the bottom of familial hierarchization: silent and dumb, seen but not heard, a stereotype of what female and child ought to be like when constituted by the complex matrix of patriarchy and colonialism—the child Victoria is represented by a dummy, possessing little or no status in the order of things.[31]

The sexuality of the female other is patriarchally conceptualized in terms of the colonized terrain. While the colonizer's wife is 'a little dove', 'delicate and sensitive' (strongly reminiscent of—but extremely funny because of the gender reversal—the scenes between Ibsen's Nora and Torvald), the woman who gives him 'an erection twenty-four hours a day, except for the ten minutes after (…) intercourse' is 'dark like this continent. Mysterious. Treacherous.' (I.ii) Notions of race and gender are mapped together and articulated in a single metaphor fusing women's sexuality with an uncharted continent which the colonizer seeks to tame and possess. The metaphor of 'the dark continent' is often used by Freud who is drawing upon a rationalist ideology of Enlightenment. Metaphors of darkness often drawn from archaeology or exploration are applied to areas of ignorance such as early childhood, but become more pronounced when Freud turns to female sexuality. The sexual life of adult women is to Freud the ultimate dark continent, conflating sexuality with the classic metaphor for Africa. Late nineteenth-century colonial discourse constitutes Africa as 'dark, moist, unknown' but amenable to penetration, a metaphor which derives from a traditional enlightenment discourse where knowledge is a matter for 'seeing into' where sight and insight are concepts which enable penetration.[32] Penetration is then a light into areas of ignorance which is a dark continent.[33] As the black servant says, 'My master is my light', I, i. Femininity, however, *is* a dark continent—dark, impenetrable, unknowable, it remains obscure.[34] Thus Africa *is* woman *and* slave, and rape, a territorial and sexual impulse.

Wife and mistress (western patriarchy's madonna and vamp) differ conceptually. Mrs. Saunders shows 'amazing spirit' but the wife is expected to be faithful and devoted: she is 'not that sort of woman' and the patriarch excuses her kissing Harry on the hypocritical presumption that 'it was a moment of passion such as *women* are too weak to resist (…) we must resist this *dark* female lust (…) or it will swallow us up.' (I, iii, emphases mine). We must tame this unruly land, or we will lose our civilized selves in this dark horror which will corrupt us against our will.[35] 'The crucial but concealed relation between gender and imperialism'[36] is revealed/explored in *Cloud Nine* as 'primordial, black degeneracy [is thought to be] usually incarnated in women'.[37]

Clive makes clear that his forgiveness is a large hearted gesture—the benevolence of colonizer/patriarch to the subject who owes him obeisance; whilst his subsequent conversation with Harry betrays the role of the male as removed from the weaknesses of the female sex:

Clive: The friendship between us (…) is not something that could be spoiled by the weaker sex. Friendship between men is (…) the noblest form of relationship. (I, iv)

The white female is subordinate to the male 'brotherhood' which seems erroneously inclusive of the black male servant who forms part of the complicity of the colonizers—in the very first scene we have Clive, whilst apparently reprimanding Joshua for having been rude to his wife, Betty, wink at his servant unobserved by the white woman. This is an act of male complicity which negates the admonition to the black slave. Forging a 'brotherhood secure' for 'the Empire to endure' no doubt.

Cloud Nine, in several ways, appears to whitewash the subtle and complex workings of imperial relations between blacks and whites. Cf. Stoler's research into the role of the white woman who holds a great deal of power over the colonized however indirectly. 'White women were not the hapless onlookers of Empire but were ambiguously complicit both as colonizers and colonized, privileged and restricted, acted upon and acting.'[38] 'The […] privileges of race […] put white women in positions of decided—if borrowed—power, not only over colonized women but also over colonized men.'[39] Churchill does break the bounds of gender but at the cost of other issues with which the English stage has a great difficulty in dealing: the issues of race and colonial relations.[40]

The colonial machine dehumanizes oppressor and oppressed simultaneously.[41] 'Feminizing the land is a compensatory gesture, disavowing male loss of [ego] boundary by reinscribing a ritual excess of boundary, accompanied, all too often, by an excess of military violence.'[42] This excess of violence impinges continually into this farce in the form of low comedy as the warring 'tribes' (which symbolize violence conveniently externalized) are held responsible for the disruption and fear.

Maud: I heard drums. We will be killed in our beds.
[…]
Clive: Of course you heard drums. The tribes are constantly at war. (I, i)

Empire seems strategically positioned to tame this violent and unruly presence which is a constant threat, yet trivialized in this farcical and comical reversal which is about white issues. ('you will be shot with poisoned arrows (…) you will be raped by cannibals' chants the colonizer as he tries to seduce his neighbour. I, ii).

'The feminizing of the land represents a ritualistic moment in imperial discourse, as male intruders ward off fears of narcissistic disorder by reinscribing, as natural, an excess of gender hierarchy.'[43] This is best seen in the nucleus of domesticity of *Cloud Nine*'s first act where woman-wife is played by a cross-dressed male, girl-child by doll. The colonial over-spill, or hyperbolic excess, is detected in Clive's speech where he reveals a 'simultaneous dread of catastrophic boundary *loss* (implosion), associated with fears of impotence and infantilization and attended by an *excess* of boundary order and [colonial] fantasies of unlimited power.'[44] As the male impersonating Betty feels diminished by the vastness of the alien horizon and the sunset, the colonial male alter-ego Clive responds, 'It makes me proud. Elsewhere in the empire the sun is rising'. As they watch yet another colonial male, the gay Harry, in the distance, he seems consumed by the enormous continent as it is Betty, once again, who comments on the loss of ego boundary : 'Harry looks so small on the hillside'. (I, i)

In the colonial contest, which is so rigidly 'male', anxieties are displaced into the passive signifier of territory which is then conflated with the passivity required of the female sex. Territory takes on a feminine aspect: it is 'virgin', 'empty', 'waiting to be conquered', a receptacle for the masculinist colonizers' imploding anxieties. The 'feminization of land is both a poetics of ambivalence and a politics of violence' as it is implicated in the notion of woman as 'earth that is waiting to be discovered, entered, named, [ploughed], inseminated and, above all, owned.'[45]

Harry, who is gay, lives outside on the land—he is 'rough' and 'male', a true conqueror of territory. The gay colonizer and the male impersonator playing the colonized wife briefly exchange metaphors as they express sexual complicity:

Betty: When I am near you it's like going out into the jungle [...] it's like going out in the dark.
Harry: And you are safety and light and peace and home. (I, i)

Here, the gay white male is feminized and anxiously displaced onto the territory signified as dangerous (a dark jungle) as the fe/male signifies male penetration ('light'), motherland/England/Empire ('home'), the comfort of the womb ('safety') and the notion of imperial domination peddled in this piece: 'peace'. As a homosexual, then, Harry is *Joshua's* equal: 'Shall we go into a barn and fuck? *It's not an order.*' (I, i. emphasis mine). It is the head of the familial nucleus who is the patriarch of all: 'I am father to the natives here,/And father to my family so dear'. Clive chastens and subdues Harry: homosexuality is 'disgusting', 'the most revolting perversion', a 'sin' that 'can destroy an Empire'—as he has Harry marry the first available white female which turns out to be Ellen, the lesbian governess.

'Lesbianism does not exist in Clive's empire. For [the white family of man] women would never want an existence apart from the sexual and social domination of [the patriarch]'.[46] Betty the patriarchal construct of dutiful wife, actively represses lesbian desire: 'You don't feel what you think you do. It's the loneliness here and the climate is very confusing. Come and have breakfast, Ellen dear, and I'll forget all about it'. (I, iv) Clum cites evidence to demonstrate 'how enlightened English peers of the nineteenth-century refused to acknowledge the existence of lesbian behaviour'.[47]

Meanwhile, the young Edward's sexuality is constituted in the matrix of the overlapping discourses of family and empire. It is interesting that Churchill's savage (Joshua) and Churchill's child (Edward) are both seduced by the colonizer, Harry (who is the equal of the racial savage as demonstrated above). Ann Laura Stoler notes that children's sexuality was similar to the discourse on race—both 'savage as child' and 'child as savage' betray an 'endangered and dangerous sexuality' which is savage and unrestrained and very much the same. 'Both representations were constructs of a civilizing, custodial mission and a theory of degeneracy whose bourgeois prescriptions would turn on the contrast and equation between the two'.[48] Children's sexualities 'was one of the principal discursive sites where bourgeois culture defined and defended its interests [and] in colonial perspective it was also one of the key sites in which racial transgressions were evident and national identities formed'.[49] Stoler contends that Foucault 'underestimated the range of other power relations' which constituted children's sexuality. Apart from the parents were 'the *relations* between those (white) family members and those who served them'. The white parents as well as the black servants and nursemaids were responsible 'for the perversions, subversions and unmanaged sentiments that contaminated bourgeois homes'.[50]

Churchill, whilst acknowledging the sexualization of the Victorian child and the surveillance practised by the family as well as the paedophilic uncle himself in a typical act of 'incorporation of perversions' also recognizes that it is, in appearance, also 'a barrier system'.[51] She extends this Foucauldian thesis to gender, as contrary to children's sexuality which is known to exist, women have been kept 'in the dark' about their own bodies and surveillance keeps them in ignorance.[52]

> Educators and doctors combated children's onanism like an epidemic that needed to be eradicated. What this actually entailed throughout the whole secular campaign that mobilized the adult world around the sex of children, was using these tenuous pleasures as a prop, constituting them as secrets (that is, forcing them into hiding so as to make possible their discovery), tracing them back to their source, tracking them from their origins to their effects, searching out everything that might cause them or simply enable them to exist. Wherever there was the chance they might appear, devices of surveillance were installed; traps were laid for compelling admissions; inexhaustible and corrective discourses were imposed; parents

and teachers were alerted, and left with the suspicion that all children were guilty (...)[53]

Stoler quotes from an unpublished talk by Foucault in the 70s entitled 'Infantile Sexuality' where he sees the emergence of a new meaning attached to masturbation [(...) and] he explicitly ties the prohibition on masturbation to a corresponding 'parental obligation' of 'incestuous intent'.[54] The incest taboo creates and sustains the desire for mother/father whilst simultaneously resulting in the compulsory displacement of that desire into auto-erotic actions.[55] In *The Logic of Sense*, Deleuze maintains that 'auto-eroticism, in its most primitive form, concerns the constitution of a pure body of pleasure, a body without organs[56], in which the co-ordination of zones of pleasure, being both actions and passions, liberates a phantasm as a surface effect that appears to produce itself as its own quasi-cause—one acts for the sake of pleasure, the action being the cause, the reason being the quasi-cause'.[57] Churchill's interventionist piece demonstrates that women have seldom been assigned control over their own bodies[58] as she has the adult female Betty in Act II recount her newly realized autoerotic transgressions to the audience.

In Act II Churchill attempts to reverse the dominant paradigms set up in Act I as she places the characters in a 'post-colonial' Britain. This is a play which attempts to negotiate with the notion of Empire in temporal and spatial terms, but doesn't deal with the fact that a post-colonial culture, especially Britain, would betray traces of immigration, and be, to a certain extent, 'riven, set against itself, in a productive, generative but difficult pattern of competing, intertwined cultures and histories'.[59] Instead, the racial white-washing continues as we get a sexually liberated white Britain which negotiates with and subverts the dominant paradigms of family, sexuality, and gender control as it completely ignores racial issues.

The second act shifts through time as the nuclear family disintegrates. The 'single global narrative' is seen at work in this piece as it valorizes and upholds the now 'liberal' and 'sexually progressive' 'White Family of Man'—an imperial narrative that eschews blacks in 'contemporary' Britain. The conservative patriarchal narrative of a long and discontinuous history is severely fractured by gender empowerment and alternative sexualities and ways of living whilst the simultaneous suppression of the once—and still—colonized blacks is firmly kept off the stage, revealing its presence only in the noting of its disconcerting absence.

The [White Family of Man] offered an invaluable trope for figuring *historical time*. Within the family metaphor, both social hierarchy (synchronic hierarchy) and historical change (diachronic hierarchy) could be portrayed as natural and inevitable, rather than as historically constructed and therefore subject to change. Projecting the family image onto national and imperial progress enabled what was often murderously violent change to be legitimized as the progressive unfolding of natural decree. Imperial intervention could thus be figured as a linear, nonrevolutionary progression that naturally contained hierarchy within unity: paternal fathers ruling benignly over immature children. The trope of the organic family became invaluable in its capacity to give state and imperial intervention the alibi of nature.[60]

It is interesting how the makers of *Cloud Nine* are able to maintain and sustain the colonial/imperial impulse within which the discourse of the western family constructs itself whilst simultaneously rupturing the patriarchal thread which is imbricated and intertwined with it. Whilst ostensibly a play which deals with synchronic and diachronic change in society, it still manages to reveal that there is no significant change at all: it is still the same old system which dehumanizes.

What serves to exacerbate the apartheid practices of the English stage is the complete disappearance of the black man in the second act by the simple 'act' of having a white actor 'play' a black part in the first act. When a black actor appears in a white role, cultural dominance and systems of representation are subverted and destabilized. However, a white actor enacting a black role *doubly reinscribes dominant colonial ideology* which negates the black body in its very absence as a negative signifier. Through the twentieth-century, the theatrical conventions of the English stage disallowed the interventionist presence of a black body for a white character, as it would have proved far more ideologically upsetting than any of the near-farcical revisions and doublings of this Joint Stock piece. The black body 'and its energies and capacities exert an uncontrollable, unpredictable threat to a regular, systematic mode of social organization.'[61] Staging 'the visibility of imperialism's racial other' is necessary 'since Anglo-European theatre has a long history of excluding non-white actors while maintaining *representations* of racial difference [...] through costume, make-up, and/or mask'.[62]

It is the dominant paradigms constructing gendering and sexuality which are subverted in Act II. A hundred years have passed but the characters have aged only twenty-five years. We have linearity ruptured in classic Churchill style, yet only superficially as the imperial/colonial impulse is still imbricated within cultural practices. Women now predominate as the males take a backseat, and the children are by no means silent spectators. The colonized make no appearance.

The act opens with four year old Cathy, the contemporary female child. Precocious and at times even obnoxious, Cathy possesses an unmistakable voice of her own:

Cathy (to her mother): They're coming to tea and we've got to have trifle. Not trifle you make, trifle out of a packet. And you've got to wear a skirt. And tights. (II,
ii)

'Cathy is played by a man, partly as a simple reversal of Edward being
played by a woman, partly because the size and presence of a man on stage
seemed appropriate to the emotional force of young children, and partly, as
with Edward, to show more clearly the issues involved in learning what is
considered correct behaviour for a girl', explains Churchill in her preface to
the play. In Cathy's process of becoming female it is not parental pressure
which strives to make her its image of female/feminine as much as it is peer
pressure and the insidious normalizing function of society; her mother, Lin
(reminiscent of the lesbian, El-len of Act I) seems to be striving towards an
androgyny but Cathy protests: 'I've bought her three new frocks. She won't
wear jeans to school anymore because Tracy and Mandy called her a boy'.
(ibid.) And the contemporary mother's confusion is mirrored in Lin's out-
burst: 'I give Cathy guns, my mother didn't give me guns. I dress her in
jeans, she wants to wear dresses. I don't know. I can't work it out (...)'
(ibid.)

Cathy's toys (mostly guns and rifles), her friends (The Dead Hand
gang), and aggressive behaviour reflect the theory that gendering is a cultural process rather than a biological one, and that aggression and crudity,
far from being innate to the male, are, rather, learned and acquired behaviour patterns. Moreover, the learning process is not confined to the home
environment: the normalizing function of society is to be found at all levels,
and the importance of peer pressure as a normative influence is emphasized.
Having Cathy played by an adult male actor reverses the subversion, and the
scene emerges at a performative level as the parody of stereotypical male behaviour, mocking and funny in dramatization.

As the characters from Act I reverse roles—Betty is played by a woman
and Edward by a man—it points to their development as persons who are in
the process of realizing their identities within their own shifting genders.
The Victorian woman's loss (lack) has been a denial of knowledge of her
body as sex has been about duty rather than desire. In Act II she quite literally 'finds her self' in the masturbatory act:

And one night in my bed in my flat I was so frightened I started touching myself
(...) and no one could stop me and I was there and coming and coming. Afterwards
I thought I'd betrayed Clive. My mother would kill me. But I felt triumphant because I was a separate person from them (...) (Act II, iv)

Betty, in the act of leaving an oppressive husband and finding a job has
found in contemporary British society an opportunity for self-integration

denied to women in the Victorian age. Now, economically, emotionally and sexually independent she is free to be a woman (signified by the sex of the actor who now plays Betty) and experiment with a newly found femaleness as well as a sexuality previously denied her. The last scene has the unresolved Betty (played by a male actor) embrace the now-female Betty in a gesture of self-acceptance.

The late twentieth-century also saw homosexuality come out of the closet and men and women are freer (though still the victims of prejudice, especially around the time of this play's first production) to pursue the leanings of an alternative sexuality. Edward, the gay gardener, is a far cry from the kind of man his father, Clive, represented and wanted his son to be. Now played by a man, Edward is depicted in a phase of search-for-identity. He is spurned by his male lover, Gerry, who plays the male to Edward's female. Gerry's male is stereotypically promiscuous, picking up strange men in train stations and saunas, which makes Edward—who plays patient wife to Gerry's truant husband—very unhappy. Edward turns to women, and in a strong bid for identification he enters into a 'sisterhood' with his sister Victoria and her lesbian lover, Lin, defining himself finally as a 'lesbian'.

The contemporary heterosexual male as represented by Martin, Victoria's husband, is also cast in a very different mould from his colonial predecessors, although the traces of some attitudes linger. He is quick to allow or offer his wife freedom and independence if she needs it within their relationship. The questions under consideration are an offer of a job in Manchester (which would take Victoria away from London where they live) and her recent experiment with bisexuality. While Martin is encouraging, he is obviously unable to offer Victoria any sexual pleasure:

> I am not like whatever percentage of American men have become impotent as a direct result of women's liberation, which I'm totally in favour of, more I sometimes think than you are yourself. Nor am I one of your villains who sticks it in, bangs away and falls asleep. My one aim is to give you pleasure. My one aim is to give you rolling orgasms like I do other women. So why the hell don't you have them? (II, ii)

And he is quick to put the blame on female passivity and a fear of male supremacy: 'My analysis for what it's worth is that despite all my efforts you still feel dominated by me'.

It is interesting that the usually vocal Victoria is silent and by implication passive during her husband's speeches whereas with Lin and Edward she takes on a more active role, especially in scene iii when they summon up ancient goddesses and culminate in a sexual orgy.

Whilst women and men strive to resolve their identities in contemporary Britain, Churchill drops a vital thread from Act I: she fails to take up the issue of the colonized black races as embodied in Joshua, as no representative of an oppressed race makes an appearance. The implication seems to be that previously colonized races which had formed part of the empire have no status in contemporary Britain, and one likens the non-appearance of Joshua to the stage presence (absence?) of the female child in Act I—represented by a dummy she occupies the lowest rung in a stereotypical hierarchy.

The implication of Act II is therefore one that allows for white men and women and children to steadily break the bounds of established traditions and norms, to transgress the confines of patriarchal restrictions on gender and sexuality, gaining a sense of self and finding identities within and without societal norms (as the communal living at the end of the play suggests) but there is no corresponding oppressed racial voice, Joshua having been abandoned, forgotten, and sunk into a relative oblivion. It may be 'upside down when you reach Cloud Nine' as the song in the play suggests, but the black man is too conspicuously absent in this colonial piece.

Elin Diamond, (an American critic who seems here newly introduced to socialism via Brecht's 'Short Organum for the Theatre'), comments that Churchill 'connect[s] patriarchy to material and sexual oppression [as she] historicize[s], present[ing] history as a complex discursive formation that is both distant and available for critique'. It is interesting that Diamond sees *Cloud Nine* as a version of Aphra Behn's *The Widow Ranter*, a text in which 'the dying Behn accedes to the ideological fantasy' of Empire, 'a new "larger world" that enlightened Europeans alone [could] improve and enrich'. Thus—she concludes, and I think quite rightly—'the foregrounding of gender inequalities in texts by women dramatists *does not [include or imply] an awareness of racism's violence*'.[63] However, for most Anglo-American critics, *Cloud Nine*'s second act signals the end of empire: 'All that is left of the British Empire is the futile, ongoing battle in Belfast'[64]; another example is Anne Herrmann who sees Churchill's socialist-feminism 'question the categories that legitimize not only patriarchy and capitalism, *but also colonialism*'.[65] These critics accept unquestioningly that the play is a 'critique' of colonialism without pausing to analyse the deeper structures which underlie the ideological formation of the authors. Just because a play is set in a colonial period does not make for an anticolonial ideology of critique. Classically, socialism is a critique of the economics of class, *and it does not automatically follow that a socialist is not (whether consciously or unconsciously) collusive with other, equally deterministic, hegemonies.*

Cloud Nine for all its revolutionary fervour in the domain of feminist subversion and western sexual liberation remains an imperial narrative as it en-acts a progress achieved by a 'civilization' which is not merely White but also English. The historical changes—valid and necessary in the context of the suppression of gender and the construction of sexualities and alternatives to the nuclear heterosexual two-parent family—are attributed to the possessors of enlightened knowledge, white man. Even as the White Family of Man changes its face its essential defining characteristic remains unchanged—it is, above all, white. The ruptured patriarchal narrative is denied the dangerous hysteric of black woman, a figure of powerful colonial desire in the imagination of the colonizing patriarchal white male as she is ultimately more passive, more malleable, *infinitely more colonizable* than the newly 'liberated' white woman who is emblematized in *Owners* and *Top Girls*, however inadvertently, as patriarchally castrating. The disintegration of the nuclear family, which is the very basis of capitalism in western societies, is, however, linked to colonialism and the rape and exploitation of the previously colonized territories: a territorialized exploitation which sustained and maintained western markets[66] and is supported, from the core, by the oedipal triangle, *dehumanizing the colonizer in his very private domain*, 'that is to say, keeping European humanity harnessed to the yoke of daddy-mommy and *making no effort to do away with this problem.*'[67] Thus Memmi's contention that the colonizer and the colonized are both simultaneously dehumanized by the colonial machine extends even into the very structures of the west as it seeps right into the familial nucleus and into the private domain of the home. In *Cloud Nine*, the transgressive nature of the politics of structural reversal (communal living, the sexual orgy in a public space) combined with the independent woman's desire (Betty's monologue celebrating autoeroticism) and the castrated man ('I'm not like whatever percentage of American men (…)') which is the beginnings of the erosion of the familial nucleus, signals the enormous threat to the very foundations of western capitalist societies posed by 'feminism' (called 'women's lib' in these early experimental days). Thus deconstructed through the triad of imbricated impulses which sustain the west,[68] means that even if Churchill's ruptural re-visioning eschews the black presence altogether, it still challenges the very structures of society by the compulsion to record the insidious intervention in the very order of things. Even as the piece (which mirrors the attitudes of not merely the British stage but also the system itself, thus functioning as a microcosm of British society at the level of the deeper structure of the text) elides the issues of black diaspora, *it inadvertently hastens the eventual displacement of the colonial impulse* (an anti-oedipal ruptural tendency) as it simultaneously attacks and demonstrates the rupture to the patriarchal impulse (gender *politics*). The deeper structures of the text, then, record the breaking of the bounds as the second act documents the fracturing of the very core of the capitalist west: the two-parent-heterosexual-nuclear family, the Freudian oedipal triangle which manufactures incestuous desire[69], the desiring-machine which keeps the fires of capitalism burning.[70]

A Collective Enterprise: Feminism in Theatre as a Consciously Counter-Normative Practice—Monstrous Regiment and *Vinegar Tom*

Monstrous Regiment was founded in 1975 as an inclusive collective feminist theatre—those were early days which saw men participate in feminism. Over a period of time, the men left, perhaps pointing to the perception of women's issues as separate from those of the general populace or, as Gillian Hanna put it, 'When men do something they speak for the human race, when women do the same thing it goes under the heading "Special Interest"'.[71]

Gillian Hanna, Chris Bowler, and Mary McCusker were with the group from its inception until it stopped in 1993 for lack of funding and a gradual loss of a politically aware audience. With the gradual incorporation of women in all walks of life came the awareness of women's issues in mainstream theatre; as more and more women wrote for the mainstream, the interest in a ghettoized women's theatre diminished. In the 60s it was radio which was the forum for neo-discursive theatrical voices; in the 70s it was the fringe which spoke for class, race, gender and sexuality; the 80s saw a gradual loss of funding but also saw previously alternative issues creep to centrestage. In the 90s it was almost usual to see all kinds of theatre in a mainstream forum such as The Cottesloe in London or The Royal Exchange in Manchester. This is not to elide these still important issues; theatre is, however, noticeably different in the mainstream today than it was in the immediate aftermath of the war and the years following.

Hanna served often as spokesperson for this politicized group of theatre workers; a group which *was* alternative fringe feminist theatre along with a few other collectives.[72] They represented theatre which was politically motivated towards changing consciousness.

> Theatre is not a revolutionary instrument in the sense that politicians or ideologies would understand revolution [but] I do think it can help people towards a change of consciousness.[73]

Hanna's statement links her to fringe feminist and gay theatres, but also to Gems' subversive theatre of ideological commitment which breaks into the mainstream in the 70s (see below). The alternative ideology represented by Monstrous Regiment explicates Churchill's sudden swing into a radical separatism with *Vinegar Tom*, and underlies the best of British feminist drama. It is

> the system [which] needs changing. The economic system, the capitalist system under which we live [...] needs changing to a socialist system [(...) also] attitudes towards women, values, opportunities, consciousness, relationships.[74]

> [O]ne of the most important questions [...] is about how things are going to change [...] the "how" is an urgent necessity [the "how" is the inseparable] dialectical relationship between socialism and feminism.[75]

It was in 1976 that Churchill's interest in 'the possibilities for change' become apparent. From personal pain and rage she moves outward to 'society, the drama, and the institutionalized theatre'.[76]

Vinegar Tom, like *Fen*, reveals women whose lives are severely circumscribed by their societies like the historic collection of women in *Top Girls*. The songs in *Vinegar Tom* highlight the plight of women past and present:

> Sometimes it's witches or what will you choose?
> Sometimes it's lunatics, shut them away.
> It's blacks and it's women and often it's Jews.
> We'd all be too happy if they'd go away.
> Find something to burn.
> Let it go up in smoke.
> Burn your troubles away.
> (*Vinegar Tom*, scene vii)

> The form of Vinegar Tom was extremely bizarre. You had a series of quite naturalistic scenes punctuated by very modern songs in modern dress. [...] we knew we had to have the music to smash that regular and acceptable theatrical form.[77]

They opine that for a woman life is not linear:

> [Men] are born into a world where they can map out life. It has a beginning, a middle and an end. It has a form, a shape. It has to do with a career (...) Now for a woman life is not like that. It doesn't have that pattern. For a woman life and experience is broken backed [...] women experience life very differently. For them life doesn't have that kind of linear overview that it seems to have for men. It's much more contradictory. And I think we've been trying to reflect that fragmented experience in what we do.[78]

Breaking the bounds of form and style was a frequent strategy as the content reflected the concerns of the female sex.

Vinegar Tom's Alice is as much of a rebel as the later *Fen*'s twentieth-century Val—both country cousins, as it were, of the Top Girl who was able to leave a milieu which demands much of its women as it entraps them. Both Alice and Val express a need to go away—specifically to the city, London—to escape a society within which both are inexorably caught up, but bound by custom or guilt—or opportunity. From the perspective of the early Alice and the later Val, Marlene's is a very significant victory in that she is able to be increasingly autonomous, freer and more liberated than those women caught up in tradition and custom.

'The Church provides the institutional mechanism for burning [...] witches; traditional prime targets are single women, economically marginal and sexually deviant' from the codes of puritanism. A 'witch' is typically a woman like Ellen who is a healer-herbalist 'who earns her own living outside of the monetary system [working] outside the sanctioned medical /male establishment'; Alice, a 'whore' because she is man's desire but not sanctioned within the code of marriage; and Susan who has an abortion. These women also internalize the *mores* and norms of their society as they are made to feel guilty as determined by their religious and social codes, unconscious of their oppression, abused and abusing.[79]

The space given to the men is small but powerful. They are the instruments of power which impose injustice and torment upon the women. The play opens with Alice conversing with a stranger with whom she has just had sex with by the roadside. Stereotypically dividing women into madonnas or whores he cannot find a category for Alice's explicit and guiltless sexuality. Although acquainted with 'the new morality' practised in London:

> (...) there's women speak out too. They smoke and curse in the tavern and they say flesh is no sin for they are God themselves and can't sin. The men and women lie together and say that's bliss and that's heaven and that's no sin. I believe it for there's such changes. (*Vinegar Tom*, Scene i)

he cannot find a space for the country girl Alice: 'What name would you put to yourself? You're not a wife or a widow. You're not a virgin. Tell me a name for what you are'. (Scene i) Although the character believes there is a place for the new morality he is also firmly entrenched in the Christian belief in sin, and the Calvinist theory of predestined damnation, which causes him to alternate between a paralysing guilt for his actions which he engages in anyway because he is sure he is damned. It is this frustration which is influential in the male condemnation of women through the play as Jack's guilt for his adulterous and ignorant behaviour translates into a condemnation of that he cannot understand—Alice and her mother—as witches. The doctor who treats Betty reveals himself as crass and uninformed as the rest of the men, as his diagnosis of hysteria and its treatment (bleeding by leeches) typifies how women were forcibly subjected to the most primitive cures for gender-based ailments which were incomprehensible to the male doctors. The only women 'doctors'—the wise old women herbalists—were hung as witches like Ellen in the play. This separationist piece indicts all men—an unusual play for Churchill to write, revealing her malleability.

The witch hunters, Goody and Packer, stand for the institutionalized and organized condemnation of women, practised as they round up women as 'witches' from every part of the country and hang them. The utter illogic with which a witch is identified is chilling: the spectator realises that any women could be proved a witch by their methods. The sheer power the witch hunters possess by virtue of their gender makes for a world filled with horror for women who are old, poor, weak and defenceless. And until the time that women could assert themselves politically, the institutionalized crime of witch hanging was one tangible manifestation of how male supremacy kept women in their place.

Janelle Reinelt points out that Churchill 'employs Brecht's episodic play structure in which each scene is isolated and has a crucial turning point'. The discrete nature of the episodes is necessary to allow the audience to interpose judgement, as each episode is a 'play' within the larger structure of the piece. Each episode in *Vinegar Tom* is 'a potentially independent vignette in which a discrete situation portrays how [...] women are controlled and socialized'. As the collusion of patriarchy and state constructs docile bodies, the audience can see that in each instance intervention could have changed the situation, 'but the isolation of the women from one another because of class made such collective action impossible'.[80]

The songs, another Brechtian device which produces distantiation to facilitate and enable audience judgement, reflect on how women and blacks and Jews have long been the scapegoats of society. In an afterword[81] to the play the Company reflected that

> the play received a very interesting reaction (...) Some men in particular were upset by it (...) some people felt accused by the songs, which in their manner of presentation—as well as the lyrics and music—were direct and uncompromising. It wasn't our intention to make people feel accused or blamed in a simplistic way, but neither did we want to let them off the hook or allow them to distance themselves emotionally from the events of the play because they were distant historically (...) when Ned Chaillet of *The Times* described it as 'a picture slightly different from the one handed down through legend and historical records', we knew we had succeeded.

This piece 'reconstruct[s] our understanding of the relationship between female image and female identity in the seventeenth-century as a means for reconstructing our understanding of the relationship between image and identity' today.[82] 'The telescoping of time makes this a play not about witches, but about how contemporary women acquire and confront the images governing their lives'. This is—as Churchill put it—'a play about

witches with no witches in it'.[83] Austin E. Quigley reminisces, 'What we remember [about *Vinegar Tom*] is the unsettling contemporary relevance of an
image, apparently archaic, that is forcefully and disturbingly reconstituted.
No one who has seen the play will ever think about witches and women in
quite the same way again'.[84]

The later Marlene's lack of guilt is atypical—her archetypal sisters, Alice and Val, are constantly caught up in the web of guilt that patriarchal society foists on women. For these women it is fear which links them to a
woman as 'successful' as Pope Joan ('*terrorem*') and as 'thick' as Marlene's
daughter Angie ('frightening'). Frightening it is too for Val, whose personal
choices form the story of *Fen*, a Joint Stock production of 1983. The women
working on the lands of the Fens are the archetypes of women who will
never make it to or in the glittering materialism of the city. Cast by determinism, these are women who have no choice.

Vinegar Tom's Women are the Contemporary Women of *Fen*

Fen's well researched rural setting documents the private lives of women and
men who are subjects of their unchanging condition and isolated environment generation after bleak generation. Exploited by the land-owning farm-
ers they work at a range of menial jobs—spud-picking, onion-sorting, stone-
gathering in inclement weather: a tiring physical labour which is as unre-
warding as it is unliberating. Val stands out as a rebel—a Marlene who
doesn't leave, more Joyce than Marlene, chained emotionally to her children and her lover. Scene ii which has women working in a field has Val
walk out in defiance of the gangmaster who threatens not to pay her. As we
learn in the next scene, she has decided to leave her husband and go to
London with her children to find a 'new life'. However, she wants also to be
with her lover Frank who decides for her that she must stay in the village
with him. Val has to choose between her lover and her children (she is
aware that the husband won't let her have them) and her anguish at leaving
them colours the happiness she might have found with Frank:

> Val: I can't hold the baby, it makes me cry. I'll do the ironing.
> Shirley: Give her here then. You don't want to be so soft. If you can't stop away
> from them, go back to them.
> Val: I can't leave Frank.
> Shirley (to the baby): Nothing's perfect, is it my poppet? (*Fen*, scene xi)

May's attitude to her daughter speaks for the community:

> May: How long is this nonsense going to last?
> Val: Don't.
> May: I'm ashamed of you.

Val: Not in front.
May: What you after? Happiness? Got it have you? Bluebird?
(silence)
What you after? (Scene viii)

The village on the Fens makes Val's life a claustrophobic hell as she is ostracized in subtle but tangible ways:

Alice: Everyone's acting funny with her.
Angela: She's the one acting funny. Leave her own kiddies. If I had my own kiddies I wouldn't leave them.
Alice: I know she's wicked but she's still my friend (…) it was sinners Jesus Christ came for so don't you judge.
Shirley: Who said anything?
Alice: Outside school yesterday, collecting time, no one said hello except me. (Scene x)

Social pressure doesn't make Val's emotional burdens any lighter, and the insular traditional community suffocates her. Her only safety valve is the Valium she frequently takes, having rejected the traditional release system of religion which, for her, is neither a refuge nor an escape.

The near isolated village on the Fens is a cradle of myth, superstition and tradition, and little seems to have changed with the passing of time. Scene xvi brings together four generations of women who have lived and worked on the Fens. Ivy, Val's ninety-year old grandmother; May, Val's mother; and Val's daughters Deb and Shona. Val is present in her absence thereby symbolizing her need to get away and cut ties. The nonagenarian's detailing of her girlhood parallels the contemporary hardship of life on the Fens—at the age of six Ivy picked beet much as the young Becky toils on the land today; Old Tewson had made life for the workers as miserable as the younger Tewson does now. If there is a sign of change it is that the owner-ship of the lands has passed into the hands of overseas investors—from one capitalist to another—but for the people of the Fens it is still 'work, work, work, which is all their lives'. Another kind of change is represented by Val: as Geoffrey says, 'Val. You're a symptom of the times. Everything's changing, everything's going down'.(Scene xi) Mechanized farming is not perceived as heralding anything new, but as a corruption of old methods of work.

Geoffrey: Don't talk to me of unemployment. They've got four jobs. Doing other people out of jobs. Being a horseman was proper work, but all your Frank does is sit on a tractor. Sitting down's not work. Common market takes all the work. (ibid.)

It isn't just Val who has repudiated religion: 'Only twenty in church on Sunday. Declining morals all around'. 'Tradition steeped and family-fixated',[85] the village on the Fens does not let Val escape its taboos. Repudiating convention Val finds no new answers and it is in death that Churchill has her united with the history of the land she has lived and worked on. That she is not allowed to break with tradition is symbolized by her only way out, death, and her subsequent reappearance as a ghost links her to the superstition and folklore which surrounded her in life. In death she becomes one with the spirits of the past, some of whom she recognizes. Frank's immediate acceptance of Val's ghost ('does it go on?') connects him solidly to the ages old superstitions of the community he lives in and the ground he works on. The imagery of bleakness and winter in Val's words merge with a faint hope for the future, which is echoed again as May grasps her 'bluebird of happiness' and sings. Present and past mingle in a destruction of traditional linearity and Nell crosses the stage on stilts bringing back the centuries old image of the once submerged Fenlands as the play draws to a circular close. The private and domestic merge with the harsh conditions of labour as Shirley irons the field. The final scene is a surreal rendition of life on the Fens, as different threads of the play interweave and coalesce to mirror the barrenness of the lives we see. The green mist is a trope for the latent aspirations of the women as it envelops them (May wanted to be a singer; the children want to be a nurse or hairdresser) but it also connects to the starkness of the opening scene which is an exposition of the matrix of capitalist greed within which their lives are imbricated. The hardship which is their determinism leaves them no agency, and it only through the surrealism of dreams that their meagre hopes are fulfilled. Their dreams are bluebirds— difficult to get hold of as they are confronted by the very real poverty they live in. These are the 'subjected subjects' of class as this play makes their issues felt on the mainstream stages.

Politics and War: *Light Shining in Buckinghamshire* and *Mad Forest*

> I go out into the blue and I sink down inside myself, and yes then I am free inside, I can fly about in that blue, that is what the church can give people, they can fly about inside that blue.
>
> —Romanian priest, *Mad Forest*, I, ix.

Fen is undoubtedly in the tradition of the class politics of Shelagh Delaney and Andrea Dunbar, and like the 1976 *Light Shining in Buckinghamshire*, betrays the influence of Joint Stock in its socialist bent. The women of *Fen* are the twentieth-century parallels of the dispossessed of *Vinegar Tom*. The politics of everyday life gives way to the politics of history and government as Churchill researched and wrote *Light Shining* and *Mad Forest*. She evokes the political climate with an intimacy of detail reflected in the lives of the common people.

Light Shining is a radical re-interpretation of history and takes its place beside the many 'history plays' of the post-war period. Simultaneous to the writing with Monstrous Regiment, this history takes account of its women in Churchill's newly found affiliation with feminism; however, the influence of Joint Stock ensures a socialist point of view, as *Vinegar Tom* remains an anomalously radical Churchill piece. The idea for a play about seventeenth-century revolution was suggested by Stafford-Clark. 'First of all, Max Stafford-Clark and I read and talked till we had found a subject in the millennial movement in the civil war. [...] though I wrote the text the play is something we both imagined'.[86] *Light Shining* was hailed as the most feminist of Churchill's earlier work as the mainstream sees, for the first time, an English history play which includes the viewpoint of women as well as the working classes. The influence of Monstrous Regiment takes possession to lead Churchill down the path of utilising her subversive theatrical tactics to the ends of feminist theatre in the British malestream. Although only a few parts are specifically for women (who numbered two of a cast of six) the device of using different actors to play the same character diffuses the spectrum of parts thereby multiplying them, whilst sharpening the impact of each scene. In effect they had, say, two women play one character at different times, or women play men's parts.[87] This device reveals that political revolutions have an all-pervasive impact; that women too, were part of the revolution, and the play was indeed a feminist history play without being merely 'herstory'. This idea, introduced as 'a joke' is actually a Monstrous Regiment technique used in *Vinegar Tom* as Kramer and Sprenger (the witch-hunters) are played by women (to indicate that patriarchy and oppression require collusion). This device was acceptable in the 'malestream' mainly, one suspects, because Joint Stock's evolving method was one which involved an ensemble of actors doubling and playing different parts.

In *Light Shining*, each character adds to the detail and texture of the whole as fragments of their lives are exposed in short Brechtian scenes, again, like *Vinegar Tom*. The play evokes a period of change, joy and subsequent disillusion. Churchill conceived the play in the form of a diagram, where 'Rigidities' led to 'Movement' which in turn led to 'Joy' leading to 'Crushings' and then 'Disillusion'.[88]

The initial pervasive rigidity is caused by class hegemony. The several 'rigidities' are the tightly constraining lives of the poorest, working people whose futures are determined by the fixed order of society. The questioning of authority in the overthrowing of the king parallels the quest for a new existence and the possibility of a new way of life. The belief in the millennial coming of Christ is a collective western fantasy; in the play we see the crush-

ing of this hope combined with the defeat of the Levellers and Diggers followed by the restoration of the throne, which leads to disillusion. 'Movement' is a brief moment of the loosening of the bonds which constrain the
people, a free flow of positive desiring-production and social-production
which leads to a shortlived 'joy' as the flow is blocked, dammed up by an
economic determinism as 'disillusion' sets in.

Scene i opens with religious rigidity: a reading of Isaiah which evokes a
universal terror by the hell-fire-pit sermonizing: 'Fear, and the pit, and the
snare are upon thee, O inhabitants of the earth (...)' As Cobbe prays, it is
apparent he is in a 'snare': his particular rigidity is the frozen terror conjured
up in his imagination by the fixed Christian belief that every 'word, thought
or faint motion' even committed 'unknowing' is a 'sin'. His rebellion against
his earthly father symbolic of the king presages his need to revolt from god's
laws (the heavenly father) as all three dictate rules which constrain him.
Subverting this trinity which forms the matrix of order which straitjackets
Cobbe prepares the ground for the movement of the play.

The next scene depicts the rigidity of economic and class hierarchy as
the Vicar 'sits at table with wine and oranges' and talks to his servant:

> Vicar: How's the baby today? Any better?
> Servant: No sir.
> [...]
> Vicar: God tries you severely in your children. It must have been a comfort this
> morning to have the Bishop himself encourage you to suffer. 'Be afflicted and
> mourn and weep'. That's the way to heaven.
> Servant: Sir.
> [He pours more wine]
> [...]
> Vicar: And if [the child] is not spared, we must submit. We all have to suffer in this
> life. [He drinks.]
> (*Light Shining in Buckinghamshire*, I, pp.192–3)

Margaret Brotherton is another of those at the very bottom of the economic ladder with no hope for movement. Caught between the pit and the
snare she is not allowed to beg, not eligible for charity, and punished for
stealing—'stripped to the waist and beaten to the bounds of [the] parish and
returned (...) to the parish where [she was] born'. (I, p.194). Brotherton, the
servant and Cobbe have no agency in a society which imprisons them in a
network of religious, economic, political and social rigidity.

The collective will to transform circumstance and the social order now
gathers momentum and flows into the piece. The pressing need to loosen
the bonds starts the 'movement'. Star, a corn merchant, recruits soldiers for
the army of saints. The promise of 'Christ [coming] in person [(...) to] rule

over England for one thousand years' is the hope (flow) which provides the forward movement. The hope for a new life of social equity and mobility is promised with the millennium (which seemed imminent by Star's calculations)—a solid comfort of eightpence a day ('better than labouring. And it's everyday (…) not just the days you fight. Every day.') held out much hope to the poor and landless. Briggs represents the hopeless; and his joining up is a celebratory gesture of hope for the men and their families. The next scene makes it clear that a woman, unmarried and poor, could share in no such hope. Her only hope for money, having been beaten for begging, is to 'lie down' with a stranger who offers her a halfpenny for the act. Brotherton understandably doesn't share in the utopian dream, preferring the solidity of a tangible and fulfilling present moment rather than a tomorrow which is not promised to her: 'If [Christ] comes tomorrow and you've not drunk your money. Sitting here with tenpence in the cold. Christ laugh at you for that'. (I, p.198).

The woman Hoskins is the antithesis of Brotherton and Claxton's wife as she provides the opposing impulse to religious patriarchy's doctrines of women's inherent wickedness and uncleanliness. It is she who reassures Brotherton in the final scenes. Hoskins is a self-appointed preacher in an age when women were not allowed to speak out. She resists the prevailing interpretation of the Bible, challenging authority in the form of an ordained minister who speaks of salvation for only the predestined few as she proclaims: 'It's a man wrote the Bible' (II, p.236). Radical in thought and action her intellectual autonomy separates her from the other women who have internalized all the guilts imposed on their gender and circumstance. Hoskins' egalitarian belief that they will all be saved, 'not one (…) is damned', is preserved even as she is hounded out of the church, publicly condemned and beaten. Admirable for the strength of her faith, she lives as a travelling preacher, stealing to make ends meet in a code of personal ethics which is echoed in the final scenes of release from fixed and unquestioning morality. The believers join to query the issues of sin, of morality, of the coming of Christ itself.

The first tremors of joy are communicated through Cobbe's vision:

> I saw a great body of light […] whereupon with exceeding trembling and amazement on the flesh, and with joy unspeakable in the spirit, I clapped my hands, and cried out, Amen, Halelujah, Halelujah, Amen. […] My most excellent majesty and eternal glory in me answered and said, fear not. I will take thee up into my everlasting kingdom. […] And I heard a voice saying, 'Go to London, to London, that great city, and tell them I am coming'. (I, p.206)

As the belief in the coming of Christ the saviour is affirmed, the joy continues in the next scene as the two women see their own reflections in a mirror for the first time in their lives. It is the landed classes who have security and a sense of identity in a society of increasingly commodified desire, and the loot acquired as landowners are overthrown and land and property claimed by the Diggers gives the poor women a sense of self they haven't known before. The mirror, symbolic of the possessions which the proletariat need to acquire so they can have a sense of identity in a material way ('property-based values'), reflects the women as they stare fascinated at their own image. Cousin points out that most of Churchill's plays affirm the self-worth of characters, which is possibly why she sees *Light Shining* as central to Churchill's *oeuvre* as it affirms the downtrodden in a very socialist fashion. In this scene the central gest is one of the affirmation of women, giving them an immediate means of establishing a selfhood they are generally denied, which they are allowed only via kinship systems. This autonomy suddenly allowed them, however brief and transitory, contributes to the wave of joy, which is a link with Cobbe's vision of hope. This is ratified in the next scene as Walt Whitman's affirmatory 'Song of the Open Road' is sung in chorus. The much condensed Putney debates close the first act. They are played by men and women actors although historically these would have all been male parts. It is scenes like these which give the whole piece a sense of an equal and participatory history for women as they are represented in contexts which even by century's end were not fully inclusive of gender. The egalitarianism which cuts across class and gender extends the feeling of a common sharing of the changes and upheavals of their society.

Act II opens with the Diggers who perform the central gest of material hope as they symbolise the need of the common people to grow their own food by tilling their own lands. This utopian vision of an economic autonomy—'There can be no universal liberty till this universal community be established' (II, p.219)—is never attained, as the army comes in to destroy what is grown and built. The crushing of all hope leads to a profound disillusion, a bleakness which is alleviated only by spiritual fervour. An increasing solace is found from religion as new sects spring up; meanwhile the people turn to venial sins such as lying or stealing to affirm a sense of autonomy—however transitory—within themselves. The only control they possess is one of minor rebellion to reassure themselves they are their own masters. The short scene which has a woman forced by stark poverty to desert her child brings alive the severe hardship endured by the poor, as the religious faith demonstrated by the poorest is queried as utopian. This is immediately followed by the short sharp scene where a butcher talks directly to the audience, his imaginary customers: 'Giving your friends dinner tonight, sir? And another night they give you dinner. You're very generous and christian to each other. There's never a night you don't have dinner. Or do you eat it all yourself, sir? No? You look as if you do. You don't look hungry. You don't look as if you need a dinner'. This gets progressively acerbic and ghoulish as the breaking of the fourth wall rouses the audience, insulting them: 'What do you need it for? No, tell me. To stuff yourself, that's what for. To make fat. And shit. When it could put a little good flesh on children's bones. [...] You cram yourselves with their children's meat. You cram yourselves with their dead children'. (II, p.227–8).

The disillusion is exacerbated with the killing of a Leveller leader as people turn from religion, as it offers no solace. Churchill said that she and Max Stafford-Clark were led to the theme by wondering and then exploring what led so many to cling to the millennial dream. The answer seems to be that poverty, lack of economic power and subjugation—a material alienation of the masses combined with abject powerlessness as their lives are determined by the fixed order of things—lead many to need the opiate of religion as a means of sustenance and escape from material conditions. The belief in the coming of a saviour is a self-sustaining drug which offered hope and respite from the numbing realities of people's lives. Hoskins' voice runs clear through the final meeting, a scene of utter abjection as she functions as the only hopeful believer whose faith is unshakeable. She reaches out to Brotherton in a sisterhood which rebuffs sexist comments as she preaches of the coming in the 'next year'. As the waves of disillusion engulf them, Brotherton is awash with guilt. This unites the gathering—christian guilt is necessary as the masses internalize the cause of their suffering, turning it back into themselves instead of outward toward the material conditions over which they have no control. However, Briggs offers assurance: 'That's not your sin. It's one more of theirs. Damn them'. (II, p.237) Denied an agency in the material world they cling to the only hope of salvation as they sing from Ecclesiastes: 'He that is higher than the highest regardeth; and there be higher than they'.

The piece closes with a scene entitled 'After' which takes place after the restoration of Charles II to the throne. The scene, typically short, reveals the general aura of a laxity in values (Brotherton) and a reconsideration of the millennium which somehow slipped them by (Hoskins). The longest speech is reserved for Briggs who symbolises the strong and fervent streak of puritanism which ran through England even as the court of Charles II was amok with values apparently imported from France. This play affirms that the power of transformative desire can bring about changes in the social order. The participation of the women in the play in scenes of political and public spaces affirms that gender can create its own space. The twentieth century offered a general social mobility in the still class ridden nation, but in this piece it is the cause of women which has most hope as they permeate the whole piece which is avowedly political, with their subversive presence.

—— ✤ ——

With *Mad Forest* (1990) Churchill attempted to step into the realm of international politics. Like *Light Shining*, this piece, set in Romania, establishes that the final instance of determinism in the material world is economic, but some rise above it by means of spiritualism. This is, however, incredibly difficult, as the basic 'needs' of the average human are fairly complex and extend way beyond mere physical sustenance.[89] Although these needs can extend into a limitless material desire they stop short of spiritual sustenance as the latter is not consonant with the subject formation under capitalism and becomes increasingly etiolated until it resolves itself into mere ritual without belief or is abandoned altogether. In *Mad Forest*, again, the stylistic method used is one which highlights typical individual private lives at a time of conflict, crisis and political instability. The movement of the play may be compared with the earlier political piece and can be summed up by a similar model where the fixity of things transform for a moment of joy and hope (which reveals the hold of capitalism rather than spirituality) to result in new rigidities and disillusion. The first act is one of Rigidities which leads to Movement. Act II is the continuation of Movement leading to Joy as Act III brings New Rigidities.

The play opens on the eve of the overthrow of the Romanian dictator Ceausescu—the piece was actually first performed on the day the miners entered Bucharest to crush anti-front demonstrations: 30 June 1990. The 'rigidities' which envelop the first act are similar to those of *Light Shining in Buckinghamshire*: they are social, political, economic and intellectual. Lacking the freedom of speech and action offered by democratic political units, the inhabitants of Romania live silent paralysed lives as they drown conversational exchanges with the sound of a blaring radio to keep from being heard. Churchill evokes life and society in a dictatorship by focusing on two Romanian families. This makes the situation immediate as the audience is immersed in the people's private lives and concerns through whose lens we get a focus on the macro-politics of state. Each personal action reveals the political climate: Flavia teaching manufactured history in the classroom; Lucia's wish to escape to 'democracy' and economic mobility by marrying an American: an act considered criminal by the Romanian regime as it is considered to jeopardise the solidarity of the state which must be maintained at all costs. This results in the family being labelled traitors and put under observation. The audience sees acts of flourishing corruption as foreign currency buys anything from abortion to eggs and American cigarettes. The scene between Lucia and the doctor is particularly revealing as their innocuous verbal exchange is contradicted by the surreptitious exchange of explanatory written notes and freedom-buying banknotes. The central gest of the hypocrisy and corruption within which the Romanians are formulated is a function of state-controlled repression. The series of short scenes lay the ground for the deposition of the dictator.

The thorough research by the students of the Central School of Drama as they went from door to door interviewing Romanians revealed material which was authentic and a supplement to what in Churchill previously figured as an empty and futile refuge. Religious belief in *Fen* was represented by the dwindling numbers at church, and *Light Shining* began with a socialist's genuine puzzlement at the collective belief in the millennial dream. These two earlier examples of oppressed social structures had a thread of 'religion' thrown in but it seemed empty and never denoted an authentic spirituality. Closest to an abstract belief was the ghost of Val which merged with the land as another woman laboured, ironing it, which is more an economic metaphor than a spiritual one. In *Mad Forest* too, Flavia 'talks' to the ghost of her dead grandmother, who significantly fails to appear after the fall of the dictator symbolising Flavia's inability to cope with the changing political landscape, having taught the supposed virtues of Nicolae and Elena Ceausescu for years. Again, the ghost is not a trope for spirituality but a metaphor for the subject's imbrication in the social and political structures of her time, a fatalistic determinism. However, the difference from earlier attempts to document spirituality lay in the research of real subjects, revealed in authentic snippets of real belief, sustaining and spiritual as in the words of the priest and the artist.

For the priest, 'church' is not voiced as a mere ritual of sacrament and mass and church attendance but a true communion which is articulated as a tangible abstract denoted by the colour 'blue' which is psychologically symbolic of 'complete calm. Contemplation of this colour has a pacifying effect on the central nervous system. [(…)The colour] is a chromatic representation of a basic biological need—physiologically, tranquillity; psychologically, contentment, contentment being peace plus gratification'.[90]

> Priest: I go out into the blue and I sink down inside myself, and yes then I am free inside, I can fly about in that blue, that is what the church can give people, they can fly about inside that blue. (*Mad Forest*, I, ix)

> Artist: Painting doesn't mean just describing, it's a state of spirit. (II)

The 'movement' at the end of Act I, however, is not from the words of the Romanian priest but set into motion as a Romanian woman marries an American citizen. This is symbolic of the systematic crushing of communism to be replaced by the forces of capitalism, a global and totalizing tendency, its permanence seemingly infinitely prolonged by its shifting and unstable base as it formulates subjects as consumers. This is accomplished by repressing desire into an infinitely plural material fantasy which infinitely defers its own gratification even as the consumers of capitalism seek to sustain it. Like the sexually mythologized Cleopatra of Shakespeare, capitalism is predicated on a 'barge' which is all glitter, 'a *burnished* throne' while both make hungry where most they satisfy.

Act II continues the movement metaphor as several Romanians, strangers to each other, introduce themselves to the audience and recount events of their personal lives from the eve of Ceausescu's speech in Bucharest (21 December 1990) until the trial on 25 December. The impinging of the personal on the political again makes for immediacy and impact, as joy mingles with pain and the difficulties of coping with change. This is the most authentic sounding section of the otherwise thin documentary-like play, as it has students, a doctor, a translator, a painter and a flower seller, a bulldozer driver, even a soldier and a representative of the formerly dreaded watchdogs of the state, the Securitate. The different perspectives coalesce as the audience receives a firsthand account of the confusion of events which led to the dictator's downfall, the army going over to the side of the people, and the period of hiatus before the election of a new government. The sense of liberation and relief when the people realize the army is one with them is intense, bringing home the severity of their bondage, which is ultimately a spiritual imprisonment. It is the artist who best describes a personal aftermath: 'Painting doesn't mean just describing, it's a state of spirit. I didn't want to paint for a long time then'. (II). The implication seems to be that the sudden freedom in the hiatus imposes a spiritual paralysis, and Act II ends with the exaction of a new rigidity.

In scene one of act three, Churchill characteristically departs into weird symbolism, rupturing the semi-naturalism of the piece almost forcibly. A 'vampire' is approached by a 'hungry dog'. Seeking to make it like itself, bloodseeking, the vampire bites the dog. As the author continues to extract an inevitably subjective essence of the Romanians' political and personal situation, she attempts to portray a failing parallel with democratic societies whose subjects assume that equity is inherent within the very structure of their societies when nothing could be further from the truth. The act unfolds to reveal the xenophobic nature of the Romanians who seem to loathe

the Hungarians, while both despise the coloured gypsies. Lucia enlightens her friends in a demonstration of the Romanian brand of racism:

> (...) in America they even like the idea of gypsies, they think how quaint. But I said to them you don't like blacks here, you don't like hispanics, we're talking about lazy greedy crazy people who drink too much and get rich on the black market. That shut them up. (III, iii).

This brief interchange raises the question of the imperfections within the so-called democratic way of life which imposes its own hegemonies inevitably dictated by capitalism. Even communist Romania seems riven between those who have and those who haven't.

The final scenes are those of Flavia's wedding. It takes place after the elections and although there is a happy buzz, the prevalent feeling seems to be one of 'they've voted the same lot in'. Murmurs of 'Jos Iliescu' mingle with jokes about Ceausescu's death, while Lucia's family harbour hopes of emigrating to the economically mobile shores of the USA. Radu is strident in his cries of 'Jos comunismul (...) Jos tiranul. Jos Illiescu', whilst the parents favour the new leader who is a communist like his predecessor. Sufficiently loosened up with alcohol, the wedding party comes to blows in a display of overt prejudice between the Hungarians and Romanians.

> Bogdan: Leave my son alone. Hungarian bastard. And don't come near my daughter.
> Ianos: I'm already fucking your daughter, you stupid peasant.
> (VIII, iii)

The play closes as the members of the wedding party dance to the lambada and revert to speaking Romanian. As each person reiterates their opinion on the political scene, divided by age (Flavia), prejudice (Ianos, Gabriel, Irina), a personal need for 'democracy' (Florina, Irina), and confusion (Mihai, Bogdan, Radu, Lucia), it is the stranger/vampire, spectre of capitalist desire who has the last word: 'You begin to want blood. Your limbs ache, your head burns, you have to keep moving faster and faster'.

Churchill's device of using Romanian to close the play and to introduce each scene would seem to have a double purpose as it would inevitably draw a Romanian audience into the theatrical space of the play even as they might be distanced by the content, which to them is of themselves and the time they are living in; whilst serving almost as a Brechtian device of distantiation and alienation for an English audience as the play ends in a babel of foreign tongues. *Mad Forest* attempts to document history in the making, and one detects the particularly English framing of the eastern European subjects as their capitalist greed and racism is offset against another 'foreign' power, the USA. The piece is too close in temporal terms to the political events which were taking place even as it was being written. Yet it works when read against Churchill's previous work as it reveals the growth and hold of capitalism, its tangible manifestation as it formulates subjects in repressive desire channelled away from the spiritual abstract (or, as Deleuze and Guattari would have it, away from the desirable 'schizzes-flows', away from lateral flights of imagination demonstrated admirably by both priest and artist, the true 'schizos' of the piece). *Fen*, *Light Shining in Buckinghamshire*, *Serious Money* and *Mad Forest* reveal subjects caught up in the last determining instance, which formulates them to desire the opposite condition, a gratuitous materialism, a flight away from the spirit which seems unable to sustain itself without gratifications of the comforts of the here-and-now. The focus is also simultaneously on poverty, deprivation and despair as no economic system seems just or fair to that class which must inevitably be at the bottom. It is, however, the 'schizos' (real people revealed by research of the students of the CSD) who seem unfettered and truly free as they frame another kind of alienation: a psychological and spiritual alienation, a kind of bankruptcy of the soul which capitalism seems to foster as it formulates its consumers in an ascending spiral of wants, ever newly created and sustained by its 'attachments' of advertising, marketing and media. Goods and services are sought by a bottomless need which replaces any movement toward an actualization of self in the masses. Thus the upward spiral of capitalism breeds the corollary of an emptiness of the soul, an alienation of the psyche—body without organs, inert without its energy machines, in need of, perhaps, the attachment of a tree or a chlorophyll machine.[91]

Here, the female dramatist critiques politics and government, democracy and communism, essaying into what has previously been the territory of the male. The issues here are not feminist, nor female, and the writing of this play asserts that the rupture affected by feminism is not merely a platform or forum for women's issues but can involve the foray into what is considered (by feminist essentialists) to be male territory.

The Surveillance Machine: *Softcops* and *Icecream*

> The perfect disciplinary apparatus would make it possible for a single gaze to see everything constantly (...) a perfect eye that nothing would escape and a centre toward which all gazes would be turned.
>
> —Michel Foucault, Discipline and Punish

1983 saw the production of *Softcops* by the RSC—an all-male examination of patriarchally-structured society's methods of punishing criminals. Following Foucault's study it is set in nineteenth-century France, and stylistically resembles the earlier *Traps* as scenes fuse into each other presenting, in this instance, a series of revue-like sketches. *Softcops* effects a subversion of Brechtian methods (there are placards but they are not interpretations of the action; Pierre, representative of Reason is preoccupied by the fact that there *ought* to be placards when not dwelling on his utopian Garden of Laws); and shares a kinship with Edward Bond in the representation of cruelty on stage and also its didacticism.[92]

Discipline and Punish[93] illustrates the fundamental transformation which had taken place in penal practices, namely, the disappearance of the public spectacle of physical punishment and the installation of what seemed to be softer methods of control. The shift was from disciplining the criminal's body to controlling the soul or the 'knowable' man conceptualized in terms of his psyche, subjectivity, personality, consciousness and individuality, which represented the emergence of a new form of power and concomitant new forms of knowledge. The body, however, was still subject to the penal process: confined in prison, forced to labour, subjected to sexual deprivation and to a series of other controls and regulations. The body was not thereby liberated from the grip of power, but rather displaced to a secondary, mediatory position by the emergence of a new technology of power, discipline, and the production—through the exercise of this new form of power—of a new reality and knowledge, that of the individual.

Softcops, although it purports to be a dramatized version of Foucault's triangulated set of concepts concerning the docile body and its articulation with relations of power and knowledge, turns out to be an indictment of the largely ineffectual nature of punishment for crime, structured by a predominantly male establishment. The play started as an idea 'about the soft methods of control, schools, hospitals, social workers'. Real life characters such as Vidocq and Lacenaire, 'the original cop and robber', add considerable dramatic interest to the theme of crime and punishment presented in near documentary fashion.[94] The play is loyal to the history of punishment in *Discipline and Punish*: the older methods of decapitation, thumbscrews, racks and execution which took place in front of a hugely voyeuristic crowd are set against later methods of chastisement. The latter include an Orwellian panopticon which enables one guard to watch hundreds of prisoners in a reversal of the spectacle of a crowd watching the misery of one condemned offender.[95]

Softcops opens with the busy activity of erecting a high scaffold for the purpose of executions. In the midst of this phallic bustle a neat crocodile of school boys enters, led by their headmaster. They are taking their lessons in discipline and duty from witnessing the morbid scene. A dark humour per-vades the scene as Pierre instructs the condemned men to make speeches of repentance before they are executed. While one prisoner, Duval, meekly acquiesces in his terror, Lafayette, a condemned murderer launches into a violent and ugly diatribe against the judges, proving in effect that punishment and the impending execution has not served to change him, but rather leads to further acts of aggression as he attacks Pierre, and the scene of the execution culminates in an ugly brawl.

Churchill lampoons justice and crime in the conversations between the minister and Vidocq—ex-criminal turned Chief of Police—and that of the two conspirators. An atmosphere of suspicion and corruption hangs over the exchanges as a clever crook becomes a police officer of rank and one conspirator tricks the other into an admission of treason for being on the side of justice.

The scene between the socialist criminal Lacenaire who is chained in his cell and the rich men who toast his downfall seems to be a political comment on the reversal of power in British politics and the capitalist-materialist Conservative attitudes which washed over 80s Britain with the appointment of Margaret Thatcher.

The procession of the chain gang once again proves that punishment—especially in front of a crowd—does not serve as a potent enough deterrent for society's wrongdoers. Foucault, after all, regarded punishment as a political tactic with a complex social function. The revolts of the prisoners is against the body politic, to be sure, but also against the body of the prison. He quotes de Guibert, 'The state that I depict will have a simple reliable, easily controlled administration' thus producing docile bodies, effects of power, which is what the prisoners revolt against. These are revolts against an entire state of physical misery; against cold, suffocation, and overcrowding; against decrepit walls, hunger, physical maltreatment. But they are also revolts against model prisons, tranquillizers, isolation, the medical or educational services, says Foucault. These are contradictory revolts: against the obsolete but also against comfort. As Churchill's prisoners chant, inciting rebellion:

> What do these people want with us,
> Do they think they'll see us cry?
> We rejoice in what is done to us
> And our judges will die.

They echo a Marxist socialism in their refrain: 'Children break your chains. Children break your chains. Children break your chains.' as Pierre, once again, falls victim to his prisoners. Pierre represents Reason, which is his 'goddess' as he envisages a Garden of Laws—not unlike Madame Tussaud's dungeons—based on the concept of heaven and hell:

> Where over several acres, with flowering bushes, families would stroll on a Sunday. And there would be displayed every kind of crime and punishment. [...] Guides to give lectures on civic duty and moral feeling. And people would walk gravely and soberly and reflect. And for the worst crime. Parricide. An iron cage hanging high up in the sky. Symbolic of the rejection of heaven and earth. From anywhere in the city you could look up. And see him hanging there. [...] Year after year. Quietly take it to heart. A daily lesson. (*Softcops*, p.14)

This vision of softcontrols which punish 'knowable man' is too avant-garde for the minister who believes in the old methods of bodily submission and control: '[we] are dealing with a wild animal and we keep it off us with raw meat and whips. We don't teach it to sit up and beg and feed it sugar lumps' (p. 16). Vidocq persists: it is 'not what the punishment is, sir, it's knowing you're going to get it. [...] nobody expects to get caught.' (p. 17). But Pierre still wants his 'little theatres of punishment' (p. 30) until Jeremy Bentham convinces him that his idea be reversed:

> Let me show you. Imagine for once that you're the prisoner. This is your cell, you can't leave it. This is the central tower and I'm the guard. I'll watch whatever you do day and night. (p. 39)

Softcops played into the year 1984 which helped stretch the audience imagination in the direction of Orwellian panopticism as Big Brother lent an evil edge to Bentham's soft method of regulation of the soul. Churchill's all-male cast emphasizes the male construction of society and the inefficacy of its institutions. The patriarchal impulse substrates the institutions which produce the effects of power, here indicted as useless in their policing function. Typically, the Churchillian piece offers no answers in a bid to stretch the satire and prompt more questions. The play implies that 'men have messed up', as policing methods are revealed as ineffective devices of regulation and control. As Janelle Reinelt puts it, 'The absence of women [in the play] is not an accident: *Softcops* is about patriarchal culture and its power relations'.[96]

The play ends with Pierre watching over some prisoners 'all on the great panoptic principle'. One of the men attacks Pierre and is immediately shot dead by a guard. Pierre, whose logical mind which has until that moment accepted panopticism, ends the play in a confused state as he reflects that there is no easy answer to discipline, crime and punishment—no perfect means of control. The society which an inefficient method of control would produce is to be found in the later short, *Icecream*, which experiments with the idea of unpunished, undetected crime, reducing violence to the level of farce. In Act II guests at a party toast and congratulate Phil for getting away with murder. After *Softcops* serious and didactic look at crime *Icecream* emerges as a rather flighty piece on crime and its causes, if any. The play begins with the feeling of rootlessness and displacement of Americans as they search for a personal history and genealogy. In production the play emerges as a comedic piece of very black humour; darkly funny it intermingles the horror of crime with the banalities of an everyday existence, connecting it in terms of style to the surreal art of Escher.

With *Softcops* Churchill reprimands patriarchal society for its use of power to constrain and infantilize: society treats its prisoners like children and its children as prisoners[97]; and, although 'the question of power remains a total enigma', 'to speak on this subject, to force the institutionalized networks of information to listen, to produce names, to point the finger of accusation, to find targets, is the first step in the reversal of power and the initiation of new struggles against existing forms of power'.[98]

The Capitalist Machine: *Serious Money*

The indictment of western society continues with *Serious Money*, a hugely successful West End play. The West is presented as one huge subsuming capitalist machine which transforms its repressed desire into greed which attaches itself to corruption as the sick socius[99] is infected with desire (now turned upon itself) for serious money.[100]

> Our societies exhibit a marked taste for all codes—codes foreign or exotic—but this taste [for 'the dollar, short-term migrating capital, the floating of currencies, the new means of financing and credit'] is destructive and morbid [...] Our society produces schizos[101] the same way it produces Prell shampoo or Ford cars, the only difference being that the schizos are not saleable.[102]

Capitalist production arrests freedom, transforming its subjects into sickness, 'not only nominally but in reality', confining heroes as madmen, keeping its artists and scientists under surveillance so as to ensure that they are absorbed by the laws of the market. Capitalism is a 'gigantic machine for social repression—psychic repression [...] a socius [...] more pitiless than any other'.[103]

The overt materialism that Tory Britain experienced in the 80s is satirized in this play which is peopled with characters who display the ideology of a cash register. 1987 saw *Serious Money* enjoy highly successful runs at the Royal Court and on its subsequent transfer to the West End. The dark comedy which examined a world simultaneously 'appalling and exciting'[104] was frenetic, fast-paced and topical in that it opened shortly after the Big Bang, the Guinness scandal and the Boesky scam. The quick-silver scenes demonstrate one of Churchill's best crafted pieces of stage art. The verse form added rhythm, comedy and movement to this high-tempo piece which opens with a scene from Thomas Shadwell's *The Stockjobbers* (1692) connecting the 80s ethos with the past with the implication that so-called 'Thatcherite' materialism was not new, merely newly visible. Reinelt comments that '[t]he similarity of the turn of the eighteenth- century with our present moment may be said to consist in part of a revolution in banking and monetary policy. The rise of the great merchant class meant that money, not just property, could dominate and control the state apparatus and that overseas markets could help insure this fiscal "revolution".'[105] The stockjobbers 'lowering and heightening of shares' in commodities real (mousetraps) and fictitious (walking under water) goes back three centuries, and as they fade the business-like reality of twentieth century wheeling and dealing comes to life.

> GREVILLE (on phone)
>
> It's quite a large placement and what we've done is taken them onto our own books, one of the first deals of this kind we've done since Big Bang, yes (...) It's Unicorn Hotels, whom of course you know, they've acquired a chain of hotels in Belgium, and the main thing is they're a perfect mirror of their hotels here, 70 per cent business, 3 and 4 star. They acquired them for sixteen million, the assets are in fact valued at eleven million but that's historic and they're quite happy about that. The key to the deal is there's considerable earnings enhancement. It was a private owner who got into trouble, not bankrupt but a considerable squeeze on his assets, and they were able to get them cheap. I can offer you a million shares, they're 63 to 4 in the market, I can let you have them for 62 ½ net. At the moment the profits are fourteen million pretax which is eleven million, the shares pay 4.14 with a multiple of 13.3. (*Serious Money*, Act I, pp.197–8)
>
> Memory has become a bad thing. Above all, there is no longer any belief, and the capitalist is merely striking a pose when he bemoans the fact that nowadays no one believes in anything any more. Language no longer signifies something that must be believed, it indicates rather what is going to be done, something that the shrewd or the competent are able to decode, to half understand.[106]
>
> With the new hotels we expect to see a profit of twenty million next year paying 5.03 with the multiple falling to 12, so it's very attractive. This is only the beginning of a major push into Europe. Essentially the frontiers have been pushed back quite considerably. (Act I, p.198)

In this piece, Churchill puts her technique of dialogue overlap to a different, equally skilful use. The ethos of the world of high finance and futures trading is well captured in the economical, technical, dialogue:

> GRIMES and his MATE in gilts dealing room of Klein Merrick.
> SCILLA on Liffe floor. Each has two phones.

GRIMES (to MATE).
I'm long on these bastards.
MATE (to GRIMES).
3's a nice sell. They'd be above the mark.
GRIMES (on phone).
Scilla? Sell at 3.
SCILLA (on two phones. To floor)
10 at 3. 10 at 3.
(On phone 2)
That's March is it?
MATE (phone).
6 Bid.
(Act I, p.198)

The productive essence of capitalism functions or "speaks" only in the language of signs—a technical means of expression—imposed on it by merchant capital or the axiomatic of the market.[107]

As the scene progresses the dialogue becomes staccato, bullet-like, rapid-fire:

JAKE (phone)
The Mori poll put the Tories four up.
SALES 1.
We're going to lose power any minute, that's official.
DEALER.
What the fuck?
JAKE (phone).
So the three month interbank sterling rate—no it's a tick under -
SALES 1.
We have Milan three months 11½.
JAKE (phone).
There's a discrepancy between band 2 and band 3 (…) I thought it might give us some arbitrage possibilities.
DEALER.
Come on come on come on guy.
SALES 1.
What's with the ECU linked deposits for Nomura?
SALES 2.
Now hurry hurry hurry guys hurry.

(Act I, p.203).

Churchill uses her hallmark technique of overlapping dialogue in yet another mode to convey the sharp sense of urgency and immediacy common to financial futures markets where time is of the utmost essence.[108]

'Far more entertaining and far more informative than a dozen textbooks',[109] *Serious Money* was a 'mixture of roulette and space invaders, the third world debt, the cocaine market, sex scandal and image boosting forays, an inquiry by the Department of Trade and Industry'.[110]

Multi-racial and dual-gendered, the world of trading and finance cuts across social class to bring together a group of high achievers whose only criteria for success are ruthlessness, greed, and an amorality which pervade dominantly over all their actions which make them serious money.

> There is only one machine, that of the great mutant decoded flow—cut off from goods—and one class of servants, the decoding bourgeoisie, the class that decodes the castes and the statuses, and that draws from the machine an undivided flow of income convertible into consumer and production goods, a flow on which profits and wages are based.[111]

Not content to satirize the children of capitalism who throng the City, Churchill's irony points with a malevolence befitting Congreve to the millionaires of the third world who, uncaring of the stark poverty of their masses, match their first world counterparts in their frenzied bid to make more wealth.

> The process of deterritorialization of the workforce goes from the centre to the periphery, from the developed countries to the underdeveloped countries, which do not constitute a separate world, but rather an essential component of the worldwide capitalist machine. [...] This peripheral proletariat generates an immense surplus value, to a point where it is no longer the developed countries that supply the underdeveloped countries with capital, but quite the opposite. Accumulation is continually reproducing itself.[112]

'My people will starve to death (...) Let them rot. I'm sick of it', mulls a Peruvian business woman (played by an Indian in the production), while the Ghanaian Ajibala has 'learnt well' from his 'colonial masters: one makes money from other people's disasters.'

The murder (or suicide) of Jake, the public schoolboy with connections, is the central backbone which holds together the 'plot'; diverse in its implications in that it serves to foreground the majoritarian attitudes of a money-making 'socius'. The social relations of the characters criss-cross in this space intensely focused on serious money as individuals, friendships and even familial connections are destroyed in the wake of the destruction of greed. While Corman cares only about the deal: 'The deal's no way affected by his death. (The deal's the priority.)' (Act I, p.217), Jake's sister Scilla's predominant motive is to locate Jake's secreted millions. Blinded by her greed she even suspects their father, a prominent stockbroker, of being 'in' on the deal, perhaps even an accessory to his own son's death. Jake's death is a scandal, and as a LIFFE dealer wonders if it's 'worth trading on', Scilla replies: 'There might be a run on sterling if you're lucky'. (Act I, p.247).

The logistics of the cleverly named London International Financial Futures Exchange, always referred to by its acronym 'Liffe' in the Capitalist

Machine, Albion, is expounded to the audience, pantomime-fashion, by
Scilla:

> Trading options and futures looks tricky if you don't understand it.
> But if you're good at market timing you can make out like a bandit.
> (It's the most fun I've had since playing cops and robbers with Jake when we were
> children.)
> A simple way of looking at futures is take a commodity,
> Coffee, cocoa, sugar, zinc, pork bellies, copper, aluminium, oil -
> I always think pork bellies is an oddity.
> (They could just as well have a future in chicken wings.)
> Suppose you're a coffee trader and there's a drought in Brazil like last year or sup-
> pose there is a good harvest, either way you might lose out,
> So you can buy a futures contract that works in the opposite direction so you're
> covered against loss, and that's what futures are basically about.
> But of course you don't have to take delivery of anything at all.
> You can buy and sell futures contracts without any danger of ending up with ten
> tons of pork bellies in the hall.
> On the floor of Liffe the commodity is money.
> You can buy and sell money, you can buy and sell absence of money, debt, which
> used to strike me as funny.
> [...]
> I found O levels weren't much use, the best qualified people are street traders.
> But I love it because it's like playing a cross between roulette and space invaders.
>   (Act I, pp.243–4)

There may be only 'one class of servants' on the floor of Liffe which
doesn't mean that women always get equal or even respectful treatment.
Sexist jokes and crude remarks abound:

> Vince: Why is a clitoris like a filofax?
> Dave and others: Every cunt's got one.
>   (Act II, p.302)

Scilla says: 'I was terrified when I started because there aren't many girls
and they line up to watch you walk.' (Act I, p.244) And the women get
propositioned. Non-inculcated women have to learn tolerance toward their
sexist colleagues. If the ethos is rude, the language is crude as the song at the
end of Act I reflects:

> You're back to front come on you cunt don't give me any strife
> You in or out? Don't hang about, you're on the floor of Liffe!

While the symbolically and double-edged named company Al-bi-on
buys and sells, Liffe goes on. The mystery surrounding Jake's death never reveals itself as the Russian roulette which serves to bind the elements which

make up the world of trading, speculation and capitalist hunger climaxes to a frenzied crescendo on stage. As Victoria Radin commented, the subject is 'the Big Bang in the City but [the] real theme is the naked ruthlessness and greed that characterizes much of life in Britain in the late 1980s'.[113]

Serious Money is a female playwright's essay into what was, until recently, male territory: a comment on the shifting ground where capitalism, power and politics meet, presaged by David Hare and Howard Brenton's *Pravda* (1985). Stylistically, *Serious Money* shares some links with Arnold Wesker's *The Journalists* (1974) although Churchill's foray into this fast-paced territory is original in its theatrical techniques which best convey the urgency and dynamism inherent in the play, outdistancing other mainstream efforts.

Capitalism and Schizophrenia: *The Skriker* as Oedipus and Anti-Oedipus

(...) it is only in history that one can discover the sole concrete *a priori* from which mental illness draws, with the empty opening up of its possibility, its necessary figures.[114]

Western society demonstrated its steadily eroding foundations of belief-systems through the twentieth century, replaced by the unstable machinating repressed desire of the capitalist impulse which turned in on itself, breeding ever-expanding markets and consumers. The latter are desirous of the material of goods and services instead of the ideal Deleuzean socius which would undoubtedly be constituted by an abstract space which would formulate itself by the coming together of intensely lived immanent social relations where each healthy individuated being is inseparable from the external natural world in a merging of the human being with all that constitutes the natural, the lived and the holistic. Here, fixed orders of society—norms, *mores*, the majoritarian view, the herd instinct, the dominant repressive constraining ideology—are freed up and cease to subjectify, cease to lead us to desire our own repression. It is when man becomes 'a chlorophyll- or a photosynthesis-machine, or at least [is able to] slip his body into such machines' when man—*Homo natura*—becomes a 'being who is in intimate contact with the profound life of all forms or all types of beings, who is responsible for even the stars and the animal life, and who ceaselessly plugs an organ-machine into an energy-machine, a tree into his body' that society will cease to breed neuroses, psychoses, schizophrenics who are ill and sick. Capitalist society breeds illness as the consumer desires material goods instead of abstract values which foster health in society, as it replaces the foundation-stones of meaning by the quest for serious money.[115] As the ancient skriker skrikes[116]:

They used to leave cream in a sorcerer's apprentice. Gave the brownie a pair of trousers to wear have you gone? Now they hate us and hurt hurtle faster and master. They poison me in my rivers of blood poisoning makes my arm swelter. Can't get them out of our head strong. (*The Skriker*, p.4).

In a sick society the schizo is really ill.[117] The psychological effects of the triadic oedipal hierarchy which manifests itself in every aspect of lived relations in society, a triangulated schema, the basic mediator of the patriarchal impulse, produces subjects who conform to the hierarchy of gender. Repressed and repressing, the two characters who nomadically traverse the stage-space of *The Skriker* (1994) are the young Lily, heavily pregnant, and her friend, Josie, mentally ill. The theatrical space of their everyday world which metamorphoses into an underworld is the domain of the skriker who is non-genderized and all-powerful. This gigantic myth opens the play; as the schizo monologue flows in both directions: schizo as a sick nation ('rivers of blood') and schizo as free ('sunlight of heart'), the space of a hospital looms, bearing the ill Josie and the deserted Lily along with Kelpie, part youth part horse, a *centaur* or the ideal Deleuzean *homo natura*.

That there is a place for myth and fairytale in the contemporary world is the statement that the writer seems to make in the grotesque and absurdist fantasy world she creates within the play. The ancient myth functions as repressed desire turning back on itself to desire its own repression as demonstrated in the figure of the skriker itself. Like her earlier plays *A Mouthful of Birds* and *Lives of the Great Poisoners*, *The Skriker* makes use of choreographed dance and music to offer an expressionist director's theatre. This effort however, is an individual one (the earlier two were collaborations) which attempts to create a setting interwoven with obscure British folklore with pseudo-realist contemporary characters who move in spaces which transform, chameleon-like from an everyday world to an underworld fusing both in the process. In a method only faintly reminiscent of the dinner scene of *Top Girls* which brought together, impossibly, several women from different time periods in a contemporary British restaurant, with this piece Churchill ventures into 'folklore and the darker parts of our collective unconscious in hope of finding fresh metaphors for that mad muddled place, England'.[118]

The skriker, a figure from ancient folklore, both 'shapechanger' and 'death portent', opens the play in a language identified variously as 'dense pun-packed Joycean prose',[119] 'children's language' and 'schizophrenic language'.[120] It does indeed sound like a Deleuzean 'schizzes-flow', and the monologue is a lateral flight from reason, a dark verbal kaleidoscope which draws its bizarre substance from the national subconscious in its eclectic mix of fairytale ('spun the lowest form of wheatstraw into gold, raw into roar (…)') to Biblical warning of the anti-Christ/anti-Oedipus which presages twentieth century environmental disaster ('the beast is six six six o'clock in the morning becomes electric stormy petrel bomb (…)'); obscenity ('or pin prick cock a doodle do you feel it?') and gruesome detail ('put my hand to the baby and scissors seizures seize you sizzle (…)').

The opening monologue is a promise of the subverted fairytale with the reminder that not every fairystory-myth-nursery rhyme has a happy ending:

> open bluebeards one bloody chamber maid eat the one forbidden fruit of the tree top down comes cradle and baby (…)

as the audience is directly addressed, provoking complicity and laughter:

> No't ain't, says I, no tainted meat me after the show me what you've got.

Through the everyday spaces of Lily and Josie roam the unconscious and hallucinatory figures of ancient folklore. Though the figures of the kelpie, the bogle, RawHeadAndBloody Bones, Johnnie Squarefoot and the others such as the thrumpins and the bluemen have a rich history which ought to have enriched the fabric of the piece as a whole, their presence upon the stage is wordless; symbolic perhaps but also superficial as each remains an unexplained figure, an obscure myth, lending by his unexplicated presence, to the sur-reality of the space conjured up and the central myth of the skriker.

The skriker is the Nietzschean anti-christ and the Deleuzean anti-oedipus but, in this piece, not merely circumscribed by figures of British folk-lore but a mythology of the island in itself as indicated by the first few words: 'Heard her boast beast a roast beef eater'. The first appearance of the skriker is as a patient in the hospital. The repressive triad is made up by Kelpie, a *Homo natura* which is completely repressed as he is boxed up, motionless, in a coffin-like prison in a corner of the set. The flow of desire is represented as dammed up, blocked in a space where everyone is sick.[121]

The skriker transforms good deeds (a positive abstract) into society's ideal abstract of repressed desire, money, as pound coins spill from Lily's mouth. Josie is similarly dealt with as her words transform into live toads.[122] Josie's time in the underworld is a brief un-noticeable instant in earth time, but the end of the play sees the removal of the parental points of reference in the oedipal triad as skriker takes Lily away, leaving her child orphaned, as it grows up to reproduce children of its own. The skriker predicts the end of the world:

> Have you noticed the large number of meteorological phenomena lately? Earth-quakes. Volcanoes. Drought. […] The increase of sickness. It was always possible to

think whatever your personal problem, there's always nature. Spring will return
even if it's without me. Nobody loves me but at least it's a sunny day. This has been
a comfort to people as long as they've existed. But it's not available anymore. Sorry.
Nobody loves me and the sun's going to kill me. Spring will return and nothing will
grow. (pp.43–4)

In this environment Josie is 'the artificial schizophrenic found in mental
institutions: a limp rag forced into autistic behaviour'. In a world without
love desire perishes into illness; we are sick with desire.[123] The play, at one
level, is the delusion of the sick schizophrenic, Josie; whereas the ideal
schizo, the skriker is genderless, ageless, timeless, and miraculous. Josie's inner world is given corporeality and substance by the characters of the play,
the manifestation of the underworldly beings representing the phantoms of
Josie's hallucinatory existence. Josie's own conviction that everyone she encounters, from the derelict hag to the child in the park is the same person
(as indeed they all are, the shapechanging skriker) validates the paranoiac
tendency of schizophrenia. As a TLS critic noted, the overlapping action on
the stage creates the illusion that the creatures are a dimension of consciousness: 'an expression of the violence and confusion in the minds of the
characters'.[124]

Conceived as a 'love story' by the author, 'a love story between the three
main characters', Josie, Lily and the androgynous shapechanging mythical
portent of death, the skriker makes up the third point of the triangulated
schema of repressed desire. The players in this love story are 'damaged' and
damaging in their attachment to each other with the skriker representing,
initially, society's repressed desire concretized as a sick person; later it is the
oedipal child, an 'angry needy demanding neglected wanting to be loved'
one who attaches her/him/it-self first to Josie, then to Lily to offer them tangible manifestation of society's repressed desires in the form of money and
filth juxtaposed with toads, which signify healing and luck in eastern mythology.[125] On this level, the play is a trope for the damaged contemporary
world, a ringing metaphor for the loss of love, and the arbitrary nature of the
meting out of rewards.

The impact of the piece in performance is an effect resembling 'an impossible object or a painting by Escher' (Churchill's description of her early
play, *Traps*), as the disparate ingredients of the work are suspended or detached from their everyday meaning: damaged. The damaged schizo language of the skriker compares with Eugene Ionesco's experiment with the
banalities of everyday speech in *The Bald Prima Donna* (*La cantatrice chauve*,
1950) where the language ultimately breaks down into nonsense syllables.
The skriker's language, like the language of Ionesco's everyday characters

makes sense in a surreal and disembodied manner, as some level of communication is achieved however damaged the sense of language. Churchill, however, sculpts a form of speech which taps the collective unconscious of the audience, bringing to the fore vestiges of forgotten myth and folklore interwoven with fragments of popular fairytale which makes it that level of language which one might term a 'constructed *langue*'. This uses disjointed aspects of communication common to a specific speech community, interweaving symbols both conscious and unconscious, enhanced by nonverbal and disembodied modes of communication such as dance, gesture, movement, music.

After a long period of politicization fostered largely by the theatre collectives she worked with, Churchill returned in 1994 to the experimental formats and eclectic content she seems to prefer when working on her own. This piece connects by way of style to her earlier *Traps* and *Owners*, an experimental fluctuating style which at its worst emerged in *Icecream* (1989) and at its best perhaps in the *Top Girls* dinner scene. At the Cottesloe platform, Churchill revealed that she had been obsessed with a surreal fantasy for more than ten years; and having written the longer passages of the skriker's speech several years earlier, she went on to write other plays which absorbed several of the ideas originally intended for *The Skriker*. As a piece the play combines two unmistakeably post-lapsarian worlds[126] where innocence and experience interweave until they become indistinguishable in a fantasy which recalls aspects of earlier plays where the reality presented on stage is far from the conventional mode of realism, bordering on the surreal and the absurd. There is no conventional rhythmic wholeness in either the structure, content or the disjuncted orchestration of movement and music which reflect the contrast of images from the different worlds of the imaginary and the 'real', reflecting even in the lone black passerby (who is surrounded by, and simultaneously part of, unexplained western myth) a trope for the confusion of coetaneous existence in contemporary Britain.

The style and form escape easy definitions; the whole fabric is rendered potent as it resounds simultaneously and at every level with a multiplicity of interpretation which is perhaps the hallmark of a really good play. It also, quite successfully, entertains.

Churchill demonstrates a strong interest in the past and its relation to the present, evoking past events with an eye on the analysis of the here-and-now as *Top Girls*, *Serious Money*, *Fen*, *Cloud Nine*, *Icecream* and *Softcops* all open with a past connection which highlights a present theme, from the influence of a colonial past, the grasping materialism of society to the position of the contemporary woman within it. These themes reveal themselves as functions of a various historical lineage as the past is revealed to be symptomatic of the future in a discontinuous continuity. Seen historically *The Skriker* emerges as a celebration of national heritage in the unearthing of ancient myth, as these unexplained figures populate the stage in a blend of man and nature, wordlessly and symbolically traversing each level of theatrical space. The lone black passerby is always on the outside, always on the fringe, a lithe dancing figure, not menacing not threatening, possessing no power not even of dance as the Green Lady moves more passionately and with more sonorous rhythm. The black person in Churchill's plays always seems neglected; here, passionless and powerless. The passerby is not indicated textually as black, and in the production appeared only briefly as a dancing figure on the outskirts.

Churchill's theatre occupies two seemingly divergent zones: one, seriously leftist and political, resulting from the influence of the two theatre groups with which she occasionally collaborated, and also that of director and founder member of Joint Stock, Max Stafford-Clark, whose many ideas found concretization in the writer's work. The other Churchill, aspects of whom are almost always present, is one of weird and dark humour, the surreal, phantasmagoria, neo- expressionistic. Her original experimental theatrical device of the stratagem of overlapping dialogue to near perfection is an interchange invested with a chameleon quality as it produces varied effects with every play: establishing sisterhood and an eagerness of sharing in *Top Girls* whilst giving that highly successful frenetic edge to the frenzy of *Serious Money*. Male academics remain embarrassingly behind in their critiques of feminist drama, as they project their sexist biases into the interpretation. Don Shiach remarks: 'The characters [of *Top Girls*] are all so taken up with their own lives and self-importance that they make bad listeners and so constantly interrupt one another'.[127] That any party of six at table would, in real life, talk across and over each other is never considered. This stratagem is actually Churchill's extension of and contribution to the convention of realism which she uses in non-realistic settings. In *Serious Money* the verse contributes to the feeling of stage(d)-reality, whereas in other plays it is the only 'concession' to realism. The investigative, querying nature of her themes result in an expressionism which is at once individual and anti-realistic. An admirer of the artist Escher, she is likewise able to take the stuff of everyday life and present it uniquely, suspended in the time and space of the stage imagination, generating new questions. Her eccentric and subjective view channels ideologically, through transformed post-Brecht British theatre, a drama of quiet protest at the values and norms of contemporary British society. Marrying newly constructed, Brechtian-influenced morphology to radical, often eccentric content in expressionistic overtures, Churchill's reper-toire of devices vary with the subject of the play: the disjointed and episodic structure of *Light Shining* and *Mad Forest* reflect the political and social up-heavals of the plays; the dreamlike and nightmarish atmosphere of *The Skriker* and *Traps* reflect the double-edged content of good/evil, ac-tive/passive, yin/yang; the ironic distancing often used puts the audience in a strange position of authority as they partake of a viewpoint denied the char-acters as in *Softcops* and *Top Girls*; other expressonistic modes are employed such as using stereotypes instead of individual personalities, as in *Light Shin-ing in Buckinghamshire*. These devices lessen the dependence on plot and character to allow this original and imaginative dramatist to continue to present some of the leading pieces in transgressive, transformative feminist malestream drama.

The evolving of the socialist writer's feminism places her alongside the informed feminist dramatists of our *fin de siècle* as she explores gender issues, the sexual and economic liberation of her generation, and a rewriting of his-tory from the perspective of the gendered other. Although she avoids deal-ing with postcolonial issues (see *Cloud Nine*, above) she successfully essays into male territory, dealing with politics and war, money and power as she breaks the bounds of mainstream drama taking it into the realm of feminism, effecting a ruptural break as male and female dramatists share common ter-rain, heralding a new equality in the making of British drama, divided per-haps only by perspective.

CHAPTER THREE

WHITE WOMEN'S MYTHOLOGIES
Pam Gems

Gems [snatches] back the truth about women's lives out of the jaws of a male-constructed history.
—Mary Remnant, quoted in *Rage and Reason*

A woman's (re)discovery of herself can only signify the possibility [...] of never being simply one. It is a sort of universe in expansion for which no limits could be fixed (...)
—Luce Irigaray, 'This Sex which is not One'

Woman un-thinks the unifying, regulating history that homogenizes and channels forces, herding contradictions into a single battlefield.
—Hélène Cixous, 'The Laugh of the Medusa'

AS JACQUES LACAN put it in *Encore*, 'Woman' does not exist.[1] Woman is not a singular category but a plurality and a diversity. In fact, it is not 'women's experience' itself but thinking from a contradictory position, that produces feminist knowledge,[2] and this chapter aims to chart the possibility of a radical plurality of voices within a specific category of gender, voices which speak from the contradictory positions of bisexuality (*Queen Christina* and *Marlene*), whoredom (*Camille, Piaf* and Stas), and the feminine/feminist split (*Loving Women*).

Born in 1925, Pam Gems came late to writing. Her experience spans three generations—the war, early inclusive second-wave feminism, and the later separationist third moment which heralded a death knell for popular feminism. Gems' non-separationist integrated approach to gender speaks for her early political commitment.[3] Her essay 'Imagination and Gender' echoes Cixous and reflects on the need for gendered writing: '[You can't] write other than from yourself. If you're a woman you're bound to write as a woman'.[4]

Perhaps it is because Gems did not write seriously for the theatre until her forties that her feminist consciousness emerged onto the British stage with a mature mixture of empathy and distance. Possibly, too, it is this mix that allowed her to make the transition from the fringe, where her work first appeared, to the established theatres where her plays have been so frequently produced.[5]

She is the only feminist dramatist in the mainstream who, despite being imbricated within the dominant heterosexual matrix, has consistently reflected on normative and regulatory ideals such as heterosexuality; and specifically, reflected on the construction of women's sexuality in the forced matrix of exclusionary political Other: the prostitute. Despite her feminist political commitment, Gems is the only woman dramatist to have been produced by the Royal Shakespeare Company five times: *Queen Christina* (1977), *The Danton Affair* (1986) and *The Blue Angel* (1991); *Camille* and *Piaf* and then *Marlene* on London's West End in 1997.[6] Her gender-based thinking is conditioned by the early 70s inclusive approach to class, race, colour; grassroots feminism for every woman.[7]

> Today's chemically mutated woman has been released from the murderous dangers of traditional childbed. We are able to begin to explore, to become aware of ourselves autonomously, to be on our own feet, and to write—and rewrite our own history. We have to discover who and what we are. We must discern our own needs, our demands [...] And of course a woman writer cannot but be involved in this vital and exciting and profound movement. Being allowed in, being asked to join is one thing. But we are half the world, and this demands proper accommodation.[8]

Gems is careful to distinguish between political polemic and subversion as a function of drama; in her work subversion becomes the means and the end of dramatic writing as she undercuts mythology, heterosexism and 'woman' as she subverts dominant ideology.

> I think the phrase 'feminist writer' is absolutely meaningless because it implies polemic, and polemic is about changing things in a direct political way. Drama is subversive.[9]

Gems did not initially see herself as a feminist writer for reasons perhaps similar to her metaphoric construct, Queen Christina, who failed to understand the blue-stockings' open hostility to men, and the separate non-integrated lives they chose to lead. Gems' subject matter is gender-based as a direct result of feeling the need to right the balance and give women a voice and presence on the masculine formulated stage; the need to see woman as centrestage in a collective solidarity which never implies a hostility between the sexes.

> The antagonism between the sexes has been painful, an indictment of our age. It is true that many women have been drawn, properly, to the Women's Movement af-

ter abuse by bad husbands, fathers [...] they have had hopes pushed aside, seeing brothers favoured from infancy. It makes for grievances, fear and resentment. But, as often, one sees men hopelessly damaged by women [...] their mothers. *We cannot separate ourselves.*[10]

In this articulation of her belief that men as well as women are both victims and perpetrators of the system, caught up within it, inexorably damaged and damaging, she echoes a poststructuralist perspective. Surprisingly, for a dramatist whose central roles are undeniably for women, she [has] 'sometimes wondered why there hasn't been more backlash, militant groups formed by men, in retaliation [to feminism]'.[11] 'There will always be the chauvinists among us, *of both sexes* (...)'[12] '[but] if we believe that there is only Us, then something is released, something egalitarian (...)'[13] Gems seems to believe in a kind of bi-sexuality in which both genders can merge and contribute toward an integrity and ethics in identity formation; a bi-sexuality which is a construction by an integration of genders: an 'Us' which is reflected in the characterization of Christina's bi-sexuality as metaphor.

Although Gems' central characters are women, it has not been her purpose unnaturally to alienate them from interacting with men. Her integrationist approach seems separate from her almost *her*storical writing, until we realise that her almost non-controversial stance to the history of drama (which has been undeniably male) emanates from the belief that writing is a gendered phenomenon. If the lineage of English drama is male it is because the writers have all been male. This may seem (almost) simple as an approach but when read in conjunction with her texts, this belief emerges as a supportive structure for writing which is always female/feminist and on the side of women, penned, undeniably, by a woman for women. She endeavours, moreover, to delineate women as a category within which lies limitless possibilities. She (re) discovers; she un-thinks the unifying regulatory history which seeks to homogenize and categorize a multiplicity of voices and gendered positions under the single rubric, 'Woman'. She is Cixous' woman writing woman.

Queen Christina: Identity Politics

I love the storm and fear the calm.[14]

[H]omosexuality is as limiting as heterosexuality: the ideal should be to be capable of loving a woman or a man, either, a human being, without feeling fear, restraint or obligation.[15]

Bisexuality unsettles certainties: straight, gay, lesbian. It has affinities with all of these, and is delimited by none. It is, then, an identity that is also not an identity, a sign of the certainty of ambiguity, the stability of instability, a category that defines and defeats categorizations.[16]

Hélène Cixous endorses an 'other bisexuality' which is multiple, variable and ever changing, an excess which arises out of a 'non-exclusion either of the difference or of one sex'. Characteristic of this 'other bisexuality' is a storm of differences which are stirred up, pursued and thereby increased. *L'ecriture féminine*, then, 'will always surpass the discourse that regulates the phallic system'; it 'can never be theorized, enclosed, coded'. This 'dynamized' writing is constantly in exchange, a bisexual process which is 'infinitely dynamized by an incessant process of exchange from one subject to another'.[17] Queen Christina is intended by Gems to be a metaphor for the bisexual and constructed gender identity of contemporary woman. She is this Cixousian storm of excess, an overspill of dual-gendered sexuality who functions as mythical sign for contemporary fe-male sexuality. Both Fe(y) and Male, Fe/Male, this is *herstory* dramaturgically contemporized by Pam Gems.

The Royal Court turned down this radically subversive playtext in 1974—'they said it was too sprawly, too expensive to do' and that '*it would appeal more to women*'. In an interview with 'Spare Rib', Gems said: 'That really got to me. I mean would they ever have said, 'We can't do this play, it will appeal to men?'[18] It was, however, the first play scripted by a contemporary woman to be produced by the Royal Shakespeare Company in 1977.

Queen Christina is historiographic in its method and approach as are the later *Camille* and *Piaf, The Blue Angel* and the 90s *Stanley* and *Marlene*. Gems undercuts mythologized figures in a Barthesian way, enabling a deconstruction of the received notions which these icons are culturally imbricated within. These mythical morphologies are 'signs' within and of western culture, cultural artefact that *is* Barthesian 'myth'. These can be defined as cultural significations which accrue on the linguistic sign, reducing the latter to a signifier which then functions alongside the cultural signified to form the associative function which postulates itself as a greater sign; a culturally specific, historically specific, constructed meaning which is *myth*. Myth functions as 'natural' meaning rather than artifice; it is naturalized in the psyche of the reception community rather than perceived as fictive.[19] Gems' focus on each myth destroys it—not, as in Barthes, by cynically making its intention obvious—but, by subversively deploying it to radical ends such as the de-construction of regulatory heterosexuality or hierarchical and dominant ideologies. This does not, as in Barthes, merely demystify or unmask, but gives it a sardonic twist which is 'allowed' onto the mainstream stages as it (the subject) is presented in the mystificatory *guise* of myth.[20] As Barthes notes, the worn-out state of each myth 'can be recognized by the arbitrariness of its signification'; just as 'the whole of Molière is seen in a doctor's ruff',[21] so all of Piaf-as-myth is signified on stage in the first strains of '*je ne regrette rien*'; but the contemporary re-presentation of gender-identity-as-construction, Christina-as-metaphor is unrecognizable as she lopes on stage as an unbecoming disabled fe/male. These myths, outworn as well as newly constructed, accrue significance as the play proceeds and become 'garrulous, a speech wholly at the service of the concept.'[22] Their meaning is distorted by the concept the dramatist is deploying each myth for; the dramatist-mythologist of gender allows a 'repetition of the concept [e.g., compulsory heterosexuality] through different forms' allowing her audience 'to decipher the myth'. 'It is the insistence [of the concept] which reveals its intention.''But this distortion is not an obliteration' but, in fact, garrulous not merely with memory, but with *new, potentially deconstructive meaning.*[23]

These white mythologies are *herstories*. Feminism is a movement which has theoretically influenced multiple disciplines, breaking, in its wake, the bounds of history. To historicize, for the feminist, would involve a re-search and a re-writing of traditional history to re-discover women where there exist records only of great men. This writing of the history of women is named herstory by separationists.[24] A few fringe dramatists and women's theatre groups have re-written historical as well as canonical drama since second-wave feminism began its task of consciousness raising, but none in so sweeping and consistent a manner as Gems' de-construction of ideology via myth-breaking.[25] Herstorians do not concern themselves merely with 'political' figures, since the feminist endorsement of the personal as political, signifying the largely twentieth century movement of women from the private domestic sphere of the home to the outer public sphere. Herstorian dramatists de-construct patriarchal cultural ideologies operative in politicized private and public spaces. The feminist endorsement of the personal as political is the crux of feminism:

> Feminism is resoundingly political. One of the slogans that is perhaps most familiar is the claim that 'the personal is the political'. By this light, it seems, feminism refuses the gendered distinction of a male sphere of public life from a female realm of domestic economy. Feminism insists that politics is not something that happens between men alone: the supposedly natural order of relations between men and women is itself political, a matter for discussion and struggle. Even traditional notions of the nature of the political, which exclude or severely restrict female participation, have a gender politics.[26]

Indeed, feminism since the movement for suffrage has been deeply political. In feminist dramaturgy too, then, the political is imbricated in every decision. Bourgeois feminist critics such as Susan E. Bassnett-McGuire have criticized Gems 'for giving a single actor such a central role and for allowing her feminist heroine to become too embroiled in her personal problems.'[27] The fallaciousness of this argument is that whilst it privileges the collective over the individual (thus Bassnett-McGuire endorses the Magdalena Project whilst condemning Gems' individual authorship) it sets store in what is, finally, a masculinist negation of emotion and feelings. Seen from a broadly feminist viewpoint, the political significance in dramaturgical terms of a single strong female char-actor is an attempt to right the balance against a history of strong central male roles. A role full of emotional turmoil also has an historical parallel: who was more full of self-doubt than Shakespeare's Hamlet?

> O that this too too sullied flesh would melt,
> Thaw and resolve itself into a dew,
> Or that the Everlasting had not fix'd
> His canon 'gainst self-slaughter. (I, ii)

Gems skilfully creates forceful women whose contradictions and conflicts parallel the self-doubt of contemporary western woman. Her mythologies are metaphors for many a contemporary dilemma of gender. Moreover, in 1996 she created a strong central male character, the artist-figure Stanley Spencer, revealing that her art and ideology embrace both genders.

The contemporary feminist search to understand the cultural nature of sex and gender identity subtexts much of Christina's dramaturgical character development. Diane Elam's summary of feminist positions on gender and sex is as follows: '[...] is "women" primarily a natural or a cultural category? The rough distinction between sex and gender can be made as follows: either sex is privileged as a biological attribute upon which a gender ideology is imposed, or sex is denied as merely the ideological mystification that obscures cultural facts about gender. [...] some feminists have argued that sex is not natural at all, that there is no natural identity behind the masks of gender, there are only the masks'.[28] Judith Butler's is the leading argument for the construction of sex. She argues that sex is a regulatory ideal which functions as a norm but is also a part of the regulatory practice that *produces* the bodies it governs. Sex is a reiterative and citational practice by which discourse produces the effect 'sex'.[29] I accept that sex is constructed inasfar as sexes are regarded as two, and anomalous cases are forced (by the medical profession which serves as the regulatory practice of society in bodies that matter, to use Butler's phrase) into occupying one or the other site. Certainly, as Butler has it, the performativity of *gender* is reiteration of a norm or a set of norms. It conceals or dissimulates the convention of which it is a repetition, making performativity a kind of citationality. Sex is imbricated within and formulated by discursive practices which compel the differentiated citations and approximations into binary sites called 'feminine' and 'masculine'. The production and articulation of sex is thus forced into *materialization* of a norm, constructing bodies that matter within the heterosexual matrix.[30]

The playtext of *Queen Christina* is Gems' attempt to portray the flux, uncertainty and instability which surrounds gender identity in postmodern culture. In a note prefacing the play, Gems explains: 'All plays are metaphors, and the dilemma of the real Christina, reared and educated as a man for the Swedish throne, and then asked to marry and breed for the succession, is perhaps not irrelevant today.' The playtext also offers a critique of western dualistic thought as it celebrates the interlinking of difference and identity. Although the ideal of unity of oppositions goes back to metaphysical foundations in western philosophy, contemporary post-Enlightenment thought is deconstructive as difference is understood to undermine the notion of stable identity; identity which is always in process, a *becoming* which is always in formation. Thus identity can never be stable nor natural as traditional western epistemology assumed it to be.[31] There is no *stable* subject: as Butler puts it, 'the "doer" is variably constructed in and through the deed.' Being constituted by discourse does not mean being determined by it nor does it imply that subjects are mired in 'culture' or 'discourse' The *supplément*, the excess of predicates which intersect to formulate feminist or gender identities is illimitable. Thus, there is no prediscursive 'I'.[32]

Queen Christina's body (sex) as well as gender refuse the conformity required of them, her privileged status perhaps activating a will to be produced differently. Perceiving male and female in terms of binary oppositions, (as western patriarchies do to make a forced classification of the sexes), leads us to a false position. It was originally Hegel's view that the laws of logic and the laws of nature are one, therefore difference should not be understood in the form of pure antinomies, of binary oppositions.[33] Diane Elam explains Hegelian dialectic as one which means 'that, within the thesis stands the difference of the antithesis, and vice versa. That is to say, neither thesis nor antithesis is purely identical to itself: within the 'I' there is always 'Not-I'.[34] Vis-à-vis Hegel, we read Christina to reject her female/ feminine biological sex (Not-I) which is simultaneous to the masculine gender she occupies at will, the 'I' of her gender/sex construction. It is Butler, however, who reveals the pitting of 'I' against an 'Other' as *a strategy of domination* particular to the western epistemological mode. 'Once [the] separation [between 'I' and 'Other'] is effected, [it] creates an artificial set of questions about the knowability and recoverability of that Other.[...] this binary opposition is a strategic move within a given set of signifying practices, one that establishes the

'I' in necessity, concealing the discursive apparatus by which the binary itself is constituted.' Thus the signifying practices of western epistemology conceal its own workings and naturalize its effects.[35]

Within signification lies the 'agency' of epistemological discourse. The 'I' of discourse is both enabled as well as restricted by the *repetition* of regulatory ideals (the feminine, the masculine, heterosexual desire). The agency of the subject is limited within the orbit of compulsion to repeat; agency, then, is merely the possibility of *variation* on the repetition. Thus the formulation of Christina's identity can only lie within the practices of repetitive signification. Her variation of sex/ gender is based upon a citational performativity of an Other which is masculine/ male in its construction, repudiating all female/ feminine performative citations. This is a result of not being offered a choice; she has to live with the consequences of being trained to be a man in every way, but eventually expected to do her duty by the throne and produce an heir as queens are expected to do. Christina's sex and gender is forced into materialization whereby she demonstrates agency in repudiating wife/mother-hood.

The idea for the play came from the Garbo film: Gems had succumbed to the myth of Christina as a 'shining, pale, intellectual beauty' until her own research proved otherwise.[36] The Garbo film was made in 1932. Garbo herself was a 'lucrative and highly commodified product of MGM'. Although the Hollywood censors stressed the importance of avoiding any tinge of homoeroticism, the film addresses 'a wide range of sexual and gender positions outside permissible [...] heterosexual limits'.[37] Both Garbo and her performance as Queen Christina are carefully constructed images of a culture's myth-making. The off-screen Garbo's aloof and sphinx-like attributes conflate with the iconic Queen to mythologize her on-screen as Gems first perceived her: glamorous, enchanting, magical myth rather than the conflictual gender-transgressive masculine bisexual of Pam Gems' 1977 play.

In history, Christina has been documented as assuming the ceremonial functions of a monarch at the age of six, and as the French ambassador Chanut reportedly realized, 'she meant to run this country herself.' She took her first step toward wresting the initiative when she was only ten years of age, manipulating the Senate's choice of guardian to suit her own preferences. She insisted on being present at the Senate's deliberations on matters of State two years before she had attained full majority. In 1647, when she came of age, she declared, 'Now the fate of this country rests entirely upon my shoulders'. Betty Millan calls her 'the most intriguing of women and—above all—the most learned of queens.' Rather than a warrior-king, Christina was a philosopher-king. Typical of contemporaries' recorded perceptions of Queen Christina were: 'nought of a child except her age, nought of a woman except her sex' (Sforza Pallavicino); 'not like unto a woman, but courageous and wise (Chancellor Axel Oxenstierna, who headed the Council of Regency that ruled in Christina's minority); 'science are [sic] to her what needle and thread are to other women' (Madam de Motteville).[38]

Pam Gems' play opens with the reigning King's necessity to 'make a man of' the child Christina. The Queen has had several miscarriages, failing to produce the much needed heir, which provokes the King to declare that his only surviving child, a daughter, be prepared for the mantle of Kingship:

King: We do have an heir.
Axel: A girl.
King: She's fit enough. Intelligent.
Axel: But the wrong sex! With a weak succession it'll be anybody's game, we can't have a woman.
King: Make a man of her then.
Axel:How?
King: Training. […] I want her fit, educated, able to lead an army if necessary. (I, i)

What we get is a 'Renaissance woman [who] hunts, fights, is bi-sexual and takes an active part in military and political decisions.'[39] Scene ii is an effective scene which incorporates a dramatic shock technique with humour, written to undercut the popular assumption of Christina as a pale shining beauty: 'Enter a German prince waiting to be received as suitor' to the now adult Queen Christina. Enter 'a beautiful young woman (…) wearing a simple but beautifully cut riding habit. Her pale ringlets fall about a beautiful but thoughtful face'. The prince, 'enchanted, moves forward, smiling with delight'. The young woman is followed closely by 'a battered figure in hunting clothes [who] appears to be slightly crippled, or perhaps it is that one of his shoulders is out of true, giving him a swivelled, crooked appearance'. The man's familiarity with the beautiful young girl, taken to be Christina, enrages the suitor who splutters: 'I see (…) I see! So this is our future consort (…) trailing a fellow about her like a common (…) a common (…) […] it is outrageous (…) bloody outrageous (…).', as the 'man' (Christina) responds, thumping the prince genially on the shoulder, sending him reeling: 'At least there's some spunk in him.' (I, ii). The prince, alarmed, is totally unprepared (as is, one expects, the audience) for the man to reveal him/ her self as Queen Christina, who dismisses him as perfunctorily as she has done all the suitors shown her. Christina dresses, looks, behaves, and thinks like the man she has trained to be; she has fulfilled the monarchical need for a male heir; she has materialized the very morphology forced on her.

Christina's personality contains both sets of dichotomous elements with which the masculine sex has been stereotyped: she is a dashing man of action but also a reflective thinker. She is always questioning: war, life, Creation, Christianity, freedom are never taken for granted but subjected to constant debate and scrutiny. In I, iii she converses with René Descartes, the French philosopher and mathematician who provided a mechanistic basis for the philosophical theory of dualism. Although their conversations in the play never veer into abstract philosophical discussion, the implication, not unfounded, is that Christina has had the opportunity and the inclination for intellectual companionship. She was a prodigious reader and drawn to scholarship; she surrounded herself with scientists and philosophers; she was a patron of intellectuals. She has a healthy appetite for the pleasures of the body as well as the spirit, surrounding herself with beautiful young girls whose bodies she delights in, as they seem to serve as an alternative, more beautiful mirror for her own self which she views as ugly, a 'freak'. As she tells Ebba, 'by God, when I'm with you I forget, *you* become my mirror, I see *your* face, *your* eyes' (I, ii). She is equally not averse to the male, as long as he does not shower her with compliments to her physical beauty, of which absence the Queen Mother has never ceased to remind her daughter. Christina's view of her own physical appearance is honest if harsh, and when Karl professes his love she rebukes him: 'Do you think I want to be desired by the likes of you? A man who fancies a long-nosed cripple? Since there's no sap of ambition in you, and I doubt you've the wit for contrivance, it must be aberration! [...] There's one freak on the throne (...) no need to perpetuate the joke. The answer's no'. (I, iii).

Christina, however, seems to possess a *jouissance* denied to her mother by patriarchal norms as the latter is forced into being a gendered societal construct of her time. The Queen mother is paradigmatic of a biological reproductive machine whereas Christina is best described by utilising the Lacanian phrase—'a *jouissance* beyond the phallus' quite literally—if only to signify her non-dependance on males for her pleasures. For Christina, 'the prospect of a royal marriage is about as effective as a forced march through mud' (I, iv). As she observes:

> We live on sufferance. To your desires. I find you a cruel sex. [...] No man follows me. They follow symmetry, and all the thought in the world won't give me that. No, I'm damned if I'll breed for them. (I, iv)

Christina's querying, philosophical nature is evident from the opening of the playtext. War, violence, destruction are already being analysed and questioned by the learned queen as she is depicted in earnest dialogue with Ebba, whom she loves:

Christina: Why are we given life? In order to suffer (…) to be stoic? If so, why the larch tree? Why you? I think! To what purpose? For to believe we're here because (…) or in order to—why that's to accept the most horrifying malignancy or the unbelievably inept! Pestilence (…) the murder of children—by design? Better no meaning at all, I begin not to believe in anything (…) oh, don't worry, I keep it to myself. (I, ii)

Christina is depicted as a blend of ideological and material doubt. In her, mind and body, abstract and physical, doubt and desire meet and blend to form an uneasy gender which, though it seems to combine the traditional oppositions, does not result in a desirable androgyny but, instead, an uneasy site of confused identity. There is no harmony in this uneasy meeting of male/female, only an intense dissatisfaction. Her strongly male gender identity combines with the refusal to marry and reproduce, as the latter is also a refusal to accept the limitations thrust upon her if she crosses the boundary of her constructed male gender.

Axel: The beauties of both sexes that you see fit to keep about you are costing the privy purse a fortune.
Christina: Oh come, a few wild oats, surely?
Axel: So far as I'm concerned, once there's an heir, you can do as you please.
Christina: I see. Tell me, how many royal confinements do you require before I'm allowed to fornicate? To secure this throne, give or take a miscarriage or so, will take the next twenty years of my life. If it doesn't put me under the ground.
Axel: The same for all women.
Christina: All the more reason to stay chaste.
[…]
Why didn't you leave me in the parlour with the rest of the women, it's what you want!
Axel: Not at all. Your unique position demands both the the manly qualities of a king, and the fecundity of a woman.
Christina: Well, you can't have both.
Axel: Why not? For twenty years I've prepared you for it.
Christina: And how? By making a man of me. A man, despising women—just like you. You've had your joke, you and nature between you. (I, v)

Christina subverts the pressing political need for an heir in her denial of her biological female sex, but perhaps the real and more personal reason is confided to Ebba: 'No man who wants a person?/ No such luck.' (I, ii) Christina's existential dissatisfaction leads her to reject 'this cauldron of ice' where she is sure she will never find the answers she seeks. Although warned by Axel:

Axel: They will not have the succession without the marriage. And if you continue to prate about choice, freedom, and all the other fashionable rubbish you'll have the Church at your throat and I shan't answer for your future, your throne or your personal safety. Have I made myself clear? (I, v) she abdicates and makes for Rome and France, looking for stimulus of mind. Christina exhibited an antipathy to Lutheranism and converted to Catholicism. Historically, she abdicated after selecting her cousin Charles Augustus as her successor and heir. Three days after the abdication ceremony, dressed as a man called Count Dohna, she left for Rome. After a notorious life she died in Rome in 1689.[40] Act II dramatizes Christina's period of self-discovery and personal growth. Her encounter with the French blue-stockings leaves her unable to identify with their separationist lifestyle. Ironically, they have long admired Christina for her independent views and freedom-seeking ways, but it is a case of misplaced admiration. They do not realize that Christina *is* a man, and does not identify with their hatred of men. It is *women* Christina does not understand, in fact frequently despises, although she loves their bodies like a (heterosexual) man. In the forced materialization of her gender, Christina is more a male misogynist than a female separationist. The construction of her 'sex' is a product of the particular power relations that she is constituted within. She is an historically specific product, but more particularly, produced by the Imperial powers which demand a *male* heir. Her 'sex' is thus an effect of power relations. Queen Christina is subject to a set of social norms—regulations—which determine her as male sexed. Her sex, gender, pleasures, desires are inevitably formulated in a binary site of opposition to female. However she overspills the site of maleness in a bisexuality of desires, while she operates and functions within the framework of intelligibility enforced by one part of a binary relation. This puts our queen in some confusion and a need to resolve her gender amongst other freedoms she questions and demands.

From France and the blue-stockings to Rome, and Catholicism and the Pope offer our queen no answers either. Of course, she manages to shock Rome with her iconoclastic views which are pronounced 'blasphemous' by the Pope. Her bisexuality and libidinal excess surface in her dialogues with the Pope:

Pope: Confession connotes repentance.

Christina: Oh, I don't repent. Best time I ever had in my life [...] that's something we're going to have to put right in your religion. Celibacy's no good—not in the bible, you know. Think again [...] no need to cut it off, Pope! (II, ii)

When Christina accepts the papal request to fight for Naples she is fully aware that the self-same Pope who denounced abortion as an act which '[turned woman] into an assassin' (II, ii), is now using her as a tool for the purpose of 'Christian warfare'. She accepts, however, more for the sake of her Neapolitan lover Monaldescho, than for Rome. It is in the course of this battle that she, in one sweeping violent motion, barbarically slaughters the traitor who was her lover.

II, vi reveals an emotional and reflective Christina repenting grievously for what she now recognizes as a brutal deed. If 'male' and 'female' were on a shifting continuum, where male occupied one end of the scale and female occupied the other end, this is where Christina's gender starts to slide from male to female. Taking place within her is the realization of the fact that she has been taught to *take* lives but born to *make* them. Close to the sights, smells and sounds of babies and women and domesticity, she heals and shifts up the continuum to being female. Living with Lucia, for the first time she glimpses what her royal masculine heritage has denied her: 'So warm down there! The smell of ironed clothes (…) linen (…)lace—Food (…)baking (…) And babies. The smell of babies. I like the smell of babies—can that be wrong?' (II, vii).

The concluding scene is forceful in its implications on her (hypothetical) future: she rejects the papal offer of the Polish throne, and having saved a child's life—in an impulse opposite to the slaying of Monaldescho—she reflects on being a woman. She lashes out at Cardinal Azzolino, the papal ambassador:

> Yet who are the poorest of all? Women, children (…) the old. Are they the fighters, the creators of war? You say you want me for the fight, and, it's true, I was bred as a man, despising the weakness of women. I begin to question the favour. To be invited to join the killing, why, where's the advantage? Half the world rapes and destroys—must the women, the other half, join in?
>
> [...]
>
> I begin to see that I have been a traitor to my sex—oh, I believed, when I commanded an army, that I fought for the weak and the helpless. [...] I don't condemn every man as a murdering brute, far from it, or we'd not have survived so far. But when I think of it (…) young men destroyed, infants burned in their cradles (…) women violated (…) how wrong, how wrong I have been to condemn women for their weakness (…) they have kept us alive!
>
> [...]
>
> Don't tell me what I can have if I fight. I won't fight. I won't fight, I tell you, I won't fight! If you want arms and legs to blow up, make them yourself. I want my children, do you hear (…) (II, vii).

Lynn Sukenik's term 'matrophobia' was defined by Adrienne Rich as 'the fear not of one's mother or of motherhood *but of becoming one's mother*.[41] Christina's prolonged negation of marriage and motherhood can be traced to this fear. In identifying childbirth and the pain and difficulties attendant upon it with her mother, who had suffered fifteen years of painful miscarriages in a vain attempt to produce an heir; coupled with Christina's masculine training to take on her future role as 'king', Christina's matrophobia prevents her from desiring anything which would make her remotely resemble her long-suffering mother. At a time when the natural process of childbirth had not been eased by the progress of medical science, when women were compelled to produce heirs even if their biological systems were especially frail, the prospect of motherhood could be daunting. Rejecting the generation-based thinking which upheld motherhood as an example and an ideal for the daughter, Christina had transgressed into a bisexuality, throwing out ideas of marriage and motherhood which had seemed synonomous at first. It is only when she has renounced her kingdom and her throne, when bearing a child is no longer for purposes of State but realized as a personal want or need, that Christina's desire has space to grow. Christina, in reaching a state of self-actualization, repudiates war and violence. In repudiating the negative (masculine), *i.e.*, the futility in taking life, she is able to welcome the positive (feminine), *i.e.*, the ability to make life. Pam Gems described the play as a 'uterine' play.[42] Christina's hysteria [Gk. *husterikós*, f. *hustéra* womb] is quite literal at the end of the play, and her final words to the departing Cardinal are an unmistakable metaphor for the female-power she has finally come to terms with (apart from being a pun on her intellectual abilities): 'I am well'.

Christina's sexuality is an excess (a well) in the play of pleasures as she crosses from male to uterine-female. The insight about violence produces the effect of womb-identification. Her 'multiplicitous sexuality' flows and is reconfigured into the 'uterine' as her 'biological duplicity' comes 'into play'. Queen Christina, textualized, is a sign of unnatural transgression which, for her, becomes fatally ambivalent. Fatal in that she cannot reproduce, her insight occurs too late, thus the transgression into the uterine is *textual* and not historical/ social. Queen Christina is ultimately the Fe-Male Bisexual who transgresses into the female uterine, becoming a 'usurper of a feminine prerogative'.[43] Her discursively produced libidinal excess is an overflow of desires. Foucault's category of sex and identity are the effect and instrument of a regulatory sexual regime. But is that regulation reproductive or heterosexual? Does that regulation of sexuality produce male and female identities within a symmetrical binary relation? Does homosexuality produce sexual non-identity? Then homosexuality no longer relies on identities being *like* one another. But if homosexuality is meant to designate the place of an unnameable libidinal heterogeneity, is this a love that cannot or dare not speak its name? The fact is that 'sex does not cause gender, and gender cannot be understood to reflect or express sex'.[44] All gender is fictive and therefore citational. 'Garbo "got in drag" whenever she took some heavy glamour part, whenever she melted in or out of a man's arms, whenever she simply let that heavenly-flexed neck (...) bear the weight of her thrown-back head (...) How resplendent seems the art of acting! It is all *impersonation*, whether the sex underneath is true or not.'[45] Queen Christina's desires are homo-social, homo-historical and overspill the binary gendered space into two kinds of bi-sexualities, 'two opposite ways of imagining the possibility and practice of bisexuality'.[46] Bisexuality can be a fantasy of a complete being. Cixous relates this idea to 'Ovid's Hermaphrodite [...] not made up of two genders but of two halves. Hence a fantasy of unity. Two within one, and not even two wholes.'[47] Thus Christina's desire for a child is an acceptance of the differently gendered script that was imposed upon her life as she finally seeks to add a dimension to it that she is able to, with the body of a woman. In repudiating the destructive energy of the male, and replacing it with the creative energy of the female, Christina's resolution is one struggling toward an identity of metaphoric androgyny—in a blend of oppositions which is perhaps the most powerful and yet, most benign; that blend of duality which metaphysics describes as 'truth' and a one-ness of being; the Hegelian dialectic which, in a metaphysics of being, blends Apollo and Dionysius.

An alternative reading has us consider another bisexuality which is an inscription of alterity within the self: it is 'the location within oneself of the presence of both sexes, evident and insistent in different ways according to the individual, the non-exclusion of difference or of a sex, and starting with this "permission" one gives oneself, the multiplication of the effects of desire's inscription on every part of the body and the other body.'[48] Thus we see her as a competitive intellectual reflective male, where Christina realizes that in bringing forth life, in creating an additional dimension to her self, she will be able to surpass the men she has always identified with. The act of creation will bring her a power which is denied the biological male, a power which surpasses the one she is used to wielding. On this reading Queen Christina is a misogynist male—this is 'an emancipation of the oppressor in the name of the oppressed', when 'the female body [...] is freed from the shackles of the paternal law [proving] to be yet another incarnation of that law, posing as subversive but operating in the service of that law's self-amplification and proliferation.'[49] Or is the resolution of Queen Christina's identity an unexpected permutation which results in difference? Does she indicate a cultural possibility in the kaleidoscope of citational choice? 'If subversion is possible, it will be a subversion from within the terms of the law, through the possibilities that emerge when the law turns against itself and spawns unexpected permutations of itself. The culturally constructed body will then be liberated, neither to its "natural" past, nor to its original pleasures, but to an open future of cultural possibilities.'[50] Butler's Fou-cauldian-Lacanian explanation posits 'the culturally contradictory enterprise of the mechanism of repression [as] prohibitive and generative at once'[51] thus enabling two readings of Christina's identity resolution. '[The] overthrow of "sex" results in the release of a primary sexual multiplicity'[52] giving Christina a new identity formulated in citational difference. For man 'what is repressed is leaning toward one's own sex.' Thus it is *woman* who is truly bisexual, 'man having been trained to aim for glorious phallic monosexuality'. Woman benefits from and opens up this bisexuality 'which does not annihi-late differences but cheers them on, pursues them, adds more.'[53] Queen Christina passes finally, on this reading, into a Cixousian excess, a 'spacious singing Flesh: onto which is grafted no one knows which I—which mascu-line or feminine, more or less human, but above all living, because changing I.'[54]

Queen Christina continues to be a powerful performance piece about gender identity which makes women—and men—confront the construc-tionality of their selves as we march into the twenty-first century.

Courtesan/Hetaira/Whore: Camille, Piaf, Stas

> We have hetairas for the pleasures of the spirit, *pallages* (concubines) for sensual pleasure, and wives to give us sons.
>
> —Demosthenes, as quoted by Beauvoir.[55]

The Second Sex is hailed by western feminists as one of the first feminist clas-sics and has been translated widely. Published in 1949 and translated into English in 1953, the book has a pre-eminent place in feminist philosophy and gender theory.[56] However, Beauvoir problematizes the category of 'woman' by perpetuating the fact that women, by the rules of patriarchy, are already labelled or stereotyped as inhabiting one or the other of the tidy categories she sets out to describe. Her categories echo patriarchy: 'The Mar-ried Woman'; 'The Mother'; 'Prostitutes and Hetairas'. Although Beauvoir's method is historiographic she seems to add to myths rather than dispel them: in the section labelled 'Prostitutes and Hetairas', having defined het-aira as 'high class' in relation to the 'common prostitute', she goes on to state definitively:

> I use the word hetaira to designate all women who treat not only their bodies but their entire personalities as capital to be exploited. Their attitude is very different

from that of creative workers who, transcending themselves in the work they produce, go beyond the given and make their appeal to a freedom in others for which they open the doors to the future. The hetaira does not reveal the world, she opens no avenues to human transcendence; on the contrary, she tries to captivate the world for her own profit.[57]

Placing creative workers and hetairas in two binary categories, she proceeds to place models, actresses, movie stars, as well as dancers as twentieth-century occupants of the space vacated by the nineteenth-century 'distinguished' high class courtesan. Whilst recognising that an amount of 'ability' is required, she continues:

But for the vast majority of women an art, a profession, is only a means: in practising it they are not engaged in genuine projects.[58]

Representation can be endless as one attempts to portray the plurality of one half of the population. The task becomes more difficult when the attempt is to re-present those regarded as un-representable: the bawd, the harlot, the whore and the vamp are only ever presented in terms of the prototypal stereotype of the fallen woman, and Beauvoir falls into the same patriarchal fallacy of describing these women as useless. This is not 'woman as the area of limitless possibility' or 'a permanently contested site of meaning' unless one is punning on their profession. Diane Elam asserts in *Feminism and Deconstruction: Ms. en Abyme*, 'her-story is not one story. An injustice is committed when any *one* history purports to speak for all women everywhere',[59] when any one label excludes women from belonging to another category as histories overlap, 'there are always several histories in several places at once, there are always several histories underway; this is a high point in the history of women.'[60] The implication for feminism today is that there is a multiplicity of voices within the category of gender, within the general category of women. Pam Gems writes several plays about a specific gender category, writing within which must surely be most difficult, prototypical as prostitution has always been of the very nadir of womanhood, pigeon-holed and derided by the self-styled expert, Simone de Beauvoir (see above). Within this category, Gems attempts to explore that radical space of indeterminacy and potentiality, the multiple voices which belong to woman-as-hetaira (Piaf), courtesan (Camille), and prostitute (Stas). Taking a stereotyped role and revealing variation within it, Gems demonstrates the limitless variety of women within the specificity of that pigeon-holed profession which even Beauvoir attaches labels to. Gems' courtesans serve as a trope for that larger category—woman—and the plurality within. The dramatist presents each as occupant of a range of categories so the courtesan overspills the prototypical space she occupies, making her more than just a stereotype.

It was Aphra Behn—the first Englishwoman to 'earn her bread' by her writing—who initially re-presented a non-stereotyped woman-as-courtesan. During the latter half of the seventeenth- century, a time when drama was as bawdy and licentious as it was in the closing years of the twentieth, the stage was still the patriarchal fold of male writers. Being a woman bold enough to write under her own name, Behn also prefaced her plays with cries against the gender-based injustice she faced. In one of her blunt epistles to the reader she declaimed:

> The play had no other misfortune but that of coming out for a Womans: had it been owned by a Man, though the most Dull Unthinking Rascally Scribler in Town, it had been a most admirable play. (Epistle to *Sir Patient Fancy*, 1678)

Behn's plays attacked several prevalent evils of her time, forced marriage being one such convention vituperatively opposed in *The Town Fop; or, Sir Timothy Tawdrey* (1676) and in *The Lucky Chance; or, An Alderman's Bargain* (1686). Behn uses the character of the prostitute 'as a weapon in her thematic attack on mercenary marriage',[61] and she figures this stock character in several plays as a foil to the good woman or the 'virgin' prototype (as is Angellica in *The Rover*, 1677). The 'Rover series' of plays illustrates the idea that prostitution may well be a more honest way to economic independence than mercenary arranged marriages. However, most of Behn's courtesans have a wish to marry, like the virtuous good woman of the play, although on a more non-stereotypical note the woman who 'wins' the man is the wittier and more generous hearted of the two, regardless of the stereotyped niche she occupies.

Gems, younger by almost exactly three centuries and as successful on the British stage, is as subversive and entertaining as was Behn. Gems courtesans range from the coarse street language of Piaf amidst the glamour of her successful career as a singer; Camille's attachment to her son revealing motherhood and whoredom as synonymous, co-existent within one woman; and the contemporary Stas—intellectual, amoral, independent.

The Myth of Camille, or the Lady of the Camellias

La Dame aux Caméllias, a novel by Alexandre Dumas, *fils* (1852), Verdi's *La Traviata* (1853). Actresses Sarah Bernhardt, Stella Patrick Campbell, and the Violetta of Verdi's opera on the stages of Paris and London, and Garbo, once again, to haunt on film. The passion, the life and the amours of the Lady of the Camellias has a long tradition in the limelight, glamorizing the lifestyle of a courtesan, 'recruiting' as George Bernard Shaw would put it, 'for

Mrs. Warren's Profession'. K. Worth accuses Gems for writing a play along the lines of the popular novel, opera and Hollywood tradition of the glamorous and tear-jerking Camille: 'Gems is in tune with her romantically minded predecessors rather than with Shaw ['s indictment of poverty which forces the underpaid, undervalued, overworked woman to turn to prostitution]'.[62] Shaw's trenchant pen wrote: 'Plays about prostitution [showed the courtesan as] beautiful, exquisitely dressed and sumptuously lodged', rather than the poor, destitute women they really were.[63] Indeed Shaw satirised the upper classes for its hypocrisies toward prostitutes and also toward the patronage of plays which portrayed the courtesan's life as one to be desired in his 1854 play, *Mrs. Warren's Profession*, which the Lord Chamberlain immediately censored. But Gems play is, like all her work, utterly subversive as it undercuts the dominant ideology from within the play.

> Viewed from the standpoint of economics, [the] position [of the prostitute] corresponds with that of the married woman. In *La Puberté* Marro says: 'The only difference between women who sell themselves in prostitution and those who sell themselves in marriage is in the price and the length of time the contract runs'.

Beauvoir, in obvious agreement with Marro, continues:

> For both the sexual act is a service; the one is hired for life by one man; the other has several clients who pay her by the piece. The one is protected by one male against all others; the other is defended by all against the exclusive tyranny of each.[64]

Yet, the path of the prostitute, compared to that of the married woman, seems one of relative independence, and this is borne out by the women of the play. Toward the close of the play, Prudence informs the grieving Armand: 'Has it never occurred to you that some of us might prefer the life—given the alternatives?' (*Camille*, II, vii) The alternatives are poverty, or the life of a married woman which to the relatively 'free' courtesan spelt slavery. However, 'neither wife nor hetaira succeeds in exploiting a man unless she achieves an individual ascendancy over him.'[65] *Camille* is the story of one woman's singular power—'individual ascendancy'—over a man. It is a story which has all the elements of a passion play and sentimental melodrama which Gems carefully avoids by the skilfully worked out structure of the play. Transposing scenes rapidly in her hallmark filmic cuts, Gems presents the play so the future precedes the past, thus presenting scenes which would make for histrionics before the causal events have occurred. The dramatization succeeds in avoiding the overwhelming melodrama of the novel and the opera by a feat of dramatic technique which closely resembles the short scenes and jump starts of film. The opening scene, set in her bedchamber in a conflation of personal and public, is an auction of Marguerite Gautier's personal effects after her death. Her lover, Armand, wanders onto a scene of what would amount to a symbolic and public rape as the auctioneer pauses significantly over her bed:

> And now (...) the lot you've all been waiting for (...) the bed. Decorated with—ah (...) (he consults his list) (...) camellias. What was it (...) twenty three days of the month she wore white camellias and for the other five days she wore red (...) (I, i)

The opening is thus a demythologizing as it demystifies the glamour by focusing on what is still a taboo of the female body: menstruation. As the bed is bid for, Armand collapses in anguish. A lover's (private) discourse mingles cruelly with that of the (public) material world of economics in the strata of the demi-monde. As Llewellyn-Jones puts it, the 'condensation of sexuality and economics' is 'indicated semiologically in the opening scene': a gest which 'underlies all the emotional transactions' of the play.[66]

The next scene moves back in time, cutting to the moment of their first meeting. Before Marguerite makes her initial and dramatic entrance, Armand is revealed as a stereotypical male, in the pursuit of women, and also cruel and given to the abuse of the courtesans whose company he seeks. A regular client, not material for a romance. Sophie, who appears to be an enchantment he has tired of, has returned from what could only have been a dangerous abortion. Bela, Armand's companion, mocks her cruelly:

> Bela: Where have you been?
> Sophie: If you must know, I've been to Dieppe.
> Bela: Dieppe? (...) The end of the universe! A long way to buy a crochet hook (...)
> (I, ii)

Armand seems to have had liaisons with most of the other courtesans as well, and, having tired of them all is ready for a new distraction who doesn't 'disappoint'. This is the moment when Marguerite appears to make a lasting impression on the rover:

> There is a long still pause as they regard each other. She inclines her head the merest fraction and walks away. He gazes after her then turns to PRUDENCE. As he does so, MARGUERITE turns to see him go. (Stage directions)

Marguerite Gautier is to all appearances the hetaira as described by Beauvoir:

> There are many degrees between the common prostitute and the high class hetaira. The essential difference is that [the hetaira] endeavours to gain recognition for herself—as an individual—and if she succeeds, she can entertain high aspirations. Beauty and charm or sex appeal are necessary here, but are not enough: the woman

has to be distinguished (...) She will have 'arrived' (...) only when the man has brought her worth to the attention of the world. In the last century it was her town house, her carriage, her pearls (...)[67]

As Roland Barthes later put it, obviously reading Beauvoir's existentialist text alongside the myth of Camille, 'the central myth [...] is not Love, it is Recognition.'[68] The existentialist position of Marguerite's class (Slave) to Armand's (Master) elicits Barthes' comparision with women from lower classes accrued onto Beauvoir's earlier parallel with the married woman: 'the alienation of Marguerite Gautier in relation to the class of her masters is not fundamentally different from that of today's petit-bourgeois women in a world which is just as stratified.' The hierarchization of society necessitates Marguerite to need Recognition from the world of her masters, Armand's class and also the middle-class audiences where 'the grateful and recognizing gaze of the bourgeois class is [...] delegated to the [audience] who in [their] turn *recognize* Marguerite.' Barthes sees the mythology of this love as two separate ideologies: it is two separate types of love which stem from two different positions in society. The master's love is 'eternal' as it is valorized by the world of the masters themselves, whilst the slave is alienated *and also aware of her alienation*. The ideology of her love is constructed as a response to the world of the masters: 'either she plays the part which the masters expect from her, or she tries to reach a *value* which is in fact a part of this same world of the masters.' This value is attained by Marguerite in the sacrifice of her love, which was also, like the love, endorsed by the same world. Thus Marguerite undergoes, in the awareness of her complete estrangement, a kind of erasure of self, as she exists only as a response to the ideals of a world to which she can never belong.[69]

In reaching the 'value' of the world of the masters Marguerite 'proves' her love is ideal: *i.e.*, non-material. Even when Armand is cut off from his inheritance she stays by him.

She may be the distinguished hetaira of Beauvoir's classification, but her origins are common. Born in poverty, sexually abused before the age of five, seduced and impregnated by her master, the Marquis (who is also Armand's father), she took her opportunity where she found it as she escaped to Paris with luxuries stolen from her master's house.

'When a door has once been broken open, it is hard to keep it shut', said a young prostitute of fourteen, quoted by Marro. [...] Now that she no longer belongs to one man, she feels she can give herself to all.[70]

Hard to keep the door shut, also, when the men in the courtesan's milieu display by word and action their lack of respect: in scene i it is the auctioneer, in scene ii, Armand and Bela, and in scene iii the valet who spits in disgust at the sight of Janine and Marguerite locked in a cat fight. Since the beginning of 'civilization' there have existed prostitutes in patriarchal societies to satisfy the prototypical man's desires. Compartmentalizing lust and love, patriarchy divided its women into virgins and whores, as the latter, though used to satiate lust, is also the repository of every negative value, and is often abused. In the repeated verbal and visual signs of abuse in the play, Gems demonstrates that—like Shaw—she is concerned at revealing the hypocrisy of society. She deconstructs the dominant ideology from within the guise of a West End show, wherein lies the genius of her subversion. The hypocrisy is revealed at its height in the words of the Marquis (the same man who had abused Marguerite and fathered her child) to his son, Armand:

> Respect? Respect?! For a whore!! You dare to talk of love (...) you dare to talk of friendship—with a whore? [...] Introduce a harlot? Into my family? Are you seriously suggesting (...) that you want (...) as your life's companion (...) before God and the Church (...) as the mother of your children (...) as my heirs (...) a woman who has felt the private parts of every man in Paris? (II, i)

Having thus posited her female protagonist within the specificity of a typecast profession in a cruel, hegemonic, masculinist culture who does not hesitate to revile her almost on cue, Gems draws the ropes of middle-class values tightly, and Marguerite Gautier with them.

Armand, in love with one patriarchal category as it were—the whore—now attempts to re-posit his love back into a prelapsarian mode. He is struck with Marguerite immediately—the myth of love at first sight—and rebukes her for the vulgar nature of the song sung by her. Her answer is in complete awareness of her alienated existentialist position; coldly, honestly she replies with irony: 'What would you have me sing? Something more elevated? Don't delude yourself, Monsieur'. (I, iii)

> Most prostitutes are morally adapted to their mode of life. Not that they are immoral congenitally or by heredity, but they feel integrated (...) in a society that manifests a demand for their services. They know very well that the edifying lecture of the police sergeant who registers them is pure verbiage, and elevated sentiments proclaimed by their clients (...) do little to intimidate them.[71]

Marguerite, typically unintimidated, distinguishes herself from the other courtesans who are too cloying for Armand. This aloofness combined with her stunning beauty make her infinitely desirable in Armand's eyes and his fascination wraps the narrative in the web of myth. Through the play, as in the last cited scene, Gems de-mythicizes 'romance, revealing it as a construct masking the exploitative nature of the traditional notions of sexuality.'[72]

The mythology of love encoded in the play is ensured by a series of devices: firstly, Marguerite's early demise whilst Armand is still in the passionate throes of love guarantees that she is instantly and forever unattainable: an impossible ideal enshrined in his passion. While she lived she swung between rational materiality and impulsive love: unwilling to abandon a carefully constructed life of comfort, economic security, and above all, independence from the tyranny of being dependant for all her wants on a single man; yet, carried away with Armand's vision of a future together. Always aware that men like Armand tired of the objects of their distraction quickly (as he indeed proved, in the first scene of their meeting) Marguerite treads warily: 'Cinderella does not always dream of Prince Charming; whether husband or lover, she is afraid he might turn into a tyrant (...)'.[73] Also aware of the vast gulf of class between them, she voices her awareness of her alienation:

> (...) no! There is no world, no way that you and I can connect (...) except in the
> moment (...) There is nothing for us. I could look over the wall at you all my life
> and never get to touch your coat-tails. Don't be a fool. Only a fool believes a lie. (I,
> vi)

'It is a very particular state of myth, defined by [...] a parasitic awareness'.[74] This awareness makes her more rather than less resistant to his charm, making her unattainable in life, elevating her far above the other demi-mondaines in his eyes.

The cause of her early death is consumption: she is that 'one in twenty [who] has tuberculosis (...) [one of the] forty per cent [who] die before the age of forty'.[75] Then as now, prostitutes were the most vulnerable to the plethora of fatal infections caught from their clients, and the beautiful Marguerite is no exception. The final brush strokes in the construction of this myth which has played for a century on European stages, include the fact that Marguerite is first a mother. Jean-Paul is her only constant in her world of ever changing affections and it is this love that the Marquis is able to buy so she can accomplish what Barthes calls 'the murder of the courtesan she is' and along with that the 'indirect murder of Armand's passion'.[76] Llewellyn-Jones accuses Gems for mythologizing 'the essentialist notion that motherhood is true fulfilment and its loss [...] inevitably tragic.'[77] Although it is true that a number of Gems' plays reflect on motherhood, it is part of women's condition, and, here, it is part of the original mythical narrative as it provides the fatal twist in the 'plot' snatching Marguerite away from Armand, as she attempts to buy her son 'the myth of respectability'.[78]

'The mismatch between the mythic construct of romance and the materialism of reality is encoded through various devices in the [...] text'.[79] Marguerite has been big business: as the appropriately named Mme. Prudence reflects, 'You keep us all afloat (...) servants, seamstresses, shoemakers (...) not a bad achievement for a girl who couldn't write her own name.' (II, iii). This is the life Marguerite returns to, as II, ii reveals the fickleness of her world. Janine is Madame's new protegée: as one star fades, a new beauty quickly replaces it; in a world where variety is of essence, the old star is quickly forgotten.

Gems maintains a delicate balance in her portrayal of Armand. His undying passion for the beautiful courtesan coupled with his illusionistic notions of an ideal life with her make this cruel, violent man maddeningly human. By presenting him at the opening scene at his most vulnerable, Gems unties him from occupying a stereotyped, gendered, masculinist role. His violence towards Marguerite when he discovers she is considering one more night with the Russian Prince for his emeralds, to enable the lovers to buy their freedom, leaves Marguerite hysterical and distraught, but the scene is poignant as the audience is aware that he will never see her alive again. This is his last meeting with his ideal love before her quiet death. Again, his sentimental desire to have her remains moved to the family vault against the advice of his closest friends, as also his marked and genuine anguish at the loss of his love, balance the hateful side to his nature.

James Redmond calls Camille 'a 'useful play' which reclaim[s] the truth about women's lives from 'the dustbins of male historians' [as Gems] offers a feminist account of the sex-war [of] violent intensity'.[80] The final deconstuction of the myth in the text's multiple interrogative strategies, reveals, however, that 'death is the penalty for those women who defy the norms of status, materialism and sex'[81] as Gems reassesses 'the reality behind the fairytales.'[82]

The Legend of Edith Piaf

Like the courtesan Marguerite Gautier, the Sparrow Piaf's origins are 'common', but she holds on to all signs of being working class with a tenacious ferocity throughout her meteoric rise to success as the highest paid woman singer in the world. The play is, as Wandor notes, about a basic 'gutter survival' and 'faith in women's basic resilience.'[83] Piaf's is a portrait of 'a woman for whom female independence means an active and vigorous sexuality, which at its most intense parallels the orgasmic satisfaction she gets from singing, and a bristly, individualistic identification with being working class.'[84] The demythologizing of the star begins, in characteristic Gems fashion, with the first scene, where, as in the later *Camille*, the playwright uses the cinematic-dramatic technique of transposition of the past into the present to capture Piaf at the downslide of her career. Her talent numbed in the web of heroin addiction, Piaf is caught in the spotlight—centrestage—unable to perform. Through the play she is constantly distanced as Other in the use of her coarse language, and her first words are the characteristic defensive: 'Get your fucking hands off me, I ain't done nothing yet (…)'

Piaf is an unsettling mix of heady glamour and backstreet crudity, enormous talent couched in verbal and non-verbal coarseness and vulgarity. Her talent enables her to be picked off the street to be given the opportunity to sing in a classy Parisian nightclub. Like Marguerite and the 1996 dramatization of Marlene Dietrich, this character escapes Beauvoir (and patriarchy)'s tidy categorization of glamorous stars—the modern-day hetairas—who feed off men to ensure their success.[85] Through the play we see Piaf surrounded by people who make their living from her talent: from her managers to the young men who want to sing with Piaf, live with Piaf, look at Piaf, they are all drawn by the lure of ringing cash registers—theirs. But the hard-headed tough-minded streetwise Piaf takes a 'genuinely greedy pleasure (…) when she [can] afford to pay for any man she desire[s], instead of having to oblige any man who desire[s] her.'[86]

In scene ii Gems transposes time to give us the young Edith walking the streets of Paris before the advent of her singing career. She has the same coarseness she will display at the height of her fame, and she responds to Leplée with her standard, '*Get your fucking hands off me, I ain't done nothing (…)*' Independent, defiant and self-willed, a woman who stands her own ground no matter what the situation, used to the hard life of working the streets, she assumes the nightclub manager expects sexual favours for the money he gives her. It doesn't occur to her or to her friend, Toine, that she has a talent for something other than selling her body for sex.

The friendship between Piaf and Toine establishes a female solidarity, and gives her personal life a continuity in the play which spans her life. They share an intimate easy rapport born of a sisterhood formed whilst working clients together.

> (…) prostitutes have a close solidarity among themselves; they may happen to be rivals, to feel jealous, to hurl insults at one another, to fight; but they profoundly need one another to form a counter-universe in which they regain their human dignity. The comrade is the preferred confidante and witness; it is she who will appreciate the dress and the coiffure intended for man's seduction but which seem like ends in themselves under the envious or admiring gaze of other women.[87]

Toine seems to be the Simone Berteaut of Piaf's acquaintance; 'Momone' who later claimed to be her sister. They were street-singers together:

in a culture where the profession has been highly honourable[88] much as India's temple prostitutes were considered sacred. There are long gaps—
sometimes years—which separate their meetings, but what binds them is
their past and their class origins. Piaf, despite herself, has acquired the trap-
pings of glamour and success, and towards the end appears different from
Toine who has ended up more conventionally—married with three children. The war years allow them to rearticulate the old camaraderie as they
are happy to do their bit for the war effort, *i.e.*, letting the soldiers have it
gratis. Her friend Marlene Dietrich, who appears in the later *Marlene* has the
same nonchalant attitude as she, too, provides 'comfort for the troops'
(*Marlene*, I, p.20) Although in the end the two old acquaintances (Toine
and Piaf) seem to have nothing in common anymore, the intervening years
having brought Piaf success beyond their youthful dreams, they still share a
strong bond of identification. Realising that

> (…) they all want a slice, even the bloody managers. Will they take the rough with
> the smooth, will they hell! (II, vi)

she, like Marlene, has her bond of female solidarity which goes back into the
past. She shares her passion for her craft with Marlene, who, after the war,
made a few more movies and then became a cabaret and concert performer.[89]

> They want the bloody product, they want that all right, all wrapped up with a
> feather in its ass, but songs—what do they know about songs! (*Piaf*, II, vi)

> Yah (…) agents, managers (…) fog, strike, crisis—"Take the Concorde, be here
> yesterday" (…) in the end, your work, the thing you dedicated your life to, denied
> yourself, lost friends for (…) the work—that becomes remote (…) immaterial.
> (*Marlene*, I, p.23)

Strong, self-willed, independent, these stars are not Garbo: 'Grrreta Gar-
rrbo. Always on the screen like she is suffering some female problem down
below' (ibid.); nor are they Beauvoir's courtesans: 'A lifetime of marriages?
Not for me. I'd rather sell pumpernickel.' (ibid., p.24) These are icons who
know where its at: '(…) Nah, pretty soon they're not going to want my stuff.
My sort's dying out. Going extinct. What they want now is discs. Canned.
In the can (…)' (*Piaf*, II, vi) Piaf knows she isn't going to be on top forever.
As at the beginning, Piaf seems to be in it for one thing—the men she will
have as a result of the fame, the success, the money. Her first thought when
she is paid as a star is for 'the little guy down the garage. I could get him a
(…) suit (…) coat, cufflinks, silk shirts' (I, v). She cheerfully shares her
earnings with Toine giving her a generous half share. Piaf never succeeds in
polishing her speech patterns or, indeed, in cleaning up her vocabulary. She

dates relatively upper class men at first, like Paul in Act I, v who attempt to 'cultivate' her:

> Paul: You don't have to stay in the gutter just because you were born there.
>
> Piaf: I feel out of place! I'm doing like what you said (...) trying to be a lady (...) [*she becomes aware of her own voice, and shrivels in her seat*] (I, v. Emphasis mine).

It is this class divide, one that Piaf is desperate to bridge at first, and later resents, which elicits from her the rage and derision she feels for the bourgeosie. Her attitude to her secretary—'that middle-class bitch' (II, iii)—is purposely mocking and scornful, as Piaf seethes with resentment.

The private self of Piaf is Piaf on stage, in a strangely class-based dis-play of a private discourse of the body and sexuality. Early on in her career, she is warned by her more sophisticated beaux: 'Piaf, your private life is your private life. Don't mix it.' (I, v). However, the public is, for Piaf, an expression of the personal, as throughout the play both are inseparably imbricated in each other. The morphology traverses the public spaces of the backstreet, the entertainment stages, the war spaces, each of which is indelibly stamped on by Piaf's private excesses. The most memorable scene, one which trans-forms this play into contemporary myth, is the one when the young Piaf, faced with an unfamiliar 'posh' setting, sips from the finger bowl arousing the waiter's scorn. Rebuffed for her *faux pas*, she defiantly lifts her skirts as she urinates in public atop the table in the restaurant: 'All right clever cock. Seen me drink—now you can watch me piss.'[90] Unable to detach herself from her art, for Piaf every performance is an orgasm, as she comes with and for the audience:

> Piaf: When I go on to do a song, it's me that comes on. They get the lot (...) they see what they're getting—everything I got.
> Josephine: Sure. But learn how to save it.
> Piaf: Nah.
> Josephine: Kid, you can't have an orgasm every single time you walk on stage.
> Piaf: I can.
> Josephine: No you can't. Nobody can. Nobody peaks all the time. Technique, baby! Trust it. Let it work for you. That way you don't exhaust yourself all the time (...) (II, i).

Yet this is the very quality which made Piaf so popular and so wanted—her complete and utter absorption in her work—an absorption which is a 'play' and a joy: a *jouissance* of the spirit-as- body as she offers 'the grain of the voice'.

The scenes in Act II are short cinematic-style cuts of Piaf's colourful life: Piaf at the height of her fame, Piaf ravaged by heroin, Piaf's young boys whose performances she tries to transfer, usually unsuccessfully, to the stage; her lover, the boxer Marcel Cerdan's death in a plane crash; the driving accidents and heroin addiction she surfaces from, time and again, to return to the stage to sing and fascinate her audiences once more. The eighth scene of the second act is a reprise of the opening scene: her dependence on drugs has finally destroyed her ability to perform. As she ruins performance after attempted performance she has to be dragged off the stage unceremoniously—'*get your fucking hands off me (…)*'. The last two scenes show Piaf with friends—she has, over the period of her life, built lasting friendships, and is fortunate to have had young men like Jacko sincerely care; and this scene has a caring Jacko ready to cancel his tour to be by her side during her hospitalization. It is here, too, that she meets the young Greek, Theo, whom she later marries and also performs with in yet another comeback. That is Piaf's career: a series of ever successful comebacks, a modern legend whose songs stir and delight. Gems' last scene shows us a Piaf who has all she longed for and more: a young man to love, her friendship with Toine as well as a lasting fame. In a profession which leaves lesser equipped mortals lonely, cynical and bitter, Piaf's is a significant victory. The play closes on Piaf as a twentieth century western myth as she sings '*Je ne regrette rien*' with characteristic raw emotion.

If it is Edith Piaf one wants, then perhaps more than any other play (including *Marlene*), Piaf is better seen in performance than de-constructed as performative possibility off the page. The quality of the songs and the absorption and emotional intensity of Piaf's stage presences make for memorable characterization read best when encoded in a discourse of 'a body that matters'. Thus the success of Elaine Paige 'materialized' as Piaf:

> Paige (…) sings (…) not in direct imitation of Piaf but with something of her fierce attention to their emotional content.[91]

> When she sings Piaf [Elaine Paige] soars (…) those of us lucky enough to have seen her in person at Olympia in Paris have always felt the same: no regrets.[92]

However, the play itself—a subversive and creative re-presentation of a successful life and a de-construction of what goes into the making of a modern legend—was dismissed collectively by a number of broadsheet reviewers as 'sketchy (…) scrappy';[93] dire with 'tripey dialogue';[94] 'fragmented';[95] a 'sketchy trawl through [thirty] years of her subject's bumpy life'.[96] Elaine Paige, more of a singer/ performer than an actor had overwhelmed the audiences with her singing which may have rather overshadowed the script.

> Why not just an evening of Paige sings Piaf? It would be ten times more enjoyable and save a fortune in scenery.[97]

(…) one of the great star-turns of the year, if not the decade. Hall and Paige (…)
[have turned the play] into a breathtaking musical triumph by the simple device of
focusing on the songs rather than the dialogue.[98]

This is where the critical strategy of reading performativity off the page
demonstrates its worth. A new play by a new dramatist—two new stars on
the horizon of English drama. However, a performance reading of the Elaine
Paige production, as demonstrated to a certain extent by the broadsheet reviewers, fails to even acknowledge an excellent dramatic text by a dramatist
who demonstrates the flair for popular acclaim with subversive political intent. For an intensive reading of the deep structure of a dramatic text, performativity must necessarily be read off the page from the multiple points of
view of a director, actor and critic. Thus in terms of reconstructing the 'better' production, it is necessary also to point the way to more possibilities.

The original 1978 production of the play had Jane Lapotaire play Piaf.[99]
She not only 'took *Piaf* from Stratford to the West End [but] to Broadway,
where she won a Tony award'.[100] Lapotaire was not a singer and the difference between the two productions was that 'at the RSC fifteen years ago,
[*Piaf*] came over as a sketchy, but authentic portrait of a gutter genius, whose
gift had to be taken on trust.'[101] Thus, for the play to 'work' the singing has
to take a back seat, and is therefore ideally 'against the grain'. Or, as the
later strategy used for *Marlene*, all the songs—what the West End audiences
actually pay for—could come right at the end. *Marlene*, another Gems act of
subversive triumph, had Sian Phillips sing—beautifully—lots of 'Dietrich'
after the play. This strategy worked well—the body of the voice, coming as
it did after the entertaining but political statement of gender, sexuality,
friendship and myth, had the audiences delay their primary gratificatory
source.

Piaf was the first play written by a (contemporary) woman to be produced by the RSC. It is a play drawn in a series of rapid sketches which reveal Piaf's rapid rise to fame and her subsequent deterioration symbolically
and efficiently. The mythical status of this star was ironically echoed in one
reviewer's comment on the closing song: 'numbingly predictable'.[102] Gems,
in fact, chose the songs with care, and most were the lesser known of Piaf's
repertoire. This made the play a success in Britain, while the same contrib-
uted to bad press in the United States.[103]

Piaf defies categorization, emerging as a subject constituted in apparently conflictual discourses—not a 'whore' (cf. Beauvoir) nor a typical 'star'.
She is a hard-headed foul-mouthed survivor who is prone to emotional vulnerability; generous hearted, insensitive, intense, she has the ability to enjoy
life to the fullest with no regrets, and a knack for bouncing back from each

catastrophe with a vigour and a verve which characterizes her dichotomousness. This is another Gems statement on womanhood which defies labels and goes against the normative grain. By positing the Piaf who walked the streets of mid-thirties Belleville on the high of success without polishing her rough edges or vulgar tongue, Gems manages to portray her as yet another woman who occupies that multifarious region peopled with characters with as much variety as human beings are capable of re-citing.

Loving Women: The Split Gestus of 'Woman'

Crystal is another portrait of the contemporary mother as was Dusa in *Dusa, Fish, Stas and Vi*. Again, Gems has her occupying several stereotypical categories at once so it is difficult to label her as either mother, wife, working woman, or indeed sex symbol. It seems too facile to name her as merely 'a dizzy working-class blonde (…) an uneducated sex-pot',[104] 'sex-crazy Crystal'.[105] These definitions undoubtedly point to the masculinist bias of the reviewers, and point also to the iconic representation of the character (which would in turn activate masculinist critiques). Crystal's development through the play reveals the serious materialism of the 80s, but equally, it is a sketch of the triumph of the working classes as they achieve social mobility. At the opening of the play she seems the stereotype of a sexy dimwitted blonde whom Frank chooses to marry over serious-thinking Susannah. Gems seems to satirise the male psyche by juxtaposing two. apparently opposite, kinds of women: the more recent stereotypes of the 'bimbo' and the 'intelligent thinking woman' where, like Alan of *Dusa, Fish, Stas and Vi* Frank makes a traditional patriarchal choice opting for 'a delicious body—and home cooking.'[106] Act I is devoted to the two women acting as a foil to each other: Crystal demonstrating a vitality and freshness to Susannah's serious level-headedness. Crystal dismisses Susannah's 'lot' as 'liberated'—which they are. They 'put [Crystal] off':

Crystal: I thought he was going to bring out the manual—Christ, what are they after, good marks or something?

Susannah: You like the man to take the lead? Crystal: Sure (…) within reason. Tell you one thing, your lot's never going to be up for rape. (I, i)

It is Susannah who had asked Crystal to nurse Frank through his illness since she was too busy working—the last thing she expected was for Frank (whom she had been with for five years) to marry what seems to be a clearly unsuitable Crystal. She confronts Frank after the wedding with bitter sarcasm:

Susannah: Well, since I'm here, you might as well fill me in. Like, why you did it.
(He doesn't answer)
Was it the breakdown?
(He looks nervous that Crystal might hear)
Well, what? Some kind of gesture (…) direct-action consciousness raising? Or did you just fall for nursey? (I, ii)

But Frank has changed. Disillusioned with communist ideals he now works as a school teacher and is a member of the Labour Party. And he more than loves his wife: he is mesmerized by her sensuality and beauty. However, he enjoys Susannah's conversation and stimulating intellect. She sums him up acidly and perhaps quite accurately:

Frank: I don't know anything. Except her. (Pause) I read to her. In the evenings. We're reading Lord Jim at the moment. Remember the opening, where he goes on about Jim's job as a tout for a ship's chandler?
Susannah: What?
Frank: After a couple of pages describing the tattiness of a tout's life he ends up (…) 'a beautiful and humane occupation'. Irony. She liked that. She got it. (Pause)
Susannah: You pompous renegade. You bloody social-democrat do-gooder.
Frank: It's real. I feel real.
Susannah: Well, good luck to you. (She picks up her bag.) What's she like in bed?
Frank: A goer. I have trouble keeping up.
Susannah: I notice she does all the cooking and shopping, all the work. What's in it for her?
Frank: She wants a husband, children. She's not after the world.
Susannah: She'd better be, or she'll end up like your Mum and mine (…) vicious. You bloody exploitative shit. I hope it rots off. (She leaves). (I, ii)

But as the scene closes on Frank and Crystal they seem genuinely happy:

Crystal: She gone?
(He nods)
Jesus.
(He doesn't reply. She contemplates him)
I had a shower.
Frank: Oh?
Crystal: Smell me.
Frank: (grabbing her and burying his face): Mmmmmm (…)
Crystal: Guess what it is.. no, you got to guess (…)
Frank: It's called 'Expensive'.
Crystal (laughing): You ain't seen nothing.
(She drops the dressing gown. She is wearing very little, but it is sensational.)
Frank: Christ!
Crystal: Thought I'd better do something.
Frank: No need.
Crystal: Really?
Frank: Look, it's old history.
Crystal: I started to feel like, you know, a fucking gooseberry in me own place.
Frank: Finished. Over.
Crystal: Right. Well (…) in that case (…)
(She sits on his lap, legs astride) Frank: Here, what about my dinner?
Crystal: It'll keep. (She kisses him)
Frank: I'm a hungry man.

Crystal: I know. (kisses him)
I've made allowances. (Kisses him)
Last course first tonight (…)
(They embrace as lights go to black) (I, ii)

Act One ends on Crystal's intense insecurity about Susannah. Act II
opens in 1984 to reverse the tables. Ten years have passed and Crystal is a
successful West End hairstylist who 'pulls a fortune'. She has successfully
mothered two children, a boy and a girl; looks sensational and well-
maintained, and supports her family practically single-handedly. Frank offers
a tribute to her fertile and sexual body in terms one would ascribe to a goddess: 'She has such a body (…) breasts (…) contours (…) valleys (…) all—
alive! It's a crime to clothe her (…) she should be decked with flowers and
worshipped. I'm a mere mortal. I deprive her. So she takes it out on me.' (II)

These two women dis-play together the central gestus of post-liberation
'woman': as two separate beings they serve to re-present the needs and desires of the male. Sensuality and sexuality is divided from intellect, both of
which the man desires: however, intellect is something he can derive from
platonic friendships and isn't something he necessarily marries. Crystal
seems to have the best of all possible worlds: Frank even ignores her promis-
cuity as long as she doesn't bring it home with her. The economic power
Crystal wields has, in effect, reversed the power nexus between the sexes:
and combined with the sexual power she has over Frank, Crystal occupies
the power-position that generations of men have had over their wives. Even
though Frank does leave in the end, Crystal is complacent: she knows he
will be back. And if he doesn't: 'Sod him! Who needs him!' she says dismissively. Frank, one suspects, would not have put up with Crystal's sexual forays
if not for the freedom her earnings offered him to pursue the path he desires:

Susannah: How's the job?
Frank: I'm supply teaching at the moment.
Susannah: Are you? I had you all dug in as senior history master. You look pretty
busy. (She picks up a pamphlet).
Frank: Socialist Combination. I've thrown my lot in, now that it's highly unfash-
ionable.
(They laugh)
Susannah: And what about freedom from party dogma?
Frank: Ah. Freedom. Plenty of that about. Freedom to sink. To go to hell. Oppor-
tunities for boys to train as butlers—I'm not kidding, there was a programme on
television.
Susannah: What about women?
Frank: Unemployment hasn't helped. The scene's changed since you left.
Susannah: Oh, how?
Frank: More polarized, I think.

I'll run you down to Greenham.
Susannah: Already been. So, you're active?
Frank: Full-time from next month.
Susannah (surprised): You're giving up teaching? Completely?
Frank (nods): I'll miss it.
Susannah: Can you afford to?
Frank: Just about. (He shrugs) Crystal pulls a fortune. (II)

Susannah the idealist do-gooder has returned from her years in Bolivia with regrets about her work, about having lost Frank, about the Pill which promised freedom to women but only seemed to delay the choice of motherhood until it was too late:

Susannah: I've gone over and over it in my mind. I should have been there. When you were ill. I realise that now.
Frank: I wasn't myself.
Susannah: I should have been there. That bloody project—God, we were so intense! We were going to change the world. Hah.
Frank: I know.
Susannah: I thought we were indissoluble. Mistake number one. We were so in step (…) at least that's what I thought. That fucking Pill.
Frank: What?
Susannah: If it weren't for the Pill I'd have been pregnant three times over, the way we went at it.
[…]
God, the agony of choice! (She groans) I mean! There's never a good time to have a baby, if you can afford it you're too old, and who needs Marmite sandwiches and little morons for ten years when you're just getting your head together—God, How I envy Crystal! (II)

Susannah returns to want the very things Crystal has: Frank, healthy children, a home, a family. Crystal's solution of a three-pronged communal arrangement appeals to Susannah—it would mean that the children would have their parents, Susannah would have Frank, while Crystal would be free to enjoy the active sexual life she seems to need. The play ends much as Churchill would end *Traps* (1977) and *Cloud Nine* (1979)—with an attempt at communal living. As Adrienne Rich remarked in a reflection on the changing institution of family in the late twentieth century: 'To seek visions, to dream dreams, is essential, and it is also essential to try new ways of living, to make room for serious experimentation, to respect the effort even where it fails.'[107]

In the 90s Gems has focussed on a male protagonist—the English artist Stanley Spencer in *Stanley* (1996). This may seem a divergence from her women-centred plays but is in keeping with her integrationist ideology. In the gamut of her work, however, Gems has given the prototypic straw women many lives and has demonstrated an ability to bring woman out from behind the veil of stereotypes infusing woman with a life long denied. In dramaturgical and theatrical terms Gems, 'the grande dame of British Theatre'[108] has retrieved woman and shattered the prototypical stereotype much as a prism shatters light revealing a bright and radiant rainbow of plurality.

———— ✣ ————

CHAPTER FOUR

FROM HETERO-NORMATIVITY TO THE VIEW FROM LESBOS

Through the Looking Glass with Sarah Daniels

Lesbian and gay experience is the lens through which heterosexual-biased society is desperately peering at its own problematic practices.

—Elizabeth Wilson

According to the laws and ordinances of the British Commonwealth as of [2001] lesbianism simply does not exist; it is not legally recognized in any form, 'deviant' or otherwise.

—Lizbeth Goodman.

SEEN FROM THE context of the groups and performers invisible to the audiences and critics of the British mainstream, groups like Split Britches and The Gay Sweatshop, Daniels' texts are 'assimilationist' texts. Looking in at her texts from these western radical-lesbian margins which parade their biographies and sexualit/ies, pleasures and partners on stage and within their performance texts[1], and for whom 'the most transgressive act at this historical moment would be representing [sadomasochistic and other kinds of pornographic performance] to excess, in dominant and marginalized reception communities',[2] Sarah Daniels is the 'conservative' mainstream dramatist who speaks of *lesbian* as a trope for bonding likened to motherhood or sisterhood. Not surprisingly, a critic as radical in her views on lesbian representation as Jill Dolan would not even take Daniels seriously enough to consider writing about her. However, it is with her words which in turn evoke bell hooks', that I introduce my analysis of Daniels as *a radical writer of the British mainstream:*

Saying "I am lesbian" has been validated in cultural feminist discourse as speech that breaks the silence of lesbian existence under heterosexual hegemony.[3]

Undoubtedly too politically correct for the radical lesbian margins of Anglo-America, Daniels undeniably 'comes out' in her writing albeit meta-phorically. The first woman to announce 'I am a lesbian' to the stages of the British mainstream she is lambasted by the (mainly male, overwhelmingly hetero-normative) critics, thereby taking her position centrestage as *the* radical lesbian writer of the *mainstream* stages of Britain. It is interesting that Elaine Aston struggles to establish that Daniels is *not* a mainstream writer because she has been performed 'on "alternative", studio stages rather than in mainstream playhouses [thus] in the "margins" of mainstream theatre.' She compares her to Churchill and Wertenbaker (whose plays have also largely played at studio venues similar to the venues at which Daniels has played, apart from the fact that they are all Royal Court writers).[4] From 1972 to 1995 (the date of Aston's article) the "most mainstream" theatre (to use Aston's nomenclature) to produce any Churchill play was the RSC's Barbi-can Pit where the—here comes patriarchy's invisible structural rule in op-eration—*all-male* version of Foucault's *Discipline and Punish, a play which had no gender content* to upset the system even unconsciously—*Softcops* was per-formed. All other plays by Churchill till the date of Aston's article were at venues such as The Dartington College of Arts (*Cloud Nine*) and Almeida Theatre (*Fen*), apart from The Royal Court which often staged the plays of all three writers. Wertenbaker has been performed at the RSC because she (even when indicting patriarchy) speaks in patriarchal high-language or the acceptable guise of classical Greek tragedy. *The Thebans* was performed in 1991 and *The Love of the Nightingale* played in 1988. The latter is a re-writing of the Greek myth of Philomel and Procne, told in the lost play of Sopho-cles, *Tereus*. Although Wertenbaker's play is an indictment of patriarchy, past and contemporary, the skilful re-working of a classical myth makes its case to the RSC. Arguably, Daniels is then the "most successful" playwright as her (undoubtedly lesbian) *Neaptide* was performed at The Cottesloe in 1986, at a time when the young writer's career had barely begun, whereas Churchill had to wait three and a half decades to be performed at the same venue. Wertenbaker is a fine dramatist, but not strictly feminist, and there-fore oughtn't be compared to Daniels at all. Churchill's case, though, makes a nonsense of Aston's observation that Churchill was more successful *be-cause* her plays moved to "more mainstream" stages. They didn't. That Churchill is, indeed, more successful, in spite of the venues Aston defines as non-mainstream, speaks for these venues being just that. They are where mainstream audiences *do* go. These are the mainstream's *adjacent stages* which form the supplement to places like the Cottesloe.

Daniels' drama gives the audiences, used to hetero-normative texts, an opportunity to step through the looking glass into a world which exists on the fringes of androcentricity. However, her dramatic mode contains a reappraisal of issues which are important to women, to feminism, to gay rights, and ultimately, to the thinking person.

> I'm not interested in feeding into prejudices or writing something that could have been done in mainstream entertainment. If there was no prejudice, no violence against women by men, I probably wouldn't be a writer.[5]

Daniels' plays are a fierce attack on and an exposure of patriarchal society as prejudiced and biased with its hetero-normative ideology which is inscribed on its very structure. She also gives us women like Jennifer (*Masterpieces*) and Tara (*Ripen Our Darkness*) who collude with men, consciously and unconsciously, to perpetuate the patriarchal order and its practices. Women in the traditional roles of heterosexual-patriarchy are exposed as trapped and guilty in play after play, as traditionally patterned relationships prove ineffectual and usually to the disadvantage of the woman as they inhibit her self-development as an individual and warp her sense of self. Daniels' lesbianism is not posited as an 'alternative' or 'the solution' to the problems of women. She uses *lesbian* as a *principle* and a *strategy* to break the boundaries of the hetero-normative traditions of British drama, to shatter or penetrate the strait/straight-lacing of our minds and bodies, by giving us a metaphor for women's need for solidarity through mutual support. She uses *lesbian* as a trope of reassurance which says there *are* alternative ways to live.

Lesbian becomes a trope for the powerless and invisible persons of society, like the deaf Dawn of *Beside Herself* who never bodily enters the discourse of the play as St. Dymphna's can't accept a person who is unable to hear (a fire alarm). Daniels unearths prejudices about gay and the mentally ill in *Beside Herself*, and also the guilt and secrecy that the abused often live with by uncovering the horror of incestual rape, as in the later *The Madness of Esme and Shaz*. Baring male minds in a pro-censorship indictment of pornography, she reveals the pervasive misrepresentation of women in the sign systems of western culture (*Masterpieces*) as *lesbian* becomes a sign of woman's awareness of the invisible oppressive text of patriarchy. *Ripen Our Darkness* and *Neaptide* lay open the hollowness and exploitative nature of traditional heterosexual relationships, as a concrete and united sisterhood is posited as the ideal utopian answer. Idealistic, wish-fulfilment endings serve as a compromise for harsher realities in several plays. It is Daniels' unique stance, which emerges from her personal and political lesbian subjectivity (which is inevitably silenced or marginalized) which makes the content of her drama seem so radical in the mainstream context. This is a brave and daring 'coming out' as she simultaneously 'outs' other silenced, marginalized and oppressed subjects by being inclusive under the sign *lesbian*. This under-lying concern for the silenced invisibles and the ability to give them a voice in the middle-class mainstream, sets her apart from what by way of differ-ence appears as Churchill's ambiguity and wavering in the face of social is-sues. Daniels does not hesitate in showing the way to solutions, offering hope mingled with a refreshing ability to infuse the most hopeless situations with laughter. It is in the offering of solutions that Daniels texts differ from Churchill. They are also, by this very quality, transmuted into a complex and utterly contemporary rendition of melodrama. Despite a rich seam of in-teresting radical and feminist lesbian theatre on the fringe, Sarah Daniels is the only lesbian-feminist to have been performed in the mainstream and its adjacent/supplementary stages through the 80s and 90s, carrying away, as she did, two awards for most promising playwright as well as the George De-vine Award. Daniels proves herself a strongly socialist dramatist, mercilessly exposing the hypocrisies which lie at the core of British society, in texts which are a series of radical political, even didactic, statements, yet main-tain a strong appeal to the mainstream audiences. In this lies her success in mainstream theatre.

The harsh, oft quoted reviews attracted by her texts betray not what the critics actually say, but rather, their pressing though unconscious impulse to function (as critics) in ways which would maintain the hetero-normatively ordered systems and its underlying structures. To maintain the regularity of discourse patriarchy deploys the subjects constituted within the system to support its regime of hetero-normativity. Their attitudes and utterances are always already inscribed and thus dictated by the invisible patriarchal im-pulse *which works against the feminist intervention* to suppress and repress any evidence of transgression, to silence the radical voice, to ostracize into obliv-ion any instance of disruption to the order of things. I cite here examples of what the critics said about *Masterpieces* (see critique below) which is a wa-tershed in feminist theatre. 'Confused the 'match with the bonfire'; 'it can't all be due to dirty books';[6] a 'crime of overstatement'; a 'rabid feminist play'; 'hysterical style and content';[7] a 'sweeping statement'; an 'irritating play';[8] and, the 'respectable broadsheet' critic, Robert Cushman of *The Observer*, dismissing the play in one short paragraph ('the argument [...] is circular and not worth much'), proceeds to dedicate the next paragraph to the three fe-male actors and a description of their bodies (legs).

The Feminist-Lesbian Appropriation of a Genre: Melodrama

'The worst thing a play can be is embarrassing. Being unintentionally melo-dramatic is equally high in the "cringe" awards', says Daniels in her preface to *Plays: One*. John Burgess concurs, describing Daniels first playscript as 'hover[ing] on the edge of melodrama.'[9] Both misunderstand melodrama to mean that which, in the colloquial sense, is 'as intellectually implausible as it is emotionally convincing'; that which, through a 'monopathy of triumph' so overwhelming brings an audience close to tears; in other words, melodrama has a tendency to be perceived as sentimental and embarrassing.[10]

I am seeking to establish that melodrama—accurately defined, and reworked to suit contemporary issues—as a dramatic form (transformed) is singularly suited to lesbian dramaturgy. As Griffiths and Woddis have pointed out, traditional drama based on conflict and difference is considered unsuitable to a single-gender experience, which leads to a need to interrogate kinds of forms which would be emergent from a dramatic focus on similarity.[11] R.B. Heilman argues that while the tragic protagonist is essentially 'divided' by 'a basic inner conflict', melodramatic protagonists are essentially 'whole'.[12] In melodrama, the protagonist remains undivided as s/he has only external pressures to fight against, as e.g., the Duchess of Malfi or the Trojan Women, in the absence of *hamartia* or *hubris*, seek self-preservation as opposed to the tragic protagonist (*e.g.*, Lear)'s progression towards self-knowledge. The Duchess and the Trojan Women are innocent victims of defeat from external forces. Melodrama, unlike tragedy, is concerned with the restructuring of relations with other people or events or things, rather than the universe at large. Smith isolates triumph, despair and protest as the basic emotions of melodrama: 'the art of working each to its highest pitch occasions the *catharsis* of the form. In melodrama we win [*The Madness of Esme and Shaz*] or we lose [*Ripen Our Darkness*: 'Dear David, your dinner and my head are in the oven'], unlike tragedy where we lose in the winning [*Macbeth*] or win in the losing [*Antony and Cleopatra*].'[13]

William Sharp identifies three genres of drama: tragedy, comedy and melodrama. Recognising that the tragic hero rises above society, and the comic hero sinks below it, he categorizes melodrama as that genre which 'focuses on the nobility of a hero who would change society [...] either [...] he [sic] is willing to change or [...] society realizes it must change'. It is because of this possibility that 'melodrama is the form used for those plays that push for social change or reform'.[14]

Daniels' protagonists (women, lesbians, the oppressed and invisible) are, by the very nature of their conflict, pitted against external adversity (in the various forms of men, social prejudices, and patriarchal structural rules which serve to normalize and regularize the constitutive subjects of the system). The resolutions are usually extreme solutions designed to produce an overwhelmingly 'monopathic' catharsis.[15] As Smith points out, this may seem naïve, trivial and second rate when compared with the rich complexities and broader moral dimensions of tragedy, but nevertheless, 'in terms of real life one often takes a side and accepts its credo: a football match, like an election campaign, must be lost or won. Melodrama is *the dramatic form which expresses the reality of the human condition as is most usually experienced by us*'.[16] Similarly, the lesbian condition and the woman condition as exposed in the plays of women dramatists, is most often fighting against external oppression from the patriarchal/hetero-sexual and normative system which is the perpetrator, and therefore a form most suited to these issues is the one chosen almost inadvertently by Daniels: Melodrama.

Smith further points out that between the mighty opposites of Right and Wrong there can be no compromise; the drama has to end in Triumph or Defeat. Either serves to rally new supporters to The Cause, and both provide a satisfying, simplified *catharsis*. Victory can be enjoyed only by blocking our sympathy for those defeated (as in the defeat of the social-welfare and criminal-justice systems by the love and commitment of a family tie, however newly forged, in *The Madness of Esme and Shaz*); while defeat arouses righteous anger at undeserved injustice (as, *e.g.*, in *Ripen Our Darkness*). The pattern of social protest can be framed exceptionally well by melodrama, and a common strategy to pinpoint a contemporary evil is to set up a blameless protagonist as a victim of the system, who is then subjected to such inhuman persecution that the empathizing audience explodes with indignation and demands an immediate repeal of laws which perpetrate such cruelties. However, such drama is effective only to the already converted, or indeed, the amenable, and effective protest takes account of the complexities which prevent a too facile and shrill denunciation of, in this case, the extant system ruled by an inflexible hetero-normative ideology.[17] To be sure, this latter is a structural principle which substrates the extant society, and as such, it is not immediately apparent that this is what is at stake in this lesbian rendition of melodrama. However, this makes the traditional melodramatic form appeal to unconscious levels (of prejudice), divesting the drama of its monopathic tone and rendering it more complex than traditional forms of melodrama can usually be. Daniels' art also makes the usually blameless victims of the system more complex than merely uni-dimensional beings, lending the melodramas a more tragic air than is commonly achieved by this genre. A further complexity is achieved by making some of the villains victims as well: Jennifer (*Masterpieces*) and Jim (*The Devil's Gateway*) are victims *and* perpetrators of unjust systems, albeit unconscious ones. Another victim is Shaz (*Esme and Shaz*), whose crime is of an extreme nature, and requires a great deal of courage (from both, the characters as well as the audience) to come to terms with, whilst Evelyn (*Beside Herself*) is a distant and aloof character who may alienate some from too close an empathy. Not all of Daniels' plays can be categorized as melodramas, but most partake of some of the best characteristics of the genre. This, combined with uncharacteristically complex, even tragic, protagonists, and an ability to infuse some of the most painful and despairing situations with well placed wit, Daniels manages to rework traditional, male, forms of drama, eliciting empathy, sympathy and pity with the genius of humour. Thus the traditional site of melodrama is restructured to create a new form suited to lesbian-feminist issues, the form of Radical and Complex Melodramas of Triumph. This restructuring of morphology (a kind of 'morphing') can also be regarded as a *citation* via Judith Butler, but, perhaps closer to my interpretation, as a strategy of camp. In *The Politics and Poetics of Camp*, Moe Meyer attempts to redefine and reclaim the discourse of Camp from what she calls the always already assimilating mainstream. Speaking of the need to account for the *decentred power* of gay and lesbian subjects, Meyer accedes that it is a power 'that is able to resist, oppose and subvert'. Daniels manages to do this well within the dominant discourse of the mainstream, and her strategy—the reappropriation of a traditional genre, melodrama—can be seen as 'camp' if approached through Meyer. She defines 'camp' as 'the strategies and tactics of queer parody' wherein 'parody is an intertextual manipulation of multiple conventions, an extended repetition with critical difference that has a hermeneutic function with both cultural and even ideological implications'.[18] Thus queer parody is derivative, a kind of dressing in drag. Just as drag entails a dependence on an already existing text in order to fulfil itself, the strategies of camp, especially parody, depend upon and feed off the dominant discourse. In my opinion, whether or not the strategy is used consciously, this dependence stems from a certain internalizing of the dominant ideology. The dominant ideology would substrate the dominant discourse, which has been reified over a period of time, the ideology being internalized by the minds and bodies which are the constitutive subjects of the discourse. Since the function of ideology is normalizing and regulatory, all subjects are imbricated within the grip of its power, and it is therefore impossible to locate oneself *outside* of it. If my explanation is interpreted with dramatic discourse in mind, we realize that every English/British dramatist writing in this moment is writing in the shadow of a long and honourable lineage of discourse which has been valorized within dramatic critical discourse since its heydey in the Renaissance. Breaking away with a centuries old tradition is difficult enough. Having no models to emulate is perhaps hardest of all. We learn from the earliest moments through emulation—thus Butler's theory of gen-

der formation as 'performance' or 'drag'.[19] In the breaking away there is almost always a citation, a reappropriation, a reformulation, as the old dominant discourse feeds into and helps formulate the new, which will in turn
serve as an early model for, in this case, camp dramatic discourse. Within
the new discourse the persistence of the old serves in part to valorize the
former but always in *sanctioning its own erasure*. Thus, writing with the conventions of a traditional drama, whether it is a lesbian reworking of melodrama as found in Daniels or, indeed, a feminist indictment of a valorized
patriarchal discourse (Greek drama) in Timberlake Wertenbaker's pieces
such as *The Love of a Nightingale*, a breaking with the old necessitates a quotation.[20] The erasure (of the old) comes from the deconstructive nature of
the strategy itself: *the old is cited in order to destruct the dominant cultural and
ideological formations and reconstruct new alternative ways of seeing*. When Alice steps through the looking-glass things appear to be the same, but she
soon finds out about the deceptive nature of the surface of things.

As Meyer puts it, 'without the process of parody, the marginalized agent
has no access to representation, the apparatus of which is controlled by the
dominant order. Camp, as specifically queer parody, becomes then, the only
process by which the queer is able to enter representation and to produce
social visibility.' This intervention into dominant discourse is double-edged:
although the vehicle is transgressive and disruptive, it 'simultaneously in-
vokes the spectre of dominant ideology in its practice, appearing, in many
instances, to actually reinforce the dominant order.'[21]

Ripen Our Darkness

Mary's defeat in *Ripen Our Darkness* has begun before the play opens. The
attitudes of her husband and son are stereotypical, conventional male attitudes to the wife/mother whose life is one of domestic servitude: a 'life
[which is] at best monotonous, and at worst unbearably painful' (The Deity
in Scene xiii). To Mary, her life is 'a half finished jigsaw while everybody
else seems to have completed their pictures' (Scene i). Mary metonymically
evokes the subtextual metaphor for the neglected Virgin as wife of the An-
glican Churchwarden David. Father and son represent the male oppression
of woman through the centuries as the woman's defeat (suicide) is transformed into omniscient transcendence as she arrives in a matriarchal heaven
where she is greeted by a female trinity. A melodrama of defeat which uses
stock characters (oppressed and oppressors) is combined with a subversion of
other stock characters (the trinity) to reverse a (real) defeat into a triumph
of almost comic wish-fulfilment. The reversal, using the principles of essentialist and separatist feminism, posits the drama successfully in the realm of
radical feminist theatre seen for the first time on the mainstream stages of

Britain. Radical by its context, it is interesting that Daniels' drama made it to the viewership of middle-class mainstream audiences as early as 1981, debunking, as it does, heterosexual and normative lifestyles. Using popular belief in the everafter as an agent of the transformation, the resolution is one of comic and sentimental triumph which, by the nature of being the converse of the traditional belief in an everafter with God made-in-the-image-of-the -patriarch, mocks the tenets of David's religion whilst it makes for a rather comic spirited feminist triumph. This achieves an effective purgation in this contemporary feminist reworking of traditional dramatic patterns.

Parallel to Mary's despair runs the story of Rene's victimized existence. Although Rene defends her violent, foul-mouthed husband (Alf) to others, when left on her own she betrays herself as trapped:

> Dear Mary Grant, I have a husband who drinks all my money away. I have two jobs to try to give him enough so he doesn't feel the need to slap me and my daughter around, but I usually fail. I have to lie in piss-soaked sheets, as my husband wets the bed every night. My daughter's severely handicapped baby has just died [...] I have dreams of doing myself in. Please don't reply as my husband rips up my mail regardless. (Scene iii)

Rene's triumph is pseudo-realistic. Again, through the use of a stock situation—here, the convenient demise of the oppressor-husband—Daniels provides for Rene's release.

By projecting Tara solely through the dramatic device of a voice-over, Daniels distances her as a potential site for (heterosexual-female audience) identification or (heterosexual-male audience) desire, using her brief speech as material for an authorial final word on heterosexual unions. If the two traditional, domestic, heterosexual women are revealed as leading unfulfilling lives, the third (Tara) is condemned as exploitative of her heterosexual marriage:

> Between you and I, Marsh has begged me to divorce him. Why should I? I don't want to live in some pokey little flat where some social worker might try and certify me for being batty. No thanks. I like being posh. Don't listen to this live without men rot. The way forward is to use them and have some fun. (Scene v)

Daniels in this first play projects lesbian relationships as ideal in a world of failed and failing heterosexual blunders. Mary's daughter (Anna) lives in lesbian union with Rene's daughter (Julie): a life ideally free from conflict. Mary, although resigned to the fact that she is 'the only mother-in-law (…)

with three sons and four daughters-in-law', appreciates, though somewhat wryly, that Anna and Julie 'can both make lunch' (scene vii). Mary, constituted as a normalized and normalizing subject of heteronormative ideology, cannot accept her daughter's lesbian life which prevents much emotional closeness between the two.

Ripen Our Darkness, as Daniels' first play, sets the pattern for most of the rest of her dramatic work. Debunking heterosexuality by revealing it as emotionally unfulfilling and disempowering for women, or (interestingly, from a lesbian dramatist) as economically parasitical on the man, Daniels projects single-sex unions as a viable alternative in this piece. Lesbianism is the central Brechtian gest at the gamut of her work: it serves as a trope for sisterhood, female bonding and emotional union, all of which are denied in heterosexual relationships. In her later plays, the mother-daughter relationship supercedes lesbian attachment, as *e.g.*, in *Masterpieces* where the only significant moments of female bonding are where Jennifer, Rowena and Yvonne share a sunny afternoon, picnicking (scene xiii) and recalling childhood memories. Similarly *The Madness* has Esme and Shaz forge and duplicate a mother-daughter bond rather than a lesbian bonding.

As a melodrama of triumph *Ripen Our Darkness* is a skilful reworking of cliched contemporary situations and characters into a fairly complex and sentimental melodrama in a lesbian-feminist mode. By the use of realism, Daniels lulls her audience into heterosexual assumptions which are then cleverly subverted.[22] By presenting lesbian union as the dominant ideological ideal within the text of the play, heterosexist cultural *mores* are challenged as the patriarchal perceptual screens from behind which mainstream audiences are used to viewing, are dismantled and an alternative, interrogatory, viewership is proposed. This visible manifestation of an alternative ideology on the mainstream stage (and the Royal Court is undeniably mainstream and establishment even as it encourages new writing) is at once provocative and political, setting the agenda for her later more mature work where *lesbian* almost ceases to be about relationships or practice, but diffuses into a metaphor for broadly feminist concerns.

Neaptide

> There is a [neap]tide in the affairs of [wo]men (…)

In *Neaptide* Daniels dramatizes the metaphor of lesbians coming out in one bold sweep, illuminating by the same token the prejudices of the heterosexual majority. *Neaptide* at its most fundamental level is about 'the performance [of] the "act" of coming out'.[23] In this act, both private/personal and

public/political fuse in performance. This is the lesbian dramatist's act of refusal: a political refusal in its rebellion against the norm of heterosexuality,
and a personal one in promoting new forms of subjectivity through the public mode of performance on the mainstream stages. The necessity to provide
a platform for lesbian subjectivity is a pressing political and personal need
which Daniels' drama courageously aims to fulfil, making her texts perform
the awkward and public act of coming out which has become central to lesbian theatre on the fringe. Inadvertently echoing Foucault, Goodman points
out 'the need to reclaim and name self', the lesbian private-become-public
self, in the face of a resistant heterosexual world order.[24] The simultaneous
double-bind the lesbian experiences as she is individualized as a woman and
totalized within a heterosexual system of normativity affects her politically
and personally. The act of coming out is a re-claiming of self, the grasping
and endorsing of a new form of subjectivity which rejects and refuses the
bind imposed by the world and its constitutive stages. As Goodman points
out, 'many lesbians do not 'come out' but lead private lives very different
from their public ones'. The act is a highly personal one, even when 'ritual-
ized into the most public of performances'.[25] Indeed, for most lesbian women
it is truistic that their choice of same-sex partner does not necessarily indicate a different life style, *i.e.*, leading a private lesbian life may not impinge
on other areas of one's life. Many lesbians do not come out, and Daniels
dramaturgy vocalizes the silence of a silent lesbian majority by stressing the
political need to do so and challenge the multitude of heterosexist prejudices.[26]

Thus, Claire and Bea Grimble's act of coming out is painful but necessary in its implications. Simultaneously Daniels cuts through the plethora of
heterosexist and normative prejudices with characteristic wit. Circumscribing the play is the Greek myth of mother-daughter bonding and patriarchal
enslavement and authority, while dominating the centre lie the modern
'myths' or falsehoods about lesbian sexuality, behaviour and lifestyles. As
long as myths about the latter exist the former (ideal) will always be a struggle for lesbian mothers who are denied control in parenting and the custody
of their children (Claire) through mis-representation and lack of understanding.

Val's opening is semi-choral in initiating the Greek origins of what per-
vades the play as subverted myth. A pun on the doctor's name (Herr/Hare
March) subliminally evokes patriarchal persecution in the dramatic text, a
metaphor of possibility which runs through Daniels work. The heterosexual
Val's insanity and her refusal to reenter the 'normal world' posits her as a
Persephone relegated to Hades—or an Alice lost through the looking glass:

Here I sit, mad as a hatter with nothing to do but either become madder and madder or else recover enough of my sanity to be allowed back to the world that drove
me mad.

(*Neaptide*, I, i)

Claire and Poppy through their reading of (Phyllis Chesler's version of)
the Demeter myth symbolise the mother-daughter bonding which is central
to this story. In the repudiation of heterosexist and normative fairytales ('I
certainly like this better than Cinderella or Sleeping Beauty') with their
stereotypical hetero-utopian and-they-lived-happily-ever-after endings, and
in the turning to a Greek myth which dwells on sister/mother/daughter
hood, Claire is educating Poppy differently. The repudiated fairytales serve
to frame the structure of Daniels tale *Neaptide* presaging the alternative ending.

The scenes set in the staff-room reveal the prevalent prejudices encountered by gay men and women. Discussing the Peter O'Toole *Macbeth*, Annette's internalized heterosexist-prejudicial response is:

(...) it brought a whole new perspective to the characters of the three witches, you
know, a hint of, er, female intimacy (...) between them (...) which gave a real
tinge of reality to their evilness. (I, iv)

The use of theatrical space which swings from public (the school) to
public/private heterosexual (the staff room) to private-lesbian (Claire and
Grimble's homes) contrasts in turn heterosexist attitudes and how they impinge upon and hegemonically disrupt private lesbian lives. The audience is
cleverly manipulated to view normalized attitudes as prejudicial revealing
the deconstructive potential of Daniels' texts as they attempt to reformulate
and displace the dominant ideology of the mainstream audiences. The heterosexual spaces of the play reveal the many misconceptions about lesbians:
that they always dress in male attire and are not 'attractive' nor biologically
natural.

The irony is that both the headmistress and the deputy lead private lesbian existences, and, by a stretch of coincidence, the two lesbian schoolgirls
discover Beatrice Grimble's secret.

Terri: (gets up and surveys the bookcase). Boring. Boring. Boring.
Diane: (finds a small framed photograph behind a plant). Hey, look at this, an old
photo of Bea with her arm around a woman.
Terri: (looking at the photo). They all did that then. Gawd, look at those shoes.
Diane: She's still got them by the sound of it. (She opens the desk drawer and ten-
tatively rummages around its contents).
Terri: (alarmed) Don't do that.
Diane: She poked her nose into our lives.

Terri: We shoved our lives under her nose, you mean.
Diane: (pulls out a card). Look, an anniversary card.
Terri: Blimey. Maybe she was married then.
Both of them look at it.
Terri}
Diane}(exclaim in unision). All my love, Florrie.
They look at each other.
Terri}
Diane} Miss Grimble's one.

(II, iv)

Grimble's sudden reversal of public attitude toward lesbianism after a lifetime in the closet signals her act of coming out, while Joyce's solution to her daughter Claire's dilemma signals an acceptance (which was denied by Mary to her daughter in *Ripen Our Darkness*), and provides the drama with a (lesbian) wish-fulfilment closure, where the father, having been granted custody, is left knocking on the door of an empty flat, while mother and daughter leave the country with grandmother's help.

It would be too facile to read the endings of Daniels' plays as patterned after traditional patriarchal forms ending in closure. Daniels' closures encode a subversive strategy as they spell new beginnings for the minoritized. However, these texts are located in the context of the mainstream, and since the majority of mainstream audiences and critics view the performance through private heterosexist screens, an audience sympathy for Claire is crucial and cleverly constructed. Daniels' strategy of melodramatic reversals of triumph for the marginalized is essential to her texts which function as alternative fairytales within the conventions of realism. Embedded within the traditional dramatic form are the seeds of its destruction as normalizing and/or regulating discourse. The conventional dramatic framework also lulls the audiences into a false complicity with a seemingly hetero-normative order which is then revealed as prejudiced and limiting. Those lulled into a complicity of empathy with Grimble and Claire would finally find themselves caught up with the lesbian Other side.

The closure is idealistic: hopefully there will no longer be a need for 'the closet' and the future seems ready for a new and equally credible ideology. In her attempt to portray that they (also) could live happily-ever-after, Daniels mixes wit with optimism and laughter. In seeking an ideal place for her characters who are constituted within frameworks of prejudice, triumphant idealized reversals seem to be a necessary ending, allowing impossible situations to be infused with a measure of hope making her dramas the fantasies of Lesbos.

The Madness of Esme and Shaz

Every [wo]man's life is a fairytale written by God's fingers.
                                                    —Hans Christian Andersen

The Madness of Esme and Shaz […] [i]s not about issues, only people.
                    —Daniels, Theatre Programme for the 1994 Royal Court production

Representing the dominant ideology once again loaded with subversive dice, in *Madness*, Daniels celebrates the role of the family as an important stabilizing factor in the often confusing and alienating modern societal structures. By the emotional bonding of a distant aunt with a long-time institutionalized niece—the only survivors of a separated family—in a sentimental melodrama of triumph over material values and state apparatuses, Daniels sketches a meritorious piece which offers hope with characteristic humour. The stereotypical psychiatrist lampooned in *Ripen Our Darkness* and again in *Masterpieces*, here proves symptomatic of the entire psychiatric welfare system, over which the strong emotional bond of family ties gains ascendancy.

Esme and Sharon could not be further apart as individual personalities: the one, devout, religious and ever conscious of her duty to society and her neighbours; the other, a foul-tongued young woman whose only knowledge of the outside world comes from television, having been institutionalized for almost her entire life. Esme's first act of taking Sharon in care is one guided by duty and a 'sign' from the Lord.

Shaz forms a relationship with Pat in a bid for love and affection, but, like Mary, Esme cannot come to terms with Sharon's lesbian relationship, and for the first half of the play her attitude is one of stoical (in)tolerance. Shaz needs demonstrations of love which Esme cannot find in herself to provide, unused as she is to emotional attachments. Although both Pat and Esme accept the fact that Shaz had been institutionalized, the former is horrified to hear the reason is because she murdered her father's baby. If she had killed the abuser she would have been 'a heroine in [Pat's] book'; to Pat's radical-separatist-essentialist thinking it would have been excusable, even, if Shaz had murdered the little *boy*, but killing the baby girl was 'killing the wrong person'. Shaz, who in her years at Broadmoor has reached a kind of self-knowledge, cannot comprehend Pat's short-sightedness: 'There is no right person, there is no fucking right person' (scene vii). Surprisingly, it is Esme who empathizes and connects:

Esme: My father, your grandfather was a -. As a Christian I don't have the words to describe him. He was one of those men. When (…) when we were children, your father and I, he wouldn't leave us alone. You know to what I'm referring?
Shaz: Yeah?

> Esme: And I suspect, I expect that my brother repeated the same pattern of behaviour when you were a child.
> Shaz: (looks down)
> Esme: That's the difference between men and women. They can't seem to help themselves. Or rather they do help themselves. We don't -
> Shaz: No, no. We only destroy ourselves instead. (Scene viii)

Although this description of gender difference with regard to child abuse is separatist and actually subscribes quite conveniently to dominant ideological beliefs, it foregrounds the reason for Shaz's action of killing her father's baby: she 'saves' the baby from almost certain sexual abuse by suffocating her to death. In destroying her father's girl-child, Sharon destroys her self, and continues to do so daily, slashing her arms in symbolic self-destruction.

Esme's inability to offer love instead of duty is distressing for Shaz, and, when she is taken back into the psychiatric care unit after her assault on a police officer, she refuses to see her aunt. However, Esme, with uncharacteristic aggressiveness born of concern for her niece, pushes her way into the unit:

> Esme: (…) Don't worry we'll soon get you out of here.
> Shaz: I love you.
> Esme: (Takes a step back)
> Shaz: I don't mean like that. I don't mean nothing sexual or nothing. I mean -
> Esme: I don't think I've ever loved anybody.
> Shaz: Yes, yes you have.
> Esme: No.
> Shaz: Jesus. What about Jesus?
> […]
> Esme: Oh Jesus.
> Shaz: Me?
> Esme: You? I don't know.
> Shaz: You took me to live with you, you must have seen something good in me?
> Esme: No, that was because of a sign from God. (Laughs)
> Shaz: Then you cared for me.
> Esme: Duty, duty, duty.
> Shaz: And now you've come all the way down here and you must have kicked up a hell of a row for her to let you see me in seclusion.
> Esme: Actually, one could argue that I did it for me. (Scene xiii)

Esme's refusal or reluctance to face her true feelings for Shaz are indicative of her repressed emotional existence and also of a wider societal disorder which a repudiation of love represents. Shaz's persistence in drawing her out is a dramatist's attempt to demonstrate what is required: an acknowledgement that love exists and must be vocalized and demonstrated within familial contexts. Esme's tentative acknowledgement of her (maternal) love is also a 'coming out', and reveals Daniels' broad use of 'lesbian' as a metaphor. Esme 'comes out' as she sees a reflection of her self in Shaz—they are, incredible as it may seem, mirror images of each other:

> Shaz: I don't want to go. [i.e., leave the psychiatric institution]
> Esme: Are you demented?
> Shaz: And I don't want to see you again unless it's only because you love me.
> (Pause)
> Esme: If love is longing for the half of ourselves we have lost, then alright. (ibid.)

Both Esme and Shaz progress toward a deeper self-knowledge, and Esme's final courage to venture into the unknown for the sake of her niece is her way of breaking the bounds, demonstrating in the process a deep insight into the necessity of and the ability to break with a lifetime of habit (constructed attitudes) when required. For Esme, Shaz symbolizes not merely her lost family, but also daring youth, both of which inspire a necessary forgiving and healing with the past. Shaz brings into Esme's life a desire to live and enjoy life to the fullest, in spite of having been a victim of abuse and after a lifetime of cautious guardedness in forming emotional attachments. In scene xiv aunt and niece almost exchange personalities as Esme, having discovered a hidden well of adventure-seeking bravado, drives recklessly, scaring the usually brazen Shaz:

> Shaz: (…) Brake!
> Esme: (Braking) Now which peddle [sic] is that? Just kidding.
> Shaz: (reclines her seat and shuts her eyes)
> Esme: What are you doing?
> Shaz: Praying.

When Shaz realizes that Esme has sold her flat to take her away to live on a faraway island, that she will never have to be taken into psychiatric care again, that she is loved, forgiven and understood, she understands that Esme's declaration of love has exceeded all her expectations. Again, the metaphor 'lesbian' frames the text, as they journey to Mytilene, which is the birthplace of the poetess Sappho and a port of the islands of Lesbos. This is where they are ready to heal and be whole again, having left the society and context which fostered their festering wounds:

> Esme: (…) will you wear a tee shirt or something with short sleeves?
> Shaz: I can't. I can't.
> Esme: Yes, you can.
> Shaz: No.
> Esme: Why?

Shaz: I don't want to.
Esme: Lots of people think battle scars are something to be proud of.
Shaz: But I ain't done nothing to be proud of.
Esme: I'm proud of you.
Shaz: Are yer?
Esme: Yes.
Shaz: But they are so ugly.
Esme: (Starts to roll up one of Shaz's shirt sleeves) How will they ever heal otherwise.
Shaz: (Starts to roll up the other one) Come on then let's go mad.
(The end)

The lesbian metaphors that frame the text—'coming out' of Broadmoor (the closet), 'coming out' to an acknowledgement of love (relationships), the journey to Lesbos—are the seeds which spell destruction within the traditional vehicles of realism and the stress on familial bonds. Daniels strategy defines lesbianism far beyond Dolan's narrow endorsement of the public representation of the gay sexual act. Same sex bonding—indeed, any human bonding—goes far beyond sex and sexuality. How subversive is the endorsement of public representation of sexual intercourse when society is a sustained by a network of other, possibly more important, kinds of intercourse? Theorists like Dolan, when they privilege the performance of sexuality over other kinds of performance fall into the trap of patriarchal reversal and take the stage into the realm of pornographic representation. Dolan duplicates patriarchy, Daniels deconstructs it.[27] Pornography in representation would only bring in a voyeuristic audience and reinforce ideas of gay and lesbian relationships as sexually deviant. Same-sex bonding, like other-sex bonding has a sexual side to it, but by foregrounding sexuality to an extent where pornographic representation is valorized reinforces stereotypical attitudes and ways of seeing (reception) whereas Daniels strategies serve to displace and reconstruct the ideology in operation.

In *Madness*, the lesbian metaphor is one of sisterhood and family ties, constructed to mean commitment, love and responsibility combined with the daring required in the 'performance of coming out'.[28] Many lesbian dramatists of the 70s and early 80s wrote coming out messages in their plays and Daniels extends this message to make it all embracing and positive thereby valorizing it in the context of the mainstream.

Daniels' plays are able to break the bounds which separate the mainstream from the alternative or fringe because they are framed within the bounds of patriarchal discourse, much as Timberlake Wertenbaker's indictments of western patriarchies are framed within the respectable guise of Greek drama. These texts achieve the task of reconstructing conventional ways of seeing in those reception communities which are most resistant to change—the mainstream which is substrated by commercialism (capitalism) the means to which lie in the age old strategies of patriarchy. Although it remains of vital importance to preach to the converted in order to support and further the practice of the alternative stage, it is perhaps more difficult to *preach to convert* as one risks being booed off the stage collectively.[29] Daniels' strategic potential then is ultimately more subversive as it skilfully manages to elicit audience sympathy for characters who are subsequently revealed as constituted within alternative ideologies. Underlying this strategy is her genius of humour which surfaces in the most despairing situations. In *Madness* she posits the most unlikely characters in the realm of audience sympathy. She reworks and re-visions the 'old maid' and gives us a foul tongued yobbish young murdereress. Both are victims of patriarchal hegemony and caught up in the cruel workings of state apparatuses which are resisted and overcome through bonding. The resultant self-knowledge, freedom and happiness (gayness?) makes for a complex revisionist melodrama—an old genre 'dragged' through the looking-glass and firmly posited in Lesbos.

Daniels demonstrates that it isn't merely gay and lesbian lives that need airing as she 'drags' out a range of issues from the British closet. The melodramas present a diverse range of characters—caricatures even—re-visioned into a contemporary feminist melodramatic mode. These are issues seldom seen on the mainstream stages, and these texts represent a dramatist's 'coming out' with a verve and ferocity of intent in order to demolish the performance of hegemony on the British stage.

More Dragged out of the British Closet: *Beside Herself*

> I don't think there are any original states of mind left to reclaim
> —Val in *Neaptide*

Shaz and Esme both broke free of the 'guilt' imposed upon them—their internalized guilt of incestual abuse: one by killing her father's girl-child and the other by leaving home in a bid to escape and form a new life. Both were victims who tried to break from the circumscription of the discourse of abuse that framed their lives. In an earlier play, *Beside Herself* (1990), Daniels personifies woman's internalized guilt in the figure of Eve in the face of what is clearly outside her self, outside the locus of the subject's control: paternal child-abuse. In a prelude which resembles the opening of *Top Girls*, Daniels gathers together Eve and wives from the New Testament in a twentieth century supermarket. The play is clearly influenced by, and yet, also a striking departure from *Top Girls* (1982) thereby demonstrating that new feminist morphologies now begin to spawn breeds which can break with the old completely. The citation of the opening of *Top Girls*, a primary ruptural text within the neo-discourse of British feminist drama, demonstrates a discursive continuity which is set in motion but, at this time of writing (2000) far too early for me to comment on at length. At this moment it must suffice to say that the rupture will have a snowball effect, and will in time account for the revisions effected in the traditional site of English/British drama.

Daniels' texts are harder hitting than Churchill's; the latter's open-ended querying morphology has an obverse side in that it is also a kind of evasiveness demonstrating that a subject can be formulated and constituted within a dominant ideology yet be alert enough to question it, remaining, however, *still located within it*. Daniels goes much further than Churchill's tentative theses: not only is she focused and specific about much elided issues such as child-abuse and pornography, thereby shattering the taboo of silence which shrouds such issues, but she goes so far as to suggest possible solutions—or a first step towards one—which places the drama very firmly in the realm of a didactic dramatic tradition which can be traced back to the mysteries and morality plays which heralded the birth of English drama, becoming, in the twentieth century, political (suffrage drama) and socialist (Edward Bond) in its role of cultural check and critique. Daniels, then, continues a tradition whilst simultaneously critiquing it and breaking with it, a strategy reflected in her choice of form and style and intent. Daniels' texts are then socialist in their aims as educative drama and, in the mainstream, the continuation of a lineage which is exemplified by Bond's texts such as *Saved*.

This is partly what accounts for the appearance of the subversive feminist texts of this thesis on the mainstream stages: they all appear, at some level, to be constituted within the ideological formation of the mainstream. This is partly true; as has been noted earlier, we don't see a single black person make an appearance in these texts. However, the texts of these female dramatists of the twentieth century are loaded with deconstructive potential as they surreptitiously effect the epistemic rupture in the site of English drama.

Daniels presents issues in a way which makes the elision of a taboo impossible by virtue of it forming the core of the dramatization. In the prelude patriarchy's elders are satirized with a wit which is characteristic of the Sarah Daniels text, and the reason for the presence of Eve is established. Eve represents 'the burden of guilt and two thousand years of misrepresentation'. Cixous' text 'The Laugh of the Medusa' speaks of the internalization of guilts by woman as classically patriarchal.[30] Thus the presence of Eve offers the audience an alternative mode of perception through which they are constructed to read the patriarchal framing of the text. Eve is the potential deconstructive tool for textual analysis. Eve is the guilty woman, Eve is the reminder of the first guilt thrust upon western woman in the originary myth of patriarchy; in the context of the play Eve is Evelyn's guilt at being sexually abused by her father, a misplaced guilt which many abused women bear through their adult lives. Eve is Evelyn's guilt concretized into flesh and blood to be made visible to the audience in a feminist-Brechtian technique which forces the spectator to continually question and assess the dialogue and action.

Evelyn is a typical middle-class woman, a classic representation of the women who comprise the audiences of the mainstream. The eventual realization that she is a victim of abuse posits child-abuse in the centre rather than invite the usual displacement/dismissal as something that does happen but not to us. Evelyn is represented as rather superficial and shallow, whose attendance at the various charity meetings is born out of a sense of a rich housewife's ennui rather than a real sense of caring. At the meeting at St. Dymphna's she is typically flippant, evading confrontation with any disturbing issues:

> Shirley: For an awful lot of people 'happy', 'home', and 'family' are not synonyms.
> Evelyn: If home is where the heart is, I'd live in John Lewis. (scene ii)

Evelyn and, like her, Teddy, seem to flit from meeting to charity meeting without any sense of participation or empathy for the issues being discussed. St. Dymphna is on par with the Working Party on Canine Control for Evelyn and the Mother's Union for the vicar, Teddy. On the surface Evelyn lives for the surface of things, which is for the most part true, so when she is visibly disturbed by Greg's remarks at the meeting and the ensuing discussion on child abuse, it signals a discrepancy within the psychological construction of the character. Moreover, Eve, who shadows Evelyn wherever she goes, functions as the vocalization of Evelyn's internal distress, first when she is with her now retired father and subsequently at the meeting when Eve tries to distract Evelyn from the conversation about child abuse. Seen and heard only by Evelyn (and the audience), Eve is the misplaced guilt that Evelyn has to confront and overcome. It is only when she can face Eve that she has the courage to unburden the guilt where it rightly belongs: on her father's shoulders. This is a dramatic and arguably honest denouement: as Greg had argued, 'blame per se is [not] a very healthy approach to rebuilding lives (…) the whole family need re-educating into their appropriate roles'. (scene ii). However, Evelyn is an adult who has lived her life bowed under a guilt which is not rightly hers, and Daniels courageous 'solution' points a way toward a healthy re-working and re-building of relationships: confrontation and acknowledgement.

It is in scene ix (entitled 'Genesis') that she unburdens herself to Nicola, and in scene x ('House Built on Sand') that she finally confronts her father, and Eve disappears, signifying the end of guilt:

> Evelyn: (calmly) There was a child who was abused by her Father for many years. It hurt. She was in pain and humiliated and eventually robbed of herself. No, Father, I don't want revenge. What could I possibly do to you that would undo what you've done to me? I've lived with it and I don't want to any longer. You can live with it. (Eve turns and looks at Evelyn and slips away). And I won't forgive you because what you've done is unforgivable.

The capital F in the articulation Father points to the larger victimization of women within the confines of an age old patriarchal regime and a similar need to vocalize grievances. It is only in reading the text off the page, however, that this is apparent, and a good theatre director would pick up on the overarching signification in the text and portray this in the sign-systems of performance and stage representation.

It is significant that the cleansing ritual that follows the confrontation is performed by Evelyn on herself and Eve, pointing to a need for personal action in the erasure of patriarchy's imposition of guilts on women. The act of cleansing is a sign for women to unburden their individual and collective guilt.

The final movement has the other victim, Nicola, come face to face with her estranged mother—who wouldn't believe her husband capable of child abuse for years—another form of denial practised in many families of abused victims. It is in the facing of facts however painful, and acknowledging that abuse can and does exist, possibly under one's own roof, that a healing is possible and relationships are able to be forged anew.

Even this starkly chilling play with its dark undertones has Daniels' characteristic ending of hope. Entwined with the central issue of parental child abuse Daniels exposes the inadequacies of state systems and its bureaucratic apparatuses: for example, the rejection of hard-of-hearing Dawn's application by St. Dymphna's because the fire regulations do not account for an inability to hear the fire alarm. (scene ii).

By presenting a taboo issue as central and solvable, something that is able to be worked through, and by involving the audience with a representative of their class, Daniels shatters the myth that child abuse is a working class syndrome characteristic of families who live on council estates. She takes the issue to the centre and demonstrates that this could be something we all have to be alert to, something that we ought to be able to contend with and confront if the need arose. In the context of mainstream theatre this is a thought provoking and challenging play. Her excellent appropriation of the Brechtian split-gest in a novel way—splitting the subject in an innovative theatrical fashion, creating two visual schizophrenic subjects who need to un-couple themselves in order to be free from the grip of the *socius*—posits Daniels among a group of accomplished and thinking feminist dramatists writing at the *fin-de-siècle*. Marrying originality of dramatic execution with a neo-didacticism on the stage which is decidedly feminist, Daniels succeeds in bringing neglected issues into the spotlight in a period of increased sociological and psychological awareness making her a dramatist of her time.

Master/Pieces

> The message? Women are pieces of meat. This is how men who use pornography learn to treat and see women
>
> —Catherine Itzin[31]

Catherine Itzin's introduction to her wide-ranging compilation of instructive essays on *Pornography: Women, Violence and Civil Liberties* (1992) locates pornography within the economic framework of capitalism.

> Why make such a fuss about pornography? Men seem to like it. It's a very profitable industry (...) It's said to be just a bit of harmless fun: entertainment for men (...) After all, it's only images. Isn't there a big difference between fantasy and reality?[32]

Daniels opens *Masterpieces* similarly. Three males, each as originator, disseminator or emptor of pornography, reveal their attitudes. The Baron projects it as 'a perfectly normal profession run by ordinary nice people, not gangsters or kinky dwarfs in soiled raincoats. That is a ludicrous myth perpetuated by the media.' The Peddler regards pornography as 'marital aids which enrich people's—men and women's—romantic lives (...) we provide the practical side to sex therapy.' The consumer opines 'Let's face it, alcohol and cigarettes can kill people, looking at pictures never hurt anyone'.

The question is pornography, and both, Itzin and Daniels use similar strategies of luring their reader/audience by lulling them into a false complicity with popular attitudes to what will be revealed as the practice of gender and racial misogyny taken to the extreme. Daniels' text is an attempt at a powerful exposition of how seemingly innocuous pornographic materials to the hard-core violence of snuff films can lead to the construction of an ingrained misogyny in men and the continued commodification of women in societies which pride themselves on having equal rights laws.

Daniels presents in the first scene, three very different men and their attitudes to women. Clive as the symbolic pater of the group, stepfather of Rowena, has enacted the three former characters, the last one—the consumer—as himself. Walking towards the group at his dinner table, he is increasingly disparaging about his wife and does not miss a single opportunity to dismiss or belittle her remarks. Ron, Yvonne's husband, holds the monopoly on misogynistic jokes. Trevor seems to be on the side of women by some of his comments, but he, too dismisses Yvonne's repulsion to the schoolboys' preoccupation with 'girlie mags' as too 'right wing' and later likens her inclination to burn the material to the Nazis who destroyed propaganda they didn't like. The feminist call for the censorship of pornographic material in the early 80s was seen as a conservative, right-wing concern with public morality. Feminisms traditional alliance with the left, its support of free speech and the abolition of censorship (see 70s journals such as 'Spare Rib') seemed to contradict with the call to censor pornographic material. It was in America that this contradiction was resolved as the Minneapolis City Council approved a new ordinance which declared that 'certain kinds of pornography violate women's civil rights.' This new law which came into being on 30 December 1983 (*Masterpieces* having opened in Britain on 31 May of the same year) is a landmark in feminist theory (even if not put into practice on any measurable scale) as it shifts the objection to pornography from obscenity to the question of *women's civil rights*. Seen as an issue of human rights, the authors, purveyors and emptors of porn are guilty of gender oppression and exploitation. The advisors to the state for this law were two feminists, Catherine McKinnon (a lawyer) and Andrea Dworkin (a teacher and author of *Men Possessing Women*, a landmark indictment of pornography).[33]

Rowena is ambivalent for the most part at first, not only because of her ignorance of the continuous misrepresentation of women in pornography but also as an authorial strategy in audience-attitude construction.[34] The tripartite reactions of the women to the misogynist jokes symbolise the three phases which an ideal reception community is led through in terms of the construction of viewership. Jennifer's raucous acknowledgement signals the first phase: a part of the audience, caught unawares, find themselves laughing, and therefore complicit with what the text will uncover as patriarchally induced misogyny. Yvonne's denunciatory response is the last phase: the site to which the audience must journey with Rowena, whose initial ambiguous discomfort should be the reflection of a large part of the attitude of an 'ideal audience' who will progress to an educated rejection of male entertainment derived from the commodification of women's bodies as a transformation achieved by this didactic interventionist text. As the play progresses we see a widening rift between all three women and their husbands, each of whom we have found guilty of some level of misogyny in the opening scene. Yvonne, who had seemed 'right wing' and 'Nazi' in her reception of what is generally considered 'soft porn' (sometimes classified as harmless 'erotica') gains the support of Rowena as the latter discovers that misogyny runs through *all* pornographic material: in fact it is the basis for pornographic representation as the dual impulses of gender and racial supremacy meet to support the economic discourse of 'advanced' capitalist societies. Just as 'for a Jew the differences between the anti-Semitism of Maurras and that of Goebbels are imperceptible' the women realise that none of them is exempt from the latent misogyny that runs through the stereotypical western male mind, fuelled by the submissive, objectified and fragmented representation of women in pornography.[35]

As Peter Baker, organizer of Britain's first national conference for men opposed to pornography (September 1990), writes on the effect of pornography on men':

> Given the nature of male power and contemporary masculinity, it is not surprising that many men find no difficulty in accepting pornography's make-believe world and its false assumptions about men and women (…) Pornography plays an important role in confirming, reinforcing and creating particular aspects of men's perceptions, especially those related to sex and sexuality (…) Pornography (…) represents women merely as sexual commodities (…) It tells men that women enjoy sex and are always available for it, even when they deny it. It tells men that women secretly enjoy rape. It tells men that women enjoy many different forms of physical abuse, including bondage, torture, mutilation and even death. The constant repetition of false information is a key part in the maintenance of any oppression: the more it is repeated, the larger the number of people (…) who are likely to come to believe that it is true (…) It is in this way that pornography contributes to the maintenance of discrimination against women *in all spheres of life, not merely the sexual.*[36]

It is when the women begin to realise that this is true, even in the context of their personal lives and their relationships with their husbands, that they turn to each other in despair. Yvonne's acute distress in class is dismissed by the other (male) teachers. 'They don't give a damn. Even the local chip shop keeps a pile of magazines for the boys to browse through at lunchtimes.' When Rowena quotes a much cited pseudo-psychological opinion in defence of pornography, that it might 'have a positive side. To enable inadequate men to act out their fantasies, save them from attacking anyone on the street', Yvonne's curt and thought-provoking response is the analogical 'Does social work for the child batterer consist of showing them pictures of parents torturing their children, with the children appearing to enjoy it—as a preventative measure?'

In Scene iii Daniels attempts direct causal links between exposure to pornography and rape.[37] A boy in Yvonne's class rapes a girl as his mother uncovers his secret collection of pornographic magazines:

> Yvonne: You and your husband had no idea?
> Irene: I supposed all young boys looked at it. As for my husband, ha, it never bothered him.
> Yvonne: You think your husband encouraged him?
> Irene: Didn't have to. He has a drawerful of his own. Only difference is, he doesn't have to hide it. (Scene iii)

Meanwhile, Jennifer is constantly subjected to Clive's misogynistic barbs and his preference for pornography over marital intimacy. As Michael Betzold puts it:

> By providing substitute gratification, it provides an excuse for men to avoid relating to women as people. It encourages unrealistic expectations: that all women will look and act like *Playboy* bunnies (...) The male consumer of pornography becomes deadened to his feelings.[38]

> Rowena: Does he still have affairs?
> Jennifer: He tries but he can't fulfil the false image in his head of how a woman should behave.
> Rowena: Because women's sexual identity has been manufactured. (scene xi)

> The more hopeless it is to find this sort of woman, the more desperate becomes the interaction between men and the women they pursue (...) ultimately, men lose because they never experience [the] true intimacy that comes from letting down and opening up with someone (...) Pornography portrays a fantasy of social communion, but in reality it leads to the desperation that leads men to abusiveness.[39]

Rowena has never really considered pornography, not having been exposed to it. Her response, when she finally does get a look at some magazines, is 'How they must hate us.' Rowena now actively seeks to find out the contents of pornographic material, and, as any woman who has seen or read accounts of what men do to women in the form of entertainment, Rowena is sickened, repelled and angry.[40]

Trevor's attitude to Hilary's 'choice of career' is stereotypically male:

> Rowena: (...) that young woman I told you about who we thought was on the game, well she wants to get off.
> Trevor: Hey, Row, you can't jump in all shining morality. If that's what she's chosen to do.
> Rowena: Choice. That seems rather an inappropriate word.

Trevor: Perhaps it's your particular values that are inappropriate (…) you choose to overlook the fact that by other definitions she is a working girl. (Scene v).

Hilary, given employment by Ron, is treated like a sex object when Ron is told (by Trevor) that she had been a prostitute to support herself. He pursues her expecting sexual gratification, not allowing her a choice to lead the life she has chosen by opting for a nine-to-five job.

Cameron and Frazer have argued that abnormal sexual behaviour is a western cultural category with a social significance. They link the writings of the Marquis de Sade and eighteenth century ideas of the Enlightenment such as 'free will' and 'transcendence' to the present century's male obsession with mastery in sex. Contending that the philosophy and art of one age become the common sense and popular culture of succeeding ages, they conclude that the notions of 'transcendence and mastery *have become sexualized*: they are part of a concept of masculine identity (…) and therefore an element in masculine sexuality.'[41] Cameron and Frazer are reluctant to isolate pornography as a causal model for abnormal sexual behaviour from the rest of western popular and 'high' culture: in their historical trajectory pornography would be one element in the matrix that constitutes male sexual mastery.

As boss Ron is automatically in the place of master. However, having objectified the woman in question, and following the urge to sexualize this mastery, as dictated by the prevalent sexual ideology of his culture, he wishes to subdue Hilary sexually, depersonalizing his victim in the process.[42] Ron is the hu-man stalking his prey, and satisfaction is achieved only by (sexualized) conquest.

Rowena: How dare you rape that woman.
Ron: That's no woman, that's my wife.
Rowena: Hilary, one of my clients.
Ron: Don't be so possessive. I was one of her clients, and do you mind, there was no force involved.
Rowena: No fucking choice involved. (Scene xii)

No force involved but no choice either. As Barthes de-constructs the Marquis de Sade in *Sade, Fourier, Loyola*: 'The scream is the victims mark; she makes herself a victim because she chooses to scream; if, *under the same vexation* she were to ejaculate, she would cease to be a victim, would be transformed into a libertine: *to scream/to discharge*, this paradigm is the beginning of choice.'[43] Thus the victim ceases to be a victim if she discharges: Discharge equals enjoyment. If Hilary, forced against her will to 'perform' (circus animals perform) for her boss, went through the motions without *physical* force being exerted on her, she is no longer a victim. Ron, in fact, 'did her a favour', he 'gave her a job'. In fact, he would 'be prepared to give her a reference'. Whilst Hilary, divested of any dignity of self, is left bitter about her first proper job:

> 'Cos you ain't ever going to know what it's like being left on the shit heap. You got enough qualifications, security and money to have some sodding choice (…) What a bloody joke and I thought working was s'posed to give you some self-respect. Ha bloody ha. (Scene xv)

Rowena, meanwhile, obsessed with the representation of women in a medium she has been hitherto unexposed to, gleans every pornographic source she can find. Daniels plays with the dimension of time in the presentation of the scenes to portray Rowena as perpetrator of a crime (murder) long before she has been introduced to pornographic material in the play. However, if Rowena's character must mirror the audience progress to the anti-pornographic stance aimed at in this didactic drama, it is essential for Rowena to achieve audience identification or at least audience sympathy. The fragmented scenes locate Rowena from the start within a criminal framework, and this leads to an unnecessary resistance in the viewer. By presenting her as a criminal in the dock for an as yet unidentified reason, Rowena's rigidly anti-pornographic stance might be rejected by the unresisting audience, who is, as established in the first scene, ambiguous about pornographic material to start with. By giving an audience who would not be inclined to identify with a criminal let alone a murderer, Daniels' Rowena is unconvincing in her final stance against pornography. In the audience rejection of Rowena lies the greater danger of audience sympathy for those very attitudes Daniels/Rowena is battling against. As early as scene ii we see Rowena in the dock, being tried for murder. It is not until the end of scene viii that Rowena confronts Trevor with his unresisting acceptance of pornography, and, given that his attitude is symptomatic of a general male view (just because he does his share of the housework, would not consider himself a rapist, and has been instrumental in introducing his wife to feminist writing—'don't forget that I was the one who introduced you to *The Female Eunuch*—the book as opposed to Yvonne') he considers himself beyond the influence of and above the intellect of pornography. Trevor's attitude is one of ambiguous tolerance and is in danger of being snapped up by the unresisting viewer precisely because of the audience wariness created by the unnecessary distancing of Rowena's character in the audience mind. Trevor's argument is not, for Rowena, a satisfactory one: that he is not willing to consider a retaliation, a joining of forces against pornography, is something she cannot come to terms with.

Rowena: You could do something (…) I don't know, write, complain, about these (…) sex shops (…)
Trevor: Sex shops? What do you know about them? They sell sex aids for men and women.
Rowena: (picking up a magazine) According to this ad they sell whips, canes, dog collars, masks, hard-core porn, inflatable life-size dolls, torsos and electric vaginas for men to masturbate into. And it must be true because there it is—the mail order form.
Trevor: All right, all right, don't lecture me for Chrissake.
Rowena: I want you to understand.
Trevor: To understand? To understand what? That you want total hostility between people in the street? (…) Well, that's what you've got in your own back garden. (Scene viii)

Rowena's antipathy towards men begins here—with her own husband in her own back garden. Scene ix (which begins after an interval) shows Rowena in a state quite close to hysteria; at the same time she is quite in control of her faculties and expresses her feeling in an articulate manner:

Psychiatrist: And you claim, Mrs. Jefferson-Stone, that looking at pornography was the turning point?
Rowena: Yes.
Psychiatrist: Enough of a turning point to make you try to kill a man?
Rowena: Yes.

It is only in the last scene that we are told that Rowena killed the man after seeing a snuff movie.

[In] snuff films (…) the death of a woman is viewed as the ultimate sexual turn-on. This poster advertises a film called *Snuff*. It reads: 'The film that could only be made in South America, where life is cheap!' In the final scene of *Snuff*, a woman is killed, her uterus ripped out of her body and held up in the air, while the man reaches orgasm.[44]

In the case of snuff films, increasingly popular as videos in the American home, the woman does not get paid and dismissed. She is, like Thomas Kasire [the black man who was tortured and killed in front of a white male audience by his employer in South Africa in 1984], dead. Or, like Linda Marciano (…) who played her notorious role in the film *Deep Throat* at gun point but survived, she is powerless to remove the film from circulation (…) For *Deep Throat* enjoys the protection of the law, as an example of 'free speech'.[45]

Snuff movies in the United States are believed to be flourishing with the use of untraceable illegal immigrants and Latin American women and children as their victims. The pornographers will force their victims to make several blue movies before they are killed as the grand finale to the last (…) *Racism like sexism is sexualized in pornography: the inequality is sexualized.* Ideas that originated in slavery are not being allowed to die, but are being retrieved and reworked into a nation's sexuality through pornography.[46]

Are snuff films available in the UK? A male reader responding to an article by Catherine Itzin in the *London Daily News* (24 April 1987) wrote: 'I saw a 'snuff' movie some years back (…) I must confess I thought it was a plain old hump 'n' bump, but then after a rather brutal rape, a young woman was tied to a table, and a hand was amputated with a Black-and-Decker type saw. Then she was raped again, and in the course of it her guts were spilled out by the rapist using a great big butcher's knife. That was nearly four years ago. I've never forgotten the horror and the certainty that it was all to real—that the budget did not cover the movie special effects required to make it a 'set-up' (…) It still fills me with horror. Some people will switch off, some like me will cry, some, like my friends, will be dismissive and think it to be all movie-tricks, but some bastard will go out and do it to somebody's wife or daughter.'[47]

Clodagh Corcoran, co-ordinator of the Irish Campaign Against Pornography and Censorship, reacted with a sense of numbness and shock to a snuff film she obtained in Dublin without any difficulty:

[After seeing the film] (…) I left the house that night in an apparently calm state, although with hindsight, I realized I had gone into shock. Shock dissolved into terror and I didn't sleep for many weeks (…) I have lived in fear ever since, knowing that while the rape, degradation and dehumanization of women is filmed and sold as entertainment, women's status in society is worthless, and our lives within and outside our homes are also without value.[48]

While some men cry, the extent of the effect of such pornography on women cannot, perhaps, be measured. Rowena's 'crime' is a measure of the complete lack of self-worth she would (like Clodagh Corcoran) have felt, followed by resentment and anger. However, it is precisely those who have known the enormity of the horror of a snuff film, like Corcoran or the unidentified male viewer, or those who are involved in researching the issue can begin to feel the context of Rowena's anger. Rowena's is an anger at men—any man. Even a stranger who comes up too close to ask for (perhaps) the time is construed as an invasion, an intrusion, a rape. She pushes him. He falls onto the track and is killed by the incoming tube train. Rowena's action is a violent and final act of the rejection and the negation of male desire which she sees herself claustrophobically surrounded by. Her push is an act of desperation to enable her to break out of a male prison which envelops her in every location. Her previous act of changing attire from skirts to jeans has been the beginning of a process of alienating the prevalent cultural objectification of women's bodies and attempting to make herself 'invisible' from the male gaze. Rowena's violent act is a push *away from* patriarchy, male desire and, for her, the now oppressive male gaze. Her complete calm reluctance to defend herself except in the offering of evidence of the men recently let off with light sentences after having murdered their wives points to the utter hopelessness she must feel after having been exposed to the most sadistic forms of pornography. A society which allows the freedom of expression to an extent where women's civil liberties are infringed, in which women can be murdered for the entertainment of some men, cannot offer her any hope of recourse. Her unconvincing defence of herself is indicative of the state of shock she is in. (Sarah Daniels obviously did not want to risk her sanity seeing a snuff film for the purposes of writing the play. In her acknowledgement she mentions her indebtedness to Dusty Rhodes 'for seeing the film and letting me use her description of it'. Not even for the sake of art.)

Rowena has turned full circle: from smiling (albeit reluctantly) at misogynistic jokes she has come to abhor any form of the 'male gaze'. Her lines close the play: 'I don't want anything to do with men who have knives or whips or men who look at photos of women tied and bound, or men who say relax and enjoy it. Or men who tell misogynistic jokes'.

The sentence imposed upon Rowena makes Daniels' point: in society, women are not the ones allowed to do the killing. Men can, and do.

Daniels, in working the multiple themes of violence, rape and misogynistic male attitudes into a case against pornography has been faithful to the politics and principles of lesbian feminism, which, in its early stages, was 'a movement that had a politics—that realised that prostitution, pornography and sexual violence could not be redefined as therapeutic, economic or sexy to fit any individual woman's whim in the name of free choice. It was a movement that recognised the complexities of choice and how so-called choices for women are politically constructed.'[49]

The bringing of issues such as the objectification of and violence perpetrated against women mercilessly to light on the stages of the mainstream, links Daniels to the very many polemical feminist and lesbian-feminist fringe plays performed.[50] However, *Masterpieces* fails dramatically in that Rowena's turnaround is too pat, too instantaneous; while the psychiatrist seems too eager in revealing his skeletons: 'you're wearing a skirt', 'you don't strike me as the type of woman to be fanatical about this sort of thing'—thus sacrificing him as a credible character for the purposes of the polemic. An unprovoked hostility from Rowena might have been more effective here. The clumsy form calls Deleuze and Guattari's comments on Kafka to mind—in their definition of 'a minor literature' they say:

> [In minor literature] everything takes on a collective value. [...] talent isn't abundant in a minor literature [therefore] there are no possibilities for an individuated enunciation that would belong to [a "master"] and that could be separated from a collective enunciation. Indeed scarcity of talent is in fact beneficial and allows a

conception of something other than a literature of masters; what each author says individually already constitutes a common action, and what he or she says or does [here, in the field of lesbian drama, *makes everything*] *necessarily political*, even if others aren't in agreement. *The political domain has contaminated every statement* (*énoncé*). But above all else, because collective or national consciousness is "often inactive in external life and always in the process of breakdown", literature finds itself positively charged with the role and function of *a collective, and even revolutionary, enunciation. It is literature that produces an active solidarity* in spite of skepticism; and if the writer is in the margins or completely outside his or her fragile community, this situation allows the writer all the more possibility to express another possible community and to forge the means *for another consciousness and another sensibility* (…)[51]

Thus, despite its dramaturgical failings, the ideological subversiveness of the play serves to uncover an important and perhaps neglected contemporary issue, and in feminist terms it is a working out of feminist ideology, principles and practice with a dramatically radical feminist finale.

The Rites of/the Rights of Birth: *Byrthrite*

(…) why are the senior IVF doctors all men? Do they want to control women's bodies and play games with their eggs? […] One of the more controversial techniques Craft uses (…) is selective reduction (…) where a multiple pregnancy is reduced to two by injecting the excess fetal sacs with lethal potassium cyanide.
—*Life*, *The Observer* Magazine, 4 June 1995

Parson: Don't be foolish, women don't make history.

(II, ii)

While Churchill's *Light Shining* might be read as an attempt to demonstrate that history might be inclusive of *her*story, Daniels' *Byrthrite* is a radical lesbian-separatist attempt at re-vision and re-presentation of what is undeniably manmade history. The retrieval of the figure of the stereotyped witch linked with a radical representment of the history of current trends in what a leading (female) IVF practitioner terms 'gynaecological plumbing'[52], takes us back in time to trace the beginnings of 'control over women's reproductive processes [which] began to change hands from women to men.'[53]

Byrthrite was damned by theatre critics (both men and women) for being 'historically unrealistic' (Mary Harron), 'a lecture' (Mark Lawson), 'ghastly', 'forced' (Michael Billington). These reactions betray the 80s and 90s social climate for lesbians as society continues to use a heterosexist perceptual screen: if we assume 'heterosexuality to be the only natural form of sexual and emotional expression' we are guilty of 'heterosexism', '*the* perceptual screen provided by our [patriarchal] cultural conditioning'.[54] Re-writing history from the perspective of women is essential to the feminist and lesbian

mind. Re-presenting women involves re-presenting the past, and the historical neglect of women's role is echoed in much critical thought in the
1980s.[55] Gillian Beer emphasizes 'the re-presentment of past history and literature to justify the present', echoing Virginia Woolf who, in A *Room of
One's Own*, spoke of the 'lack of facts' about past woman: 'History scarcely
mentions her'. Speaking of the possibility of 'a supplement to history', 'call-
ing it, of course, by some inconspicuous name so that women might figure
there without impropriety',[56] Woolf presaged the feminist writing of 'herstory'.[57] A re-ordering of the past might be crucial to understanding the present, but it is also important to posit this retrieval in the *fictions* of the
present. If a fictive re-present-ment of the past becomes necessary to provide
the neglected genderized Other with a sense of causal history, it becomes *imperative* to the lesbian in the complete absence of their history. Thus the lesbian critical tradition has been one of 'peering into shadows, into the spaces
between words, into what has been unspoken and barely imagined' because
past lesbian writers have had to resort to 'coded and obscure language and
internal censorship' for fear of censure.[58] Zimmerman speaks of the lack of
role models for lesbians and Daniels' creation of lesbians in the seventeenth
century reflects the lesbian critics search for 'the mythic presence of lesbians
in fiction'.[59]

Daniels creates a mythos which interlinks the persecution of single, old
and/or helpless women with a radical overview of the history of reproductive
technology, creating a legitimate, if fictive, herstory in which lesbianism is
natural for women.[60] Daniels delineates a group of women who are periph-
eral to a persecutionist patriarchy. At the core of the company is Grace: a
re-working of the stereotype of the witch figure, here re-presented as an educated and wise old woman who is also a competent herbalist. Grace demonstrates her wisdom in diverse ways: the young Rose, who, demonstrating a
hatred for her developing body which attracts the unwanted sexual atten-
tions from the farmer, requests a potion to 'rather wilt than grow', is gently
rebuked—'The farmer is the problem not your body.' (I, vi) In the creation
of Grace Daniels provides lesbians the figure of an alternative archetype: a
gentle matriarch reworked from the domineering models of witches handed
down by androcentric historians and mythmakers. Grace is a strong depend-
able woman who believes in the cohesion of the sisterhood they have
formed: this is indicated by her sadness at their fragmentation (I, viii). The
separation of the diverse group as each woman's dream takes her where she
desires, serves as a metaphor for the individuality and plurality of womankind. Grace's education received from her father 'when [he] saw he wasn't to
have no sons' (Rose, I, v) makes her position precarious in the cultural con-

ditions of her time. By locating the old and wise matriarch's words within contemporary lesbian-feminist discourse, Daniels effectively creates a feminist mythology:

> Jane: How can it be women of our time are stronger than ever before and yet persecuted worse at the same time?
> Grace: When those who are accumbred kick back, the oppressor kicks harder.
> Jane: But they pick on frail, defenceless old women (…)
> Grace: First there is your reason, is easy. Second, some have power, such as they see it in health and advice over women's bodies, particularly in childbearing. And they want power over that. [...] New inventions and persecutions step together, in time.
> (I, iii)

> Grace: Our sex with its single power to give birth, pose a threat to men's power over whole order of villages, towns, counties and countries. That control depends on women cur-tailing to men's ideals of how they should behave.
> Rose: So, if it is fact you want from me, happen there was women enough to cause trouble against each other.
> Grace: Because not only are men set against the woman named wicked, but also the women and children whose livelihood depends upon the approval of the men.
> (II, viii)

In a reversal of the then unformulated theory of phallic envy, Jane, the soldier, discourses on creation-envy—the feminist reversal, womb-envy:

> Jane: So then, and I've been thinking of this, maybe is compensation for their inabilities. Alarmed that they cannot give life they do find glory in death (…) 'tis envy of birth (…)(II, i)

That patriarchy was seen as a repressive and regulatory structure by women of the seventeenth century cannot be disputed on the basis that recorded history reveals no such readings. The androcentric recording of history and the subsequent silencing of women's voices is dramatized in Part II, ii as the parson chronicles 'plain statement of fact':

> Parson: (reads as though delivering a sermon) 'The war has rid us of many evils not least of the evil embodied in some of the female sex who were weighed in the balance and found wanting. Suitably dealt with through rigorous court procedures and brought to justice either swum or hung.'
> Helen: (curtly) You've repeated the word 'evil' twice.
> Parson: (casually) 'Tis part of women's nature since life began with Eve.

Although the parts for men are few (played by a single actor) and rendered necessarily restrictive, they represent the reified spectre of patriarchy as tyrannical in its influence over every aspect of the women's lives. The fictions that surround the androcentric concept of witchcraft (that witches 'fly'; the idea of 'carnal copulation with Satan'—Part I, scene iii), and the terrorist 'pricking out' of 'witches' demonstrate this, as did Churchill's *Vine-gar Tom* (1976) which seems to have served as a model for this radical text. Daniels continues Churchill's mythological theme of the male fear of control over their (male) sexuality: Jane jokes about this almost as if she might have heard the Jack of *Vinegar Tom* (scene xii) complain that he had 'heard how witches sometimes get a whole boxful and they move and stir by themselves like living creatures and the witch feeds them oats and hay':

> Jane: (to Mary and Rose) They are of firm belief that women collect male organs and keep them in bird's nests where they move about by themselves and eat corn and oats. (I, iii)

The arrival of Jane in the group composed of diverse women—the young Rose, the old Grace, married Helen—transforms female affectionality into lesbian togetherness. Lesbian critical discourse, which in its early stages sought to be integrated with feminist discourses, is varied in its definition of the lesbian body. Lillian Faderman defines 'lesbian' as

> a relationship in which two women's strongest emotions and affections are directed toward each other. Sexual contact may be [...] entirely absent. By preference the two women spend most of their time together and share most aspects of their lives with each other.[61]

Whereas Adrienne Rich sought to establish the idea of a 'lesbian continuum' which would include

> a range—through each woman's life and throughout history—of woman-identified experience; not simply the fact that a woman has had or consciously desired genital experience with another woman [(...) the lesbian continuum includes] the sharing of a rich inner life, the bonding against male tyranny, the giving and receiving of practical and political support (...)[62]

The group might be seen in Rich's sense as a lesbian category, as each occupies a position on 'the lesbian continuum' and pledges a lasting oath of sisterhood. Faderman's definition of lesbian (which is subsumed by Rich's continuum) would map the relationship shared by Rose and Jane. By cross-dressing they break the bounds of their time; in transgressing they search for equality and discover the futility of the (male) violence of war (Rose, II, iii) but men's attire gives them a power, 'a wonderful freedom to go charging about where I want' (Rose, II, iv) they would not otherwise had access to, as women.[63] Rose's guise enables her to rescue Grace and the deaf Ursula from gaol, but she later regrets her absence from the village in 'Rosie's song' (II, iv):

(...) what they have got is a soldier to fight
And one woman less to defend her birthright.

The freedom to pass as a man is a curse -
No woman would choose that for her life -

Helen's search for equality leads her to reject everything the Parson stands for to become a preacher herself: a legitimate Quaker unlike Hoskins of *Light Shining in Buckinghamshire*. Women's search for power where they had known only servitude is traced historically: 'woman shall laugh till she cries at the very notion of being pinned down to man' (Helen, ibid.) as twentieth century parallels, echoed by the contemporary songs, reverberate to the metaphors encoded in these seventeenth century women.

The central mythos of *Byrthrite* is the history of the origins of reproductive technology re-viewed from the lesbian perspective and forecast to the end of the road: the creation of wombs in men and/or total extra-corporeal gestation. The fear is that once men secure total control over the birth process, the survival of women will depend upon what has proved a centuries-old patriarchy. With the 80s and 90s controversy over lesbian-mothers this surfaces as a lesbian fear of being kept on the fringes. (The NHS still assists only heterosexual couples with IVF technology). With international examples of state control over women's bodies the control of reproductive processes by an outside agency translates into a very real fear for women *as well as men*.[64]

Byrthrite's mythology is a lesbian feminist one. Faced with an irrecoverable past, recourse to an imaginary history becomes essential to the lesbian feminist dramatist who creates a mythical text in order to provide women with role models and archetypes posited historically. The dialogue in Part II, viii is a form of dramatic meta-discourse. Rose's playtext is a metaphor for the greater text of Daniels' playtext. Both are 'stories' 'to entertain' and Daniels' attempt to re-present the lives of seventeenth century women is not an attempt at historical realism but, rather, a need to *contemporize* lesbian history and establish continuity with an unrecorded past unheeded by androcentric history. As Rose puts it: 'Is not s'posed to be a list of facts and dates. There must be other women interested in recording exact history. I cannot do all. Is a story I've written, out of my imagination, to entertain. Not a bible.'

The burying of the playtext symbolizes the buried gifts of women through the ages. As Adrienne Rich puts it:

(...) we all know women whose gifts are buried or aborted. Our struggles can have meaning and our privileges—however precarious under patriarchy—can be justified

only if they can help to change the lives of women whose gifts—and whose very being—continue to be thwarted and silenced.[65]

Daniels' well placed wit might alleviate a heterosexist discomfort in the
radical presentation of controversial issues in this re-visioning of history essential to her alternative perspective. In the gamut of her work she manages
to elicit laughter in the most critical or pensive situations making for a ca-
thartic effect, and here it cuts through the didacticism, making the issue-
based play entertaining. That *Byrthrite* was performed in a mainstream venue
at all is surprising because it typifies gay fringe plays addressing a selective
audience.[66] The radical feminist-Brechtian distancing created by the provocative songs should help to get past the patriarchal perceptual screens in
mainstream audiences, but the severally bad reviews the play received are
indicative of the pervasiveness of normative rationality. Men and women
are not accustomed to men being elided or kept on the fringes of (even) a
play. The effect of this patriarchal expectation extends to women in the audience who are culturally conditioned to accept that women might be on
the fringes or even entirely absent from 'great' contemporary drama—from
Look Back in Anger (1956) to *Arcadia* (1995, revived 1999). In spite of the
overwhelmingly bad press it received, *Byrthrite* remains a play with depth
and intensity as it tells the slanted truth about women's right to the rites of
birth and takes mainstream audiences through the looking-glass and beyond.

In terms of content, Daniels' texts are radical in their placement on the
centre(s)stage, and it's not surprising that in the end she proved a force too
radical for the mainstream and was boo-ed off the stage to write television
drama. However, she did have the opportunity to stage her confrontation
with straight society with its manifold prejudices lurking behind their patriarchal heterosexist perceptual screens bringing such drama out of 'the
ghetto'. This served to create an awareness of issues which are usually elided.
Daniels broke the bounds of heterosexist society by bringing her texts into
the arena of confrontation: the mainstream stages of Britain thereby rupturing forever the heterosexual matrix within which these stages are constituted.

CHAPTER FIVE

SOLILOQUIZING WOMAN
Clare McIntyre and Anne Devlin's Subjects of Desire

MOST FEMINISTS READ Foucault as denying the subject a space for resistance;[1] that Foucault's subject is always 'subjected'.[2] Foucault himself declared:

> Maybe the target nowadays is not to discover what we are, but to refuse what we are. We have to imagine and to build up what we could be to get rid of [a] political 'double bind', which is the *simultaneous individualization and totalization* of modern power structures. The conclusion would be that the political, ethical, social, philosophical problem of our days is not to try and liberate the individual from the state, and from the state's institutions, but to liberate us both from the state and from the type of individualization which is linked to the state. *We have to promote new forms of subjectivity through refusal of this kind of individuality which has been imposed upon us for several centuries.*[3]

Here it is clear that Foucault believes in the subject's ability to overcome and transgress normalization; but as Rabinow points out, the implications of this refusal of constructed subjectivity have not been developed by Foucault;[4] it remains for us however, to continue his project as he himself asked others to do[5], and this is an important quotation in light of the subsequent feminist indictments of Foucault which accuse him of denying his subject agency and subjectivity.[6] Sawicki rightly reads Foucault as

> presupposing the existence of *a critical subject*, one capable of critical historical reflection, refusal and invention. This subject does not control the overall direction of history, but it is *able to choose* among the discourses and practices available to it and to use them creatively. It is also *able to reflect* upon the implications of its choices as they are taken up and transformed in a hierarchical network of power relations. Finally, this subject *can suspend adherence* to certain principles and assumptions, or to specific interpretations of them, in efforts to *invent new ones*. Foucault's subject is *neither entirely autonomous nor enslaved, neither the originator of the discourses and practices that constitute its experiences nor determined by them.*[7]

It is crucial here to attempt a definition of 'the subject' and it is Butler who proves helpful. The subject is not an individual but

> an abstract structure of human longing [...] a conceptual configuration of human agency and purpose whose claim to ontological integrity is successively challenged throughout its travels.[8]

The Female Subject and the Soliloquy/Monologue[9]

Although the soliloquy can be traced to Attic and Roman drama and thence to medieval England's mysteries and moralities, it is Shakespeare who has been the greatest influence on modern day drama. His soliloquies have been regarded as 'refined soliloquies of character' with a psychological function.[10] It is much later, with Samuel Beckett, that we get women characters who soliloquize. (*Happy Days* 1961 and *Rockaby* 1980). However, it is in the hands of contemporary women dramatists that the function of the soliloquy and the monologue is transformed as it becomes a tool to explore the psyche of the female subject constituted within discourse allowing the dramatist to trace the process of her subjectivity and agency. Not only is the female subject centrestage in the presentation of her hopes, conflicts, desires and limitations, the audience is allowed a glimpse into her inner worlds—her hopes, passions and desires. Woman now reveals her private and personal life in the theatrical space.

Clare McIntyre: Subjects that Matter

> I sing the Body Electric
>
> —Walt Whitman

Subtly wreaking havoc on the structures of patriarchal society and patriarchally constructed sexuality, McIntyre fragments the female subject's social self in *My Heart's a Suitcase* and her sexual self in *Low Level Panic* and points to the patriarchal agents of their construction. She demonstrates theatrically a tripartite response to gender conditioning by presenting three women who inhabit three culturally delimited zones where sexuality and greed (both a desire) are constructed in the image of western capitalist patriarchy's desires.

Low Level Panic. McIntyre's *Low Level Panic* is a fine example of writing-the-body for theatre. The three women are the fragmented female subject—their sexualization is a fabrication constituted by patriarchy's needs. The three women's attitudes to sex and sexuality make up the play. Although their notions of sexuality differ, they are all ultimately influenced by male constructions of female sexuality within the larger context of society and culture.

Cameron and Frazer's constructivist view allows them to posit sexuality as a 'social or cultural construct' emphasizing that 'it has not to do with instinctual need but with desire; and that forms of desire are cultural rather than natural (…)"In human culture sex is always [sic] overlaid with sexuality'.[11] Cameron and Frazer opine that it may be 'wrong' to frame pornography as a direct cause of male violence. Rather 'feminists should (…) concern themselves with forms of representation that exist in culture'.[12] McIntyre's play points to these other aspects of culture which work on woman as well as pornography: the role of the advertisement and the media which objectify sexuality; televisual means of sensationalizing the everyday violence done to women; and the entire apparatus of culture which normalizes.

Anglo-American feminist theorists tend to ignore the presence of desire in women. It is Luce Irigaray who writes: 'female sexuality has always been theorized within masculine parameters', that 'woman and her pleasure are [never] mentioned' and, critiquing Lacanian phallocentricism, that '[Woman's place is] within the dominant phallic economy'.[13] Women *do* desire. But that desire is formulated and expressed through those constructions of personality which are formed by patriarchy's cultural norms. The sexual mirror for women is inevitably the advertisement, the commercial film, the pornographic material which holds up the female subject quite consistently as patriarchy's sex-object: an object of desire materialized for the viewer. Thus the sexualization of the female and her desire is male-controlled. 'Desire, say the psychoanalysts, is simply a function of the law of the Father: one enters into desire when one enters into the relationship with the father. […] if we [women] enter into desire by becoming objects of the desire of/for the father, what do we know about our identity and our desires?'[14] 'Desire for [women], her desire […] is what is forbidden by the law of the father, of all fathers […] they always intervene to censor, to repress'.[15]

The three women are fragmented responses of the female subject's objectification in western culture. If Celia's response represents acceptance, Jo's is a wholehearted assimilation, while Mary's is the rejection of cultural representation. There is (almost) no room for the expression or a formulation of an autonomous or quasi-autonomous site for women's desire.

Scene One of *Low Level Panic* opens with Jo who is obsessed with her body. She internalizes the objectifying male gaze as she assimilates the sexuality desired by the stereotypical male found in advertisements and in the apparently ubiquitous porn magazine. The latter insidiously governs women's actions and thoughts as its ideological premise is internalized (see the three women in the opening to Daniels' *Masterpieces*, above). Women's sexuality is manufactured and objectified in the media, and this constructs the consciousness of women:

> Jo: (...) I'd go to swanky bars and smoke menthol cigarettes and I'd wrap my new legs round cocktail stools and I'd smooth myself all over with my delicate hands and I'd have my hair up so you could see my neck (...) I'd go out and buy silky underwear with lots of lace on it and suspenders and that's what I'd wear (...) I'd wear that and a lot of make-up and I'd snake my way around bars and hotels in Mayfair (...) and I'd really be somebody then. (Low Level Panic, Scene i)[16]

Jo's desires are trapped within this culturally constructed world of female sexual fantasy, her articulated desire is framed by the received idea of male-constructed womanhood. She aspires to being the muted woman of male fantasy, 'I could be dumb. I could be a mute. He might like that'. (Scene i); a modern Philomele desirous of the sexual violence of Tereus: 'Then the next one pushes me on to the floor and he has to tear my dress all over again'. (Taped monologue in Scene vii).

The influence on Mary is quite the opposite. Her resistance puts her in a site of refusal; however it makes her non-sexual or frigid: 'Many women are guilty, unhappy, paralysed, say they are frigid, because, within the norms of a phallocratic economy, they do not succeed in living their affects, their sexuality, whereas they could do so if they tried to go back to a *jouissance* more in keeping with their bodies and their sex'.[17] Mary's is a revulsion. Like Yvonne and Rowena in *Masterpieces* the cultural representation of women's desire makes her feel like 'a thing', 'We're all just things to fuck', 'It's the whole world, the whole world of men obsessed with schoolgirls' knickers'.

Celia remains an underdeveloped character more concerned with the right colour of eyeshadow for green eyes: the inference is that this is an attitude constructed by the magazines which keep women 'informed' about what is desirable; an aesthetics that 'matters'.

> The objectification of women's appearance is now so central in western culture that the relationship of women to fashion appears in itself to be fetishistic, or at least fixated on certain parts of the female body. Modern women often see themselves in fragments—a good pair of legs, tits or eyes, etc. [sic] Some women get fixated on emphasizing their lips (by constantly putting on lipstick) [...] This behaviour appears to be linked to the overall effect of objectification of the female form.[18]

Gamman and Makinen quote John Berger who points out that women *commodify* themselves as a direct response to having internalized male ways of seeing.[19]

Scene ii opens with Mary's monologue in which she internalizes the guilt of her aggressors' violent sexual assault on her. The scene points to the cultural malaise which is fed by cultural apparatus such as pornography.

Mary: Maybe if I'd been wearing trousers it wouldn't have happened. I was only wearing a skirt because I'd just come from work and it's the kind of place where they like you to wear a skirt [...] Anyway I wasn't even on the bike: I was going to get on it. I was going to. It's not as if I was cycling along with my skirt up my ears. [...] I could have worn whatever I liked. But I'd still have been there, on the edge of the road at midnight, about to get on my bicycle or into a car or just been stuck there waiting for a taxi whether I'd been in a skirt or not, whether I had good legs or not, whether I was fifteen or menopausal or lame, I'd still have been there.

Like Rowena of *Masterpieces,* Mary pushes away her aggressors by way of a Brechtian distancing technique; pushing away at the male gaze in an attempt to free herself from an intrusive and violating male sexuality which the assault itself serves to foreground. In the dramatization of the scene of sexual assault, it is the actor herself who enacts the gestures of violence upon her own body, and encoded in this solitary enactment is her subsequent self-deprecation and recrimination. Try as she might ('She then holds her arms away from herself, disassociating herself from what is happening to her and screams') she cannot distance or disassociate herself from the experience which will continue to colour her behaviour through the play. The lone enactment emphasizes the internalized nature of her subsequent 'guilt' as Mary takes on the guilt for having incited the attack by word or attitude, dress or gesture.

Mary: It was because I was dressed up.
Jo: We've been over this before Mary: you weren't dressed up. (Scene v).

She is restrained, guilty and afraid of her own sexuality because it is portrayed as the objectified commodified location/construction of male desire. Like the assault which is inseparable from her self, male fantasy has inscribed itself on her body, materializing it into what seems to be *her* desire.

On the other hand, Jo's sexual fantasies are revealed in a monologue which indicts pornographic material as an influence. Dressed in 'men's (...) baggy pyjamas', her verbalized fantasy posits her as an occupant of the fictitious constructed space given to women as objects of male desire in the cultural media. Unlike Mary, she invites the 'male gaze' as she enacts the female need to be visible, to matter within the structures of masculinist ideology. The scene is also an exposition of a woman's sexual fantasies and how they are influenced by the needs of male sexuality: 'I think about hitchhiking in a flowery skirt and a very sexy top (...) I always imagine my body a different shape to the way it is. I'm always very thin and light and *what I think people think* is the most desirable thing possible' (Scene iv, emphasis mine).

It is important that we discover the singularity of our *jouissance*. Of course, it is possible for a woman to come [*jouir*] in accordance with the phallic model, and there will never be any shortage of men and pornographers to get women to say that they have amazing orgasms [*jouissent extraordinairement*] within such an economy. The question remains: aren't they being drawn out of themselves, left without any energy, perceptions, affects, gestures or images to relate them to their identity? For women there are at least two modes of *jouissance*. One is programmed in a male libidinal economy in accordance with a certain phallic order. Another is much more in harmony with what they are, with their sexual identity. [...] If we are to discover our female identity, I do think it important to know that, for [women], *there is a relationship with jouissance other than that which functions in accordance with a phallic model.*[20]

The set (a bathroom dominated by a bath) serves to defamiliarize the commonplace, indicating a private space for the women to disclose their sexuality and desire. It is the space for a sharing of women's fantasies, secret desires and fears. In certain scenes, as in scene iii it becomes the space where a spiritual and physical cleansing is performed or denied. Scene iii which follows the assault has the cleansing ritual withheld from Celia. The three women thus serve as aspects of each other; and like the bathtub, Mary is rendered unclean and uncleansable from the molestation. As the materialized female subject of desire—torn into three—appraises its physical self in an imaginary mirror, it faces the audience. In unison, the three women, for that brief moment, check their appearance as mirrored in the audience gaze—in the gaze of society's expectations of gender, constructed and reflecting its norms, prejudices and practices. The women are in bondage to the patriarchal construction of their desire, denied a *jouissance* beyond the phallic domain.

McIntyre's bodies are not formulated within social forces that determine the parameters and indicate the possibilities of agency—instead, they deny the female body constituted in desire an agency or an autonomy. Woman as subject is trapped and lacks a choice outside the parameters of patriarchal desire—there is no *jouissance* beyond the phallus; there is no agency accorded the female subject.

Scene v reveals two young women getting dressed to party with all the insecurity of youth:

Mary: Do I need anything else?
Jo: It suits you down to the ground.
Mary: Do you think?
Jo: I know it does.

However, the excited mood is dampened by Mary's earlier experience:

Mary: I can never think straight in clothes shops (...) You can see straight through it.

Jo: You can't. You can't see anything. I'd have told you.

Mary: We're going to walk down the street and get whistled at by blokes who'd stick their fingers up your vagina as soon as look at you and they don't even know who I am.

The gesture of dyeing the party dress black to make it opaque is her need to make herself invisible to the penetrating phallic male gaze. By doing something concrete—however useless the gesture—she tries to gain control over herself and her violated body.

The anxiety of the three women in this piece stems from an oscillation between two subject positions: 'Women are expected to construct themselves as objects, as well as to experience themselves as subjects, and to oscillate between the subject/object dichotomy in order to maintain a notion of successful femininity.'[21]

It is in Mary we see a struggle to be autonomous—the only one who is possessed of an agency. In her monologue in scene vi she recounts the scaling of a gigantic poster of a semi-naked woman and a gorilla:

I was walking past a poster one day.

It was an absolutely huge poster.

[...]

And there was a gorilla in the picture and he was holding on to a woman in a bikini.

He had one hand through her legs [...] and he had one thumb which was sort of half pulling off her bikini top.

[...]

And I looked at her and then looked at her face.

And she had absolutely no expression at all.

[...]

She didn't in her body look like anything at all either.

She didn't look like she was trying to get away. She just looked like she was posing there and the gorilla was holding onto her.

And I just wanted to ask her what she felt.

[...]

So I climbed up on this picture and I was standing on her knees and I could just use all the relief bits to get me right up. And as I got towards the top I had to hold on to the gorilla's hand and I was levering myself up and finally I was standing on her breast and hanging on to her neck and then I got a knee on one of her shoulders.

And as I got up there I was face to face with her and her eyes [...] weren't focused. They weren't looking at me. I don't, I don't think they were looking at anything at all.

And as I got up there her head gently fell back and her mouth opened.

So I pulled myself up on both of her shoulders and looked into her mouth. And I just screamed and screamed and I nearly just fell off the picture because inside there wasn't anything at all.

She was completely empty.

Here Mary reveals her coming to consciousness as she realizes that the patriarchal construction of women's sexuality—here, as it materializes into a gigantic advertising poster—is meaningless and empty, not a *jouissance* at all for a woman who is conscious of being formulated to concord with masculinist desire.

In McIntyre's *Low Level Panic* the body of woman is a target and vehicle of normalization as disciplinary regulatory practices act on and formulate the 'subjected' subject. The play speaks of the enslaving of the female subject, the assumptions which underlie the manufacture of her sexual identity. Theirs is an expression of the needs of patriarchal sexuality: formulated within it they are allowed no exit. Their retaliatory techniques are frustrated and rendered impotent by the prevalence of the very ideology they seek to oppose. The singular lack of space for *women*'s desire is made visible through its complete absence in this play which won the 1989 Samuel Beckett Theatre Award.

My Heart's a Suitcase. McIntyre's 1990 piece, *My Heart's a Suitcase*, has been described as a 'female Chekhovian version of *Look Back in Anger* mediated through *The Tempest*'.[22] A play which effectively blurs the boundaries between the real and the imagined, it is about spiritual, physical and emotional paralysis. It is also about anger.

Fragmenting the social selves of women—and men—much as women's sexual selves were split in *Low Level Panic*, McIntyre circumscribes two women within the space of a friend's large empty house:

> Hannah: He has to have money to burn to have this place and a home as well.
> Chris: He has.
> Hannah: It's another world money isn't it? I suppose it's an investment.
> Chris: Knowing Colin it will be. Or it'll be tax deductible. Or it'll be in his wife's name and it'll be a fiddle. Or the company had to lose some money and it'll just sit here, empty, increasing in value till they sell it. Whatever it is it'll be about making a killing, that's for sure. (*My Heart's a Suitcase*, Scene i)

Hannah is cheerful and adventurous, but Chris is paranoid:

> Chris: Let's go and stay in a hotel. It's bloody derelict. [...] The whole building's empty. There's no one in the flat downstairs is there? [...] At least bed and breakfasts aren't creepy: they've got signs of life about them like other people and carpets and curtains. (ibid.)

The space is surreal, as it becomes a trope for the women's lives; to Chris it is empty and inert; for Hannah it is a place where her repressed and tormented memories find concrete existence.

Chris' paranoia is reflected in her soliloquy: 'When I walk down the street every third car parked beside the pavement has a bomb in it and just as I'm passing it explodes right from the centre out. Bang (...)' (Scene ii).

The chaos of the outside world impinges upon their inertia in the form of reported television violence and Chris' real and imagined memories terrorize her and bring on an emotional paralysis. A spiritual malaise symptomatic of a diseased capitalist economy predominates and Chris speaks as a frustrated consumer: 'If they're gloomy about the stock exchange or their lack of suntan they can go on holiday. What about the rest of us? If you haven't got money you can't buy yourself out of anything. How are you meant to cope?' (ibid.)

It is Hannah who is philosophical and optimistic, displaying a personal agency as she refuses to be shackled by socio-political determinism:

> Hannah: I have never thought I was poor.
> Chris: There's no one else in the whole of Western Europe who could live like you and say that.
> Hannah: It's true. What matters to me is my own personal happiness (...) (ibid.)

My *Heart's a Suitcase* is a play about the 1980s, 'a time when everyone was supposed to be getting richer but Chris, who is middle class, articulate, has a degree, and could presumably earn money [...] is paralysed' while her friend Hannah faces a real paralysis in the form of multiple sclerosis.[23]

'Luggage' is Sisyphus endowed with faith in God despite the injustice of the heavy burden. S/he is a trope for the world's most oppressed; those who carry the heaviest burdens. Abused by her father (patriarchy) and punished eternally by an unforgiving mother (society) Luggage's attitude speaks for those who bear their burdens with grace and fortitude.

Tunis is rich, upper-class, supercilious. Her expensive tastes highlight the economic situation of Chris and Hannah while her words are an exposition of how the rich live:

> I'm going to drive round listening to very loud music. I'm going to look in the antique shops and I'm going to spend money. It's what I'm expected to do. It's what I like doing and why shouldn't you do what you like? That's what's essential to me: my car. I'd die without my car. (Scene iv).

Elliot's wine-buying business has collapsed to leave him broke, and his wife has left him. Now no more than a tramp, he meets Luggage who tries to introduce him to faith and spirituality. The coldness and bareness of the house reflect the lives of the characters as they are caught up in socio-economic determinism; they are immobile in the race of the upwardly mobile (Elliot, Chris) or beset by an empty ennui which is the result of having too much wealth (Tunis). While the absent Colin stands for power and authority attained through the accumulation of wealth, for the others life will always be less than: 'I've finally realised this is my life. I'm not going to be living it soon. I'm living it now. This is it'. Combined with this insight, Chris takes stock of herself: 'I've never been anything. I've just had jobs'. (Scene vi). Hannah's utopian-socialist answer fits their needs as they feel they never will be anything significant in the larger scheme of things; ordinary individuals who are not necessarily poor but not necessarily power crazy either; people who drift along rather than work hard and play hard as the rules of capitalism invariably demand:

> You don't have to own where you live. There's thousands of ways of being [...] we've got it into our heads that the only way to be is like everyone else, scared and timid and pathetic like everyone else: feeling we've got to own things to exist (...) [...] I don't want to own things. How can you share something when you own it? It's a contradiction in terms. Can't you see that? (ibid.)

Although this is a healthy questioning of deterministic socio-politics and the assumptions it bases itself on, it's impossible to overturn the apparatus itself. To be the ideal consumer in an advanced capitalist society one must kow-tow to the rules, and both Tunis and Hannah's analysis of Chris' predicament is pointedly knowing:

> Tunis: Chris doesn't want to work. She wants to be well off.
> Hannah: And look what it's doing to her head. Why greed isn't recognised as a major illness of our time is a mystery to me. (ibid.)

Chris' amorality points to her status as capitalism's subject; subjected by the repressive desires turned toward the material of goods and services: 'I didn't expect not to have things'. Like Stas of *Dusa, Fish, Stas and Vi*, hers is a kind of freedom but delimited, indeed, constructed by capitalist-desire.

This play serves as a comment on the class situation within a thriving capitalism, which, being a world-wide phenomenon, invited one reviewer to remark that it was 'an illumination of the human condition'[24] while for another it sat 'comfortably in the honourably incensed and censorious tradition of *Look Back in Anger*'.[25]

The space of the large cold room of the flat is a trope for the lovelessness of capitalist society for those like Chris who are 'in a rage at the state of the world' and 'in a rage at [their] own circumstances' (Hannah, Scene ix). Pest stands for the terror and 'the unspeakable peril in the day to day' (Chris, scene vii) while Luggage is a reminder of the increasing breakdown of belief systems and the absence of spirituality in the western world. Tunis, representative of the power of the capitalist in capitalist patriarchy has the final word as she firmly clears out Elliot (the loser) and Luggage: the space of capitalist subject-formation does not have time for either.

McIntyre rails against the constructed nature of society and culture which constitutes its subjects to be so subjected; she brings to the stage an understanding that the subjects of the west are all implicated in the insidious workings of culture as *capitalist* subjects who desire as consumers must, to make possible the conditions of western existence; she holds a mirror up to western society on the mainstream stages and mediates the image through the soliloquizing female subject thereby giving the audience a unique and different viewpoint.

A Theatre in Exile: Anne Devlin's Subjects with Agency

The dramas created by Anne Devlin may not on the surface resemble those wrought by McIntyre, Devlin being an Irish dramatist whose psychological portraits of women are set against the backdrop of the conflicts of Northern Ireland. It is in the dexterity of the rendition of the experience of the female body, in the skill of the use of the construction of women's intimate dialogue, and the use of the female soliloquy that the similarity becomes apparent. Both create dramas which are undeniably those of female experience: these are theatres of emotion and feeling in an intimately female space. As Andrew Rissik put it: in theatre such as McIntyre and Devlin's

> there has been a discreet but unmistakable insistence that life is fickle, random and subjective; that we can make sense of it not by doing anything but by feeling and reacting, by scrutinizing the emotionally-charged thoughts which external action inevitably prompts in us. Drama of this kind [...] has lent the conventional stage play a new vantage point. It has retrieved the soliloquy, and diminished the importance of [conventional modes such as] melodrama.[26]

Ourselves Alone

> Her art of crossing the whole of history and its little histories and the contests of the sexes, and of crossing unscathed the foul economies, in a spirited stroke (...)[27]

Anne Devlin's plays involve 'a recognition of the power of patriarchal values in Irish society'[28] and here, the women of Northern Ireland are the subjects of the dramatist's exploration. These are the Trojan women in a contemporary landscape as it is through their lives and hopes and desires and personal tribulations that we are confronted with a socio-political structure which is rigidly dominated by a warring, masculinist ideology.

Until the late 50s 'the Irish State enforced by law the teachings of the Catholic Church, which emphasized the woman's duty was to uphold the family. Contraception, divorce and abortion were illegal. There was a marriage ban on women working after they married. Single mothers and women living apart from their husbands had no right to social welfare.'[29]

This rigid patriarchal order rules that woman, if Protestant, is 'divinely ordained [...] to provide service and succour to her husband' as the Catholic woman's role model is the Virgin Mary, and Mother Ireland, a grieving and plundered mother. 'Whether Catholic or Loyalist, the role of the woman is to serve and suffer. While her image is sublimated, her voice is suppressed'.[30] The Irish female subject is formulated within the pressures of the rigorously rigid belief systems of the Church which are reified as social structures as the state apparatus transforms them into law.

The contest between the sexes is exacerbated by the intense political conflicts which have raged in Northern Ireland for decades, separating the men and women into two dichotomous zones. The genders are polarized, thrown into binary oppositions. The need for peace and harmony conflict with war and violence, armament and control, as the material conditions are targeted as responsible for this severe opposition. The British occupation since 1969, the increasingly factious political structure, riots, raids and daily violence impinge on the seldom-still centre of the women's domestic and child-bearing and rearing lives.

Ourselves Alone valorizes the tenets of 'cultural feminist theatre', a counter-tradition which is based on the 'revelation of women's experience and intuitive, spiritual connection with each other and the natural world [which] is idealized'. It views women as instinctually more natural because they can give birth:

> more natural, more closely related to life cycles mirrored in nature. Men are seen as removed from nature, which they denigrate rapaciously. Since women are nurturers, they are seen as instinctively pacifistic. Men, on the other hand are viewed as instinctually violent and aggressive. [...] Cultural feminist theatre stands as a counter-tradition to theatre history. In what Rosemary Curb defines as 'woman-conscious drama', 'the necrophilia of the patriarchy is unmasked (...) '. The gender dichotomy is strictly adhered to: the death principle in patriarchy is replaced with the life-affirming ritual of cultural feminist theatre.[31]

This is the area of feminist theatre that *Ourselves Alone* inhabits, as indeed it must, as the severely fractured socio-political structure is riven by a polarized gender distinction.

The agency of the female subject seems almost impossible given the attitudes in society; yet Devlin gives us Frieda, whose song opens the play. She is the apolitical free spirit, a singer whose need for freedom and personal empowerment through her art are increasingly stifled. Donna is the mother who loves the insensitive and violent Liam, brother to Frieda and Josie. The latter is an activist, closely involved with her party's activities, until she feels the stirrings of a child in her womb which transform her and reclaim her to the traditional sisterhood of domesticity.

The 'old assumptions' are in play in Andersonstown: 'either you stay at home where you can hope to express tenderness (...) or you enter the male world and play the game like a man: the game being control, impassivity, ends above means, exploitation'.[32]

The three women seem like pawns in a masculinist chess game and they appear destined to live their lives patterned after the existence of their parents: 'My mother spent her life listening. My father was picked up four times'. (Josie, I, ii).

It is in the central gest that Devlin strives to break the bounds of her particular patriarchy: the women's need for personal (and political) freedom is symbolized by Frieda's rebellion and the play achieves its subversive aim by presenting these issues in a different culture thereby juxtaposing a rigid patriarchy within another which feminism's ruptural tendency has transformed enough to allow a woman's play to be produced frequently enough in the mainstream without it seeming almost anomalous. The comparison alone is a comment on feminism's transformative influence. Devlin gives us subjects with a personal agency even as they are formulated in socio-political and economic oppression; theirs is a need for freedom from the framework of masculinist domination which is at once extreme (in the figure of Liam) and mellowed by the presence of the kindly patriarch Malachy. Even Josie, 'active' within the passive nucleus of women has to finally depend upon her father to shield her from Liam's rage.

On the other hand, 'Mother, or the absence of her, became, in the face of the violence, a major force for good. Josie and Frieda have no mother; their friend Donna is a mother substitute.'[33]

Their mutilated Auntie Cora, 'blind and deaf and dumb and she has no hands' represents what is expected of Ireland's women—to be able to be sacrificial victims in the face of political adversity:

> Frieda: They stick her out at the front of the parades every so often to show the women of Ireland what their patriotic duty should be. But I'll tell you something—it won't be mine! (I, ii).

It is Frieda who recognises that to fully realise her creative potential she must leave the scene of conflict. While Frieda seeks to escape from the imposition of the dominant ideology, Josie has been complicit with the dominant masculinist framework until she finds that it cannot accommodate her self as a pregnant woman. Devlin based the three women on her own experience in Andersonstown, thus dividing the three as aspects of herself at different moments in time:

> I found the three women representative of the three paths available at different stages of life, my own essentially. I have been all three women, both political [Josie] and non-political [Frieda], yet when I began writing this play (…) I had never been a mother (…) [the subsequent] fact of [Devlin's] motherhood changed my whole perspective on the script.[34]

Act I subversively charts the similarities between the two apparently diverse sisters. While Frieda, hungry for love and affection, throws herself at any available man, Josie has spent ten tormented years of her life as the mistress of a married man, only to give him up when she succumbs to the charms of Joe Conran. Both are unhappy, and their political decisions are submerged in emotional undercurrents. Frieda changes her political affiliations with every new lover—an emotional opportunist where her brother is a political one—while Josie recruits Conran into the IRA on the basis of what seems to be an emotional calculation. Josie never gets a direct answer to a crucial question in the interrogation:

> Josie: […] Now did your wife leave you because she realised you were working for Counter Insurgency Operations? *We think she did.* (I, vi. Emphasis mine).

Joe answers in emotional terms without directly answering the question:

> Joe: […] When Rosa left me, she said she regarded all her association with me as a betrayal of her tribe (…) I was deeply mortified and ashamed (…) (ibid.)

The presence of Malachy and O'Donnell seems not to be of a supervisory or cautionary nature which seems odd in such a rigid gender hierarchy; they accept Joe on the basis of Josie's decision.

Donna meanwhile looks after the home and child, waiting for Liam's release from the Kesh, terrified but ever vigilant for raids: she spends her life listening.

Donna's soliloquy in Act II reveals the strong hold of the Church on the Irish psyche:

> Donna: The devil's back. He was lying with his head on my pillow this morning. When I woke up I recognised him immediately. Even though it's been years. (pause). The first time I ever saw him, he was standing in the corner of the room. I could feel something watching me. […] I felt so sick at the sight of him because I knew I didn't have the strength to struggle any more. I said: 'Please leave me alone'. I was very surprised when he replied. He's never spoken to me before. He said very quietly, 'All right, Donna'. And do you know—he vanished. But I don't believe he's really gone. He never really goes away.

Donna's belief that the devil is always at her shoulder echoes the sense of sin and guilt which figure equally strongly in Greta's search in *After Easter*. Liam enters as Donna completes this reminiscence bordering on religious doom. Liam is jealous, abusive and paranoid about Donna's love for him. In Donna's life, at least, Liam seems to be the devil who abuses her love and questions her loyalty. It is Josie who leaves Donna with a smile at the end of the scene, emphasizing once more that it is the women who are each other's support.

The relationship that Joe offers Josie seems superficial and shallow compared to her serious intensity:

> Josie: Have you ever loved anyone so much you would die for them?
> Joe: This is fun, Josie. I want what there is between us to begin and end in this room. And then on another occasion we could go to another room and have some more fun. (II, iii).

Josie's soliloquy reveals her as vulnerable and lost: in running away from O'Donnell she has sought refuge in the first responsive man; official work and emotions merge in their relationship. Like the other men Joe seems to be using Josie, and the ambiguity about his loyalty at the end, as also his unresponsiveness to Josie's pregnancy, cast him in an unsupportive role.

Meanwhile, Frieda and McDermot try to 'catch' happiness in an atmosphere charged with political suspicion. The policeman's presence is intrusive and symbolic of the loss of spontaneity and freedom. The scene is typically indicative of the emotional unrest felt by the people of Northern Ireland, and Donna's words to Frieda come to mind: 'happiness requires all your intelligence'.

Donna is a figure of unconstrained domesticity, bound by convention as well as the constant political disturbances. In the raid the soldiers are brutally intrusive causing Donna untold emotional upset. The constant pressure from the threat of raids from 'the Brits' is a strain on the women invariably left behind at home. Josie too is feeling the strain:

> I'm tired. Tired of this endless night watch. I've been manning the barricades since 'sixty-nine. I'd like to stop for a while, look around me, plant a garden, listen for other sounds; the breathing of a child somewhere outside Andersonstown. (II, vii).

Like all the women in the play, Josie is haunted by memories of an unceasing vigil that has been their lot combined with the incessant and pervasive hold of their religion: 'Back then (…) somehow rid myself of that dark figure which hovered about the edge of my cot—priest or police I can't tell (…) (Josie, ibid.). The oppressive and repressive apparatuses of state grip the women of Ireland in their power infiltrating and regulating their minds as they must conform and acquiesce as required.

The men are all violent, albeit on differing scales. McDermot seems to love Frieda but he is as violent as Liam is to Donna. The socio-political circumstance seems to make the men aggressive exacerbating violent traits. Both women leave their men, and scene ix has the three women together again, and news of Josie's pregnancy turns their meeting into a celebration.

> Donna: So let's have a toast.
> Frieda: To?
> Donna: To Josie's baby (…) To Frieda's return (…) To my love! (II, ix)

The agency of the female subject in the most rigidly deterministic situations makes this play a celebration of the power of feminism. To indicate that this agency is fragile and difficult to sustain, there is almost immediately news of the betrayed shipment and the raid at the club, as Joe Conran is suspected of being a double agent. Liam insists Josie get rid of the child but Malachy interposes: 'This baby's my blood. If anyone harms a hair on its head (…) ! (ibid.) Like Donna, their father believes that 'a child doesn't belong to anyone. It's itself'. Donna and Frieda remain behind to reminisce about their days as youngsters when they broke the bounds:

> Frieda: First Liam and then John, and my father in a temper because we'd left our swimsuits on the beach. And the shouting and the slapping and the waves breaking over us. We raced for cover to another part of the shore. We escaped into the shadows and were clothed again before they reached us. We lay down in the sandhills and laughed.
> Donna: I remember.
> Frieda: I have not thought of that night in years.
> […]
> Oh, it is not him; it is Ireland I am leaving. (ibid.)

Donna and Josie stay behind: having left their lovers they too, have achieved a kind of freedom from oppression; while Frieda takes the cause of her unhappiness further than blame assigned to an individual partner—it is the entire system that has failed her. It is Ireland she must leave in order to fully realize her creative energies.

'Anne Devlin's plays […] work against the mythology of heroism promoted by both sides and thereby contribute towards dismantling the myths that obscure the political, social and economic issues'.[35]

The play offers a unique vantage point as we see how imperative the need for personal and political freedom is, through the eyes of the women of Northern Ireland, a perspective seldom encountered. It also forms a trope for those subjects subjected to cruel and oppressive systems everywhere, as Devlin demonstrates we can be masters of our own fate. Deleuze's schizo is not a nomad without reason: deterritorialization and reterritorialization is of essence here.

This is a political theatre inasmuch as the women's personal lives are constantly and severely circumscribed by the political climate. Although the men are located off-centre their influence is pervasive not merely by means of the controlling ideology but also by the women's need and dependancy on the men, thereby re-positing the latter at the centre of events even though women's bodies seem to dominate the real centre. The levels of freedom each woman attains even as she is a patriarchal subject is the task the dramatist sets her hand to, as the state of Northern Ireland is defamiliarized by being viewed through the lives of the women. This makes the situation at once new and bitterly real, transporting us to a more human area of experience: that of interpersonal relationships and gender-power differences in a land torn by religious differences and warring and factious socio-political structures. The production of this play at the Royal Court in London makes for a juxtapositioning of patriarchies, and the agency of the female subject makes this an important play of hope in the midst of—what are, for women—repressive regimes.

After Easter

> Her art of living her abysses, of loving them, of making them sing, change, resounding their air with the rhythms of her earth tongues, regardless of the littoral and acoustic delimitations of their syllabysses.[36]

In the course of the decades of strife in Northern Ireland a number of people left their homeland to relocate elsewhere simply because, not unlike Frieda, they could no longer countenance a life so filled with violence, rioting and dissidence. Out of such experience and self-enforced exile—a deterritorialization and a reterritorialization—comes the writing of *After_Easter*, resulting in a quest, both spiritual and psychological, for roots and identity and meaning.

Devlin describes herself as 'continually torn between writing about the 'Troubles' and wishing to ignore them; resenting the grip of history and bowing to its inevitability.'[37] The trauma which surrounds the impossibility of severing the umbilical cord with the motherland is psychologized in the subjectivity of Greta as much as it is in the psyche of her creator. Greta's is an anguished quest complicated by a Catholic ascendancy to which she is spiritually (and psychologically) wedded even if she is consciously a rationalist and an agnostic. Displaced from the homeland she finds acceptance and assimilation difficult in England: 'I don't resent being Irish—I only resent it

being pointed out to me' (Greta, Scene i). She finds herself able, in difference, to identify with other dislocated minority groups within hostile larger
cultures: 'I'm a Catholic, a Protestant, a Hindu, a Moslem, a Jew'.

Greta's experience is supported by McClintock's research which reveals
that English discourse (newspapers), at the turn of the 19th century, consistently analogized the Irish with the 'Negro', rendering them a kind of 'Celtic
Calibans'. The English stereotyped the Irish as a 'simianized and degenerate
race' which destabilizes Spivak's later trope of Otherness—'chromatism'—
making it an imprecise and inadequate marker of power.[38] '[T]he English middle-class male was placed at the pinnacle of evolutionary hierarchy'; he was
'racially superior'.[39] 'English racism [towards the Irish] concentrated primarily
on the "barbarism" of the Irish accent.'[40] This dictates that the Irish in England must disguise themselves if they can, and Helen's comments shed light
on Greta's psychological distress:

> Helen: London isn't a good place to have an Irish accent right now. I find when I'm
> buying or selling an American accent gets me through the door. Whereas an Irish
> accent gets me followed round the store by a plainclothes security man. I'm not ex-
> aggerating. (Scene ii)

In the light of the experience of Devlin's female subject in England, it is
hard to accept Homi Bhabha's analysis of the act of mimicry as a sophisticated strategy which knowingly and consciously involves a 'representation of
a difference *that is itself a process of disavowal* [...] an immanent *threat* to [...]
'normalized' [does Bhabha mean Anglicized and/or English?] knowledges and
disciplinary powers' as it destabilizes 'the authority of colonial discourse.'
Problematic, then, to describe mimicry as 'a resemblance and menace' to the
colonizer. Jacques Lacan's words, cited by Bhabha at the opening of the essay, are closer to the experience of the 'mimic man': 'The effect of mimicry
is camouflage (...) It is not a question of harmonizing with the background
[Helen uses an American accent], but against a mottled background, of becoming mottled—exactly like the technique of camouflage practised in human warfare.'[41]

And a battle it is; Greta's 'banshee' wail feels as if 'the whole of Ireland
was crying out to me' (Greta, scene ii) and is symptomatic of her increasing
distress at the estrangement from her mother country, an alienation which
began soon after she left Northern Ireland—articulated as a dying, a death of
the self. She tells her sisters: 'I left Ireland in 1979, but I never arrived in
England. I don't know where I went.' (ibid.) Genuinely distressed and hallucinatory, disturbed, incoherent, half-believing in the visions and voices
which mingle with childhood memories, Greta is directed to Elish, her
cousin who is now a nun in Ireland. Together with her homeland Greta has

also renounced the Catholic faith which has induced an unconscious guilt which finds an outlet in hallucinations and visions which are the nun's envy: 'I have lain awake for nights on end to achieve this state of grace that you so artlessly fall into.' (Scene iii).

Devlin establishes that 'sanity' is relative to the beliefs one holds, and gives us a protagonist who is intelligent enough to know so: 'If I tell a doctor I'm having religious visions, he will tell me that I'm ill; and that is closure. If I tell a nun I am having religious visions then we can agree we are both ill and at least begin the conversation on an equal footing'. (Greta, scene iii).

It is also established that Greta is the only one of the family who has completely cut herself off from the motherland; even Helen has ties: she sends gifts of money to the children's orphanage.

Scene iv brings the family together as calamity strikes: the father has been hospitalized for an attack as Greta is gathered together with Aoife and Helen and their brother Manus and their mother Rose. In this scene, set in Ireland, we see Greta's psychosis accelerate: the visions take on a new significance as she deludes herself that she is somehow responsible for the killings and violence around her. Internalizing the external events of violence, she experiences guilt, self-deprecation and a sense of misplaced responsibility which seems to stem from the rejection of mother (land). 'I feel compelled. I feel as if it were running away with me. The voice. […] I wanted to stop the killings. I thought if I obeyed the Voice it would all stop'. (Greta, Scene V). Again, Devlin juxtaposes 'sanity', this time with reference to a country's political agenda: 'In England they lock her up if she's mad but let her go if she's political. In Ireland they lock her up if she's political and let her go if she's mad'. (Helen, ibid.)

It is after her father's death, as his body is laid out in the coffin, that Greta begin to come to terms with her own desertion: 'Funny how people who leave their own country stop living, in some part of themselves, in the same year in which they left'. (Greta, Scene vi). In identifying once again with those who bewilderingly grope their way through the sounds and signs of a newly adopted and strange culture, Greta sees herself in the illiterate man from Mayo and the Hindu child who could not write his name: 'Father, I recognise them, the man from Mayo and the Hindu child, because I am the same. I too am a copier. I do it out of fear'. Mimicry here is camouflage and self-defence in an attempt to 'normalize' within an alien and hostile culture.

Greta's fantasies and hallucinations impose on the linear and realist structure of the drama as her father rises from the coffin to converse with his daughter. The family gathers round the coffin as a Freudian undercurrent surfaces in the oedipal nucleus:

> Aoife: (To Helen) You're wearing his sweater.
> Helen: I was cold. I put it over my night-dress.
> Aoife: Give me that, it's mine.
> [...]
> Rose: (...) I'm the wife here. Nobody gets anything without my say so.

And:

> Aoife: He was my daddy. I can touch him if I like.
> (She goes over to kiss him)
> (Rose pushes her away)
> Rose: He's my husband. Not yours!
> Aoife: I'm his daughter. You're only his wife [...] We're his blood love, not you!
> (ibid.)

In terms of Ireland's social dynamics as depicted in the play, we see they are cast in a rigidly bi-polar hierarchy, a dynamic which doubly inscribes itself on the social body by replicating the hierarchy of the nucleus—the family:

> In the Imperial formation, *incest has ceased being the displaced represented of desire to become the repressing representation itself.* For there can be no doubt: this way the despot has of committing incest, and of making it possible, in no way involves removing the apparatus of social and psychic repression (*l'appareil répression-refoulement*). On the contrary, the despot's intervention forms part of the apparatus (...)[42]

And the father has intervened in the daughter's desire to turn them away from the mother, a rationalist-materialist seen as exploitative by the family. The father is the 'ideal'—a utopian socialist, and in acknowledging a 'blood-love' with their idealist nurturer they hope for an ideal state of things denied them so long. The flow of their desire is blocked by the capitalist mother and it turns back as a negativity as the funeral becomes a time for recriminations and accusations:

> Rose: But I kept you. I educated you. We came up from the country with nothing and your father couldn't get work and I started knitting and then I did dressmaking and I made my money fairly and squarely. And when they couldn't pay I lent them the money. There's nothing wrong with that. I paid for your music lessons. Remember that.
>
> Manus: My father thought there was something wrong with it.
>
> Rose: He was unrealistic.
>
> Manus: He wasn't unrealistic; he was ashamed! I mean, you had a captive community here, didn't you. No communion dress, no First Communion. It was either a

new communion dress or damnation and your interest rates stood between them and their souls. (ibid.)

In this play the mother, whom Greta and her siblings seem to have cauterized, is the capitalist machine while the dead father stands for a hope never to be realized, and it is in his direction that desire flows only to be stopped by the figure of the mother, who represents the land itself.[43]

Scene vii takes the two expatriated sisters back to England and Greta's concerns seem to be getting more localized, less distant. It is her children and her estranged husband who are in her thoughts as she scatters her father's ashes into the Thames. It is the materialist Helen, though, who undergoes a transformation: '(…) the worst thing I did was to squander a great gift, which was very powerful and I used that power to seduce and dominate. When I should have used that power to create and free'. (ibid.) Greta's is not so much a story of transformation as it is an examination of the material conditions which underlie the psychosis of an exile. Greta is an extension of the earlier Frieda, and the irony is that the sisters are twice alienated: aliens at home and in their adopted country as they adapt themselves to England.

The last scene is typically Irish in the content of the story Greta tells her child and the placing of the traditional empty chair beside her. The play ends with autobiographical overtones: 'So I got on the stag's back and flew with it to the top of the world. And he took me to the place where the rivers come from, where you come from (…) and he took me to the place where the rivers come from, where you come from (…) and this is my own story.'

Devlin's plays perform a kind of schizoanalysis of the female subject. 'Destroying [normative] beliefs and representation' is the task of schizoanalysis; 'a disengage[ment of] the deterritorialized flows of desire […] [l]eaving, escaping, but while causing more escapes'.[44] In terms of Deleuzean thought, the nuclear family, site of repressed desire, is the site of reproduction and dispersion of patriarchy's bi-polar hierarchization, and thereby formulates and sustains the attitudes to women in society. It is 'a restriction, a blockage, and a reduction that the libido is made to repress its flows in order to contain them in the narrow cells of the type "couple" [and] "family" [(…) N]o matter how well grounded the love blockage is, it curiously changes its function, depending on whether it engages desire in the Oedipal impasses of the couple and the family in the service of the repressive machines [patriarchy and patriarchal apparatuses and structure, in this context], or whether on the contrary it condenses a free energy, capable of fueling a revolutionary machine.'[45]

Devlin's female subject, appropriately pluralized and individualized, is empowered to act out agency whilst caught in the grip of a starkly repressive regime (highlighted by way of contrast when compared to the geographical location of the performances). Donna, Josie, Frieda, Greta and Helen all decode their patriarchy's regulative and oppressive structures as they recode themselves differently, achieving a limited but, yet, substantial freedom. Some reterritorialize into a woman-centred space as they sustain themselves (Donna, Josie) the others accept that they must be, in different ways, nomadic and reterritorialize geographically. They become, in Deleuzian terms, the 'schizo'—a kind of positivity, an *élan vital*, a subject with agency:

> The schizo knows how to leave: he has made departure into something as simple as being born or dying. But at the same time his journey is strangely stationary, in place. [S/he] does not speak of another world, [s/he] is not from another world: even when [she] is displacing [he/r]self in space, [he/rs] is a journey in intensity, around the desiring-machine that is erected here and remains here. For here is the desert propagated by our world, and also the new earth, and the machine that hums, around which the schizos revolve, planets for a new sun. These men [and women] of desire—or do they not yet exist?—are like Zarathustra. They know incredible sufferings, vertigos, and sicknesses. They have their [spectres]. They must reinvent each gesture.[46] But such a [wo/]man produces him [or her]self as a free [wo/]man, irresponsible, solitary and joyous, finally able to say and do something simple in [he/r] own name, without asking permission; a desire lacking nothing, a flux that overcomes barriers and codes, a name that no longer designates any ego whatever.[47]

CHAPTER SIX

RECAPITULATION

> [...]theatre [...] is about ways of employing the force of art in the service of change, about ways of putting the levers of change in the hands of those who would otherwise be its victims.
>
> —Tim Prentki, *Popular Theatre in Political Culture*

BREAKING THE BOUNDS has been not so much about a transgression as about a gradual *transformation* in western discourse. The twentieth century has been a period which signals an epistemic break in western patriarchal and cultural knowledges as the numerous marginal discourses of sexuality, race and gender seep into the mainstage and affect socio-political space.

Specifically, of course, this book has looked at feminism as *the* transformative force, as it implies (monolithically speaking) the *revolutionary desire* of half the population. The conscious act of consciousness raising—in the suffrage era as well as post-war second wave feminism—demonstrated *the agency* of the female subject.

Within feminism, I have focused on drama created by five British women who—for different reasons and in different ways—managed to rupture the apparently seamless enclosure of patriarchal mainstream theatre. These feminists have stepped *severally* into traditional territory and addressed topics such as politics, war, money, capitalism, power, which were male prerogatives for centuries. Most importantly, they have destabilized malestream discourse to incorporate *herstory*. They have *broken open* the British closet with issues ranging from domestic abuse and pornography—male control over women's bodies—to 'coming out'. They have demonstrated that the *personal is indeed the political* as the political influences the personal lives of women. They have subverted traditional morphologies to create drama which is experimental and neo-avantgardist in *subject matter*. These feminist dramatists have *collectively* broken the bounds of traditional male-dominated dramatic discourse.

At the beginning of the new century, it is too early to tell in which direction new writing will go. However, the mainstream looks very different today than it did twenty years ago, or indeed, a hundred years ago. Today, there are far more women writing in the public spaces of theatre. The fight still goes on, but the women's movement has finally intervened in all sorts of writing, carrying with it, in its third wave, the *public* discourse of women's dramaturgy, changing forever the writing which formulates the mainstream stages of Britain.

> You do not have to be me in order for us to fight alongside each other. I do not have to be you to recognize that our wars are the same. What we must do is commit ourselves to some future that can include each other and to work toward that future with the particular strengths of our individual identities. And in order to do this, we must allow each other our differences at the same time as we recognize our sameness.
>
> —Audre Lorde, *Sister Outsider.*

APPENDIX

PLAYS & DATES

Caryl Churchill (b. 1938)

1972 *Owners*
The Royal Court Theatre Upstairs
Directed by: Nicholas Wright

1976 *Vinegar Tom* (written with Monstrous Regiment)
Humberside Theatre, Hull
Directed by: Pam Brighton

1976 *Light Shining in Buckinghamshire* (written with Joint Stock)
Traverse Theatre, Edinburgh and
Royal Court Theatre Upstairs
Directed by: Max Stafford-Clark

1977 *Traps*
The Royal Court Theatre Upstairs
Directed by: John Ashford

1979 *Cloud Nine* (Joint Stock)
Dartington College of Arts and
The Royal Court Theatre
Directed by: Max Stafford-Clark

1982 *Top Girls*
The Royal Court Theatre
Directed by: Max Stafford-Clark

1983 *Fen* (Joint Stock)
University of Essex Theatre and
Almeida Theatre, London
Directed by: Les Waters

1984 *Softcops*
The Royal Shakespeare Company (Barbican Pit)
Directed by: Howard Davies

1987 *Serious Money*
The Royal Court Theatre
Directed by: Max Stafford-Clark

1989 *Icecream*
The Royal Court Theatre
Directed by: Max Stafford-Clark

1990 *Mad Forest*
Central School of Speech and Drama, London
National Theatre, Bucharest and
The Royal Court Theatre
Directed by: Mark Wing-Davey

1994 *The Skriker*
The Royal National Theatre (Cottesloe)
Directed by: Les Waters

1998 *Blue Heart* (*Heart's Desire* and *Blue Kettle*)
Royal Court & Out of Joint
Theatre Royal, Bury St Edmunds and
Traverse Theatre, Edinburgh
Directed by: Max Stafford-Clark

2001 *Far Away*
Royal Court Theatre Upstairs
Directed by: Stephen Daldry

Pam Gems (b. 1925)

1973 *Piaf* (first performed in 1978)
The Royal Shakespeare Company (The Other Place)
Transferred to the West End; produced on Broadway; Tony Award to Jane Lapotaire
Directed by: Howard Davies

1976 *Dead Fish* (later renamed *Dusa, Fish, Stas and Vi*)
Kundry Theatre; Hampstead Theatre Club

1977 to West End
Directed by: Caroline Eves; Nancy Meckler

1976 *The Project* (re-written and renamed *Loving Women*: 1984)

1977 *Queen Christina*
The Royal Shakespeare Company (The Other Place)
Directed by: Penny Cherns

1984 *Camille*
The Royal Shakespeare Company (The Other Place)
Director: Ron Daniels

1984 *Loving Women*
Arts Theatre
Director: Philip Davis

1996 *Stanley*
The Royal National Theatre
Directed by: John Caird

1996 *Marlene*
Oldham Coliseum; 1997 The Lyric Theatre (West End)
Directed by: Sean Mathias

1998 *The Snow Palace*
Wilde Theatre, Bracknell
Directed by: Janet Suzman

2000 *Natalya*

Sarah Daniels (b.1956)

1981 *Ripen Our Darkness*
Royal Court Theatre Upstairs
Directed by: Carole Hayman

1983 *Masterpieces*
Royal Exchange (Manchester) and Royal Court Theatre Upstairs
Directed by: Jules Wright

1986 *Neaptide*
The Royal National Theatre (The Cottesloe)
Directed by: John Burgess

1986 *Byrthrite*
Royal Court Theatre Upstairs
Directed by: Carole Hayman

1988 *The Gut Girls*
Albany Empire
Directed by: Teddy Kiendl

1990 *Beside Herself*
Royal Court Theatre
Directed by: Jules Wright

1994 *The Madness of Esme and Shaz*
Royal Court Theatre Upstairs
Directed by: Jessica Dromgoole

Awards: Most promising Playwright London Theatre Critics Award
Most Promising Playwright Drama Magazine Award (*Masterpieces*)
George Devine Award (*Neaptide*)

Clare McIntyre (b. 1953)

1986 *I've Been Running* (as a radio play: 1990)

1988 *Low Level Panic*
Royal Court Theatre (in association with The Women's Playhouse Trust)
Directed by: Nancy Meckler
Winner of the 1989 Samuel Beckett Award

1990 *My Heart's a Suitcase*
Royal Court Theatre
Directed by: Max Stafford-Clark

Anne Devlin (b. 1951)

1985 *Ourselves Alone*
Liverpool Playhouse Studio and Royal Court Theatre Upstairs
Directed by: Simon Curtis

1994 *After Easter*
The Royal Shakespeare Company
Directed by: Michael Attenborough

NOTES

INTRODUCTION

1. *Critical Theory and Performance*, eds. Janelle G. Reinelt and Joseph R. Roach, University of Michigan Press, 1992. p.225.

2. Jill Dolan, *The Feminist Spectator as Critic*, University of Michigan Press, 1988. p.3; *Critical Theory and Performance*. p.225.

3. See the Methuen series *Plays by Women, Volumes I–X*, introduced successively by Michelene Wandor, Mary Remnant, and Annie Castledine, published between 1982 and 1994, for plays written by women since the 50s. Also see Lizbeth Goodman's excellent and concise Introduction to *Contemporary Women Dramatists*, ed. K.A. Berney, St. James Press, 1994.

4. Michelene Wandor, *Understudies: Theatre and Sexual Politics*, Methuen, 1981. p.62.

5. Compiled by Michelene Wandor, 'The Impact of Feminism on the Theatre', in *Feminist Literary Theory: A Reader*, ed. Mary Eagleton, Basil Blackwell, 1986. p.106.

6. See *How the Vote was Won and other Suffragette Plays*, ed. Dale Spender, Methuen, 1985; and *A Stage of their Own: Feminist Playwrights of the Suffrage Era*, ed. Sheila Stowell, Manchester University Press, 1992.

7. For plays by women written in the interim, see Fidelis Morgan, ed., *The Years Between: Plays by Women on the London Stage 1900–1950*, Virago, 1994.

8. Jane Gallop, *Feminism and Psychoanalysis: The Daughter's Seduction*, The Macmillan Press, 1982. p.14.

9. Bonnie Zimmerman, 'What has Never Been: An Overview of Lesbian Feminist Criticism', in *Making a Difference: Feminist Literary Criticism*, ed. Gayle Green and Coppélia Kahn, Methuen, 1985. p.179. Zimmerman endorses reading with a 'double vision' which would make the critic more aware of reading as a lesbian, and defines heterosexism as 'the set of values and structures that assumes heterosexuality to be the only natural form of sexual and emotional expression'. Heterosexism, I would argue, is but one aspect of regulated awareness, of normative rationality.

10. See Michel Foucault's *Afterword*, 'The Subject and Power', to Hubert Dreyfus and Paul Rabinow, *Michel Foucault: Beyond Structuralism and Hermeneutics*, University of Chicago Press, 1982. p.208.

11. A good contemporary critique of Stanislavski's system is to be found in Colin Counsell, *Signs of Performance*, Routledge, 1996.

12. Richard Schechner, *Performance Theory*, Routledge, 1988.

13. Michel Foucault, 'Preface' to Gilles Deleuze and Félix Guattari, *Anti-Oedipus: Capitalism and Schizophrenia Volume I*, trans. Robert Hurley, Mark Seem, and Helen R. Lane, 1972, The Athlone Press 1984. p.xi.

14. Roland Barthes semiological critiques were more in the area of music, film and photography and other elements of daily European life than in theatre. See 'Literature and Signification' in *Critical Essays* [1963], trans. R. Howard, Northwestern University Press, 1972. pp.261–79.

15. For semiological approaches see Keir Elam, *The Semiotics of Theatre and Drama*, Methuen, 1980; Elaine Aston and George Savona, *Theatre as Sign-System: A Semiotics of Text and Performance*, Routledge, 1991.

16. Karen Finley, a strip-tease artist, defends and endorses pornography. Performance artists like Finley are defended by highly placed academics such as Professor Jill Dolan who received the American Association of University Women Educational Foundation's Emerging Scholar Award in 1992 and teaches at the University of Wisconsin in Madison. Critical anthologies such as the ones cited below carry interviews, essays and articles on performances of pornographic content declaring them 'subversive' and 'transgressive' over and above black women's performance art or what is regarded as more conservative lesbian performance which is seen as not quite transgressive enough. Whilst recognizing the need to transgress the dominant ideology and open up our repressive cultural closet/s, feminist critics, academics and students have to beware of leaning too far over the boundaries which separate titillation in sexual dis-play from the need to possess knowledge long denied of the female body. What necessitates the re-presentation of the female body as staged discourse, is the ignorance with which it has been shrouded, and feminists everywhere need to acknowledge and endorse a lifting of the veil. However, a serious commitment to the discovery and re-presentation of the female body is being confused in the realm of physical and visual performance with pornographic representations disguised as art. Karen Finley, a former strip-teaser who abuses her body on stage in an alternative pornography is hardly the sort of performance art we would want to bring into academe. Yet she is easily researched well within the boundaries of our own libraries. See *Acting Out: Feminist Performances*, ed. Lynda Hart and Peggy Phelan, 1993; *Critical Theory and Performance*, ed. Janelle G. Reinelt and Joseph R. Roach, 1992 and Jill Dolan's *Presence and Desire*, 1993. All University of Michigan Press publications, all mandatory on every feminist and gender performance art bibliography.

17. 'Introduction' to *Performativity and Performance*, eds, Andrew Parker and Eve Kosofsky Sedgwick, Routledge, 1995.

18. '[A] performative utterance will, for example, be *in a peculiar way* hollow or void if said by an actor on the stage, or if introduced in a poem, or spoken in a soliloquy. This applies in a similar manner to any or every utterance—a sea-change in special circumstances. Language in such circumstances is in special ways—intelligibly—used not seriously, but in ways parasitic upon its normal use—ways which fall under the doctrine of the etiolations of language. All this we are excluding from consideration. Our performative utterances, felicitous or not, are to be understood as issued in ordinary circumstances.' J.L.Austin, *How to Do Things With Words: The William James Lectures 1955*, Cambridge University Press, 1975. p.22.

19. 'Writing' is 'a *means of communication*'. It is 'a powerful means of communication which *extends* very far, if not infinitely, the field of oral or gestural communication'.

Jacques Derrida, 'Signature Event Context' in *Margins of Philosophy*, trans. Alan Bass[1972], Harvester Wheatsheaf, 1982. p.311, 325.

20. For an appraisal and application of the theories of Judith Butler, see section on Sarah Daniels below.

21. Patrice Pavis, 'From Page to Stage: A Difficult Birth' in *Theatre at the Crossroads of Culture*, Routledge, 1992. pp.24–47. I have developed my theory of the *performativity of the dramatic text* in conjunction with this essay.

22. Cf. John Rouse's notion of the interweaving of two texts, 'Textuality and Authority in Theater and Drama: Some Contemporary Possibilities' in *Critical Theory and Performance*. pp.147–8.

23. As quoted in 'From Page to Stage'.

24. See Peter Brook, *The Empty Space*, Penguin, 1972.

25. The comment is Foucault's as he remarks on the text of *Anti-Oedipus* in the preface. Gilles Deleuze and Félix Guattari, *Anti-Oedipus: Capitalism and Schizophrenia* Volume I [1972], trans. Robert Hurley, Mark Seem and Helen R. Lane, Athlone Press, 1984. p.xiv.

26. cf. Tim Miller and David Román, 'Preaching to the Converted', Theatre Journal, Vol.47 No.2 May 1995. pp.169–88.

CHAPTER ONE
Patriarchy and the (Western) Patriarchal Impulse

1. By 'post-discursive cultural practices' I mean those cultural practices which are reified and concretized in institutional frameworks, either consciously or unconsciously, *e.g.*, apartheid or gender discrimination.

2. Cf 'Two Lectures', in *Power/Knowledge*, ed. Colin Gordon, The Harvester Press limited, 1980. p.93. 'We are subjected to the production of truth through power and we cannot exercise power except through the production of truth.'

3. This example helps us securely grasp the conceptual apparatus of Foucauldian discourse: it exists as a matrix of fields (the discursive matrix); the boundaries of each amorphous discourse in the matrix are able constantly to shift and be re-allocated and appointed to another discourse whilst still being circumscribed by the original discourse. The entire in a given (historical) moment forms the *episteme*.

4. *régime* can be variously translated as flow, force field, rule or law.

5. See Michel Foucault, *The History of Sexuality: Volume I*, trans. Robert Hurley, Penguin Books, 1990. pp.97–102. Cf. Foucault, 'Two Lectures'. Foucault speaks of the use of psychoanalysis as a totality which has 'proved a hindrance to research'. He goes on to speak of the need for and the validity of local criticism/s which are 'not dependant on the approval of the established *régimes* of thought'and the need to valorize subjugated knowledges. p.81.

6. See Michel Foucault, *The Archaeology of Knowledge*, trans. A.M. Sheridan Smith, Tavistock Publications, 1972. p.74.

7. *Archaeology*, p.27.

8. Cf. 'Two Lectures', p.109.

9.   See Fredric Jameson, *The Political Unconscious*, Methuen, 1981 and W.Dowling, *Jameson, Althusser, Marx*, Methuen, 1984. Jameson argues that the 'master code' of any interpretative method is the ideology it works to perpetrate. Ideology is the repression of those underlying contradictions that have their source in history. Jameson conceives of ideologies as strategies of containment, and of literature as an ideological production mirroring such strategies at the level of individual works. (Jameson claims that political criticism is the absolute horizon of all interpretation. Literary works are to be grasped not primarily as objective structures but as *symbolic* practices.) He tries to subject literature to symptomatic analysis, a mode of interpretation that reveals the specific ways in which works deny or repress history. Symptomatic analysis is also able to show that critical approaches usually assumed to be in competition with one another (the Freudian, the formalist, the structuralist, etc.) share at the deep level an identical set of assumptions, they deny history in an identical way. This method has some similarities with Foucauldian or Nietzschean 'genealogy', which elicits from the structure of a cultural text that unexpressed subtext or *hors texte* it cannot acknowledge. What Jameson tries to do is to find certain patterns which represent strategies of containment; he looks at gaps or absences as specific signs of the way the text denies or represses history. Cited with reference to Madan Sarup, *Post-structuralism and Postmodernism*, Harvester Wheatsheaf, 1993. pp. 179–80.

10. *The History of Sexuality:Volume I*, p.93.

11. cf. Foucault, *The History of Sexuality:Volume I*, pp.92–3.

12. *The History of Sexuality: Volume I*, p.93. Here, Foucault is speaking of attitudes to and the regulation of sex and sexuality. These would be constituted as part of, and as an effect of, I would argue, *the same strategy*, that same invisible text which inscribes the patriarchal impulse with, as this case reveals, rules prescribing heterosexism.

13. cf. Foucault—the *level* of the archive and its rules. *Archaeology*, p.130. Also see 'Truth and Power', where Foucault explains that it is not a matter of locating everything on one level, but realising that there is a whole order of levels of events 'differing in amplitude, chronological breadth, and capacity to produce effects'. In *Power/Knowledge:Selected Interviews and Other Writings, 1972–1977*, ed. Colin Gordon, Harvester Press Ltd, 1980. p.114. Reprinted in *The Foucault Reader*, ed. Paul Rabinow, Penguin, 1984. p.56.

14. *The History of Sexuality:Volume I*, p.93.

15. Foucault often uses war, battle, politics as points of reference as his concept of history is one 'of struggles, of strategies and tactics' rather than language (meaning), semiotics (communication) or a dialectic (which he sees as an evasion of conflict). See 'Truth and Power', pp.56–57. Cf. the earlier 'Two Lectures'where he explains history as a form of war. p.114.

16. Louis Althusser, *Lenin and Philosophy and other essays*, trans. Ben Brewster, Monthly Review Press, 1971. see pp.127–186. Althusser calls ideology a social formation and, in a conflation of Marx and Freud, said ideology had no history (was 'eternal'). Foucault himself acknowledges this when he remarked on the question of power in an interview: 'on the Marxist side, [power] was posed only in terms of the state apparatus.' 'Truth and Power', p.57.

17. And, indeed, by Robert Young's extension, a reading, also, of colonialism, which is imbricated within my notion of the Western patriarchal impulse. See *Colonial Desire:*

Hybridity in Theory, Culture and Race, Routledge, 1995. pp.166–174.

18. *mass* can be read as body (of knowledge), volume.

19. See Gilles Deleuze and Félix Guattari, *Anti-Oedipus: Capitalism and Schizophrenia, Volume I*, [1972], trans. Robert Hurley, Mark Seem, and Helen Lane, Athlone, 1984. pp.22–36.

20. This lucid explication is offered in his interview with his Italian translators and editors, Alessandro Fontana and Pasquale Pasquino. 'Truth and Power', in *Power/Knowledge*. p.112. Cf. Lois McNay who defines Foucauldian transformation as a 'sudden and complete rupture'. *Foucault: A Critical Introduction*, Polity Press, 1994. pp. 64–5 and 56–7. This is a complete misreading; Foucault emphasizes that '[t]he idea of a single break suddenly, at a given moment, dividing all discursive formations, interrupting them in a single moment [...] *such an idea cannot be sustained*'. *Archaeology of Knowledge*, p. 175. My emphasis.

21. *The History of Sexuality:Volume I*, p. 96.

22. See, *e.g.*, Jane Gallop, *Feminism and Psychoanalysis: The Daughter's Seduction*, Macmillan Press, 1982.

23. Although of course, Kristeva has been read as aiding that very phallocracy she seeks to subvert by valorizing the maternal body and reinscribing the institution of motherhood as compulsory for women. This gives the institution a permanent legitimation in which 'the female body is required to assume maternity as the essence of itself and the law of its desire'. Judith Butler, *Gender Trouble: Feminism and the Subversion of Identity*, Routledge, 1990. p.92–3.

24. Richard Rorty (Spivak's 'trivialist') speaks of what feminists term 'masculinism': 'so thoroughly built into everything we do or say in contemporary society that it looks as if only some really massive intellectual change could budge it. [...] Masculinism [or e.e.cummings' 'manunkind'] is a much bigger and fiercer monster than any of the little, parochial monsters with which pragmatists and deconstructionists struggle. For masculinism is the defense of the people who have been on top since the beginning of history [sic] against attempts to topple them; that sort of monster is very adaptable, and I suspect it can survive almost as well in an anti-logocentric as in a logocentric philosophical environment.' 'Feminism, Ideology, and Deconstruction: a Pragmatist View', *Hypatia Vol. 8 No. 2*, Spring 1993.

25. See Werner Sollors, 'The Idea of Ethnicity' (from *The Invention of Ethnicity*), in *The Fontana Post-modernism Reader*, ed. Walter Truett Anderson, Fontana, 1995; Werner Sollors, 'Who is Ethnic?' (from *Beyond Ethnicity: Consent and Descent in American Culture*) and Aijaz Ahmad, 'Jameson's Rhetoric of Otherness and the "National Allegory"', in *The Post-Colonial Studies Reader*, ed. Bill Ashcroft, Gareth Griffiths, Helen Tiffin, Routledge, 1995.

26. Immanuel Kant, *Anthropology from a Pragmatic Point of View (1796–98)*, trans. V.L. Dowdell, Southern Illinois University Press, 1978, p.236. As quoted in Chetan Bhatt, 'Primordial Being', *Radical Philosophy*, No.100, March/April 2000, p.30.

27. Sollors, 'The Idea of Ethnicity'. The racial theories of Gobineau and Agassiz have also been excellently de-constructed in Robert Young's *Colonial Desire: Hybridity in Theory, Culture and Race*, Routledge, 1995.

28. The genealogy of what I call the colonial impulse or imperative which substrates 'culture' is to be found in *Colonial Desire*. Young unearths the colonial impulse ('colonial

desire') as a text which substrates western 'culture' (see chapters 2, 3 and 4), 'the conflictual structures generated by […] imbalances of power are consistently articulated through points of tension and forms of difference […] transformed into mutually defining metaphors that mutate within intricate webs of surreptitious cultural values that are then internalized by those whom they define'. p.xii. Also see p. 60 where Young describes the transference of genderized cultural values onto race, thus establishing colonial desire (the colonial impulse/ imperative) as a subtext imbricated within western patriarchies (p.162).

29.   There has been a great deal of research into what has been variously defined as 'man-made language'. See Dale Spender, *Man Made Language*, Hélène Cixous' *'écriture féminine'* in 'The Laugh of The Medusa', as well as Suzanne Romaine, Julia Kristeva, among others.

30.   Churchill was 'politicized' in 1976, see section II below.

31.   'Anyone making a profound study of Brueghel's pictorial contrasts must realize that he deals in contradictions. […] In the great war painting *Dulle Griet* it isn't war's atmosphere of terror that inspires the artist to paint the instigator, the Fury of War, as helpless and handicapped, and to give her the features of a servant.' p.157. Brecht reads Dulle Griet as 'The Fury defending her pathetic household goods with the sword.' p.158. *Brecht on Theatre: The Development of an Aesthetic*, ed. and trans. John Willett, Methuen, 1964. Reprt.1978. pp.157–159. Contrast Brecht's (masculine) reading of Dulle Griet with Churchill's (feminist) representation of the figure in the dinner scene. Also see Ruby Cohn, *Anglo-American Interplay in Recent Drama*, Cambridge University Press, 1995. p.115.

32.   See *Anglo-American Interplay*. Cohn cites Eva Figes' *Patriarchal Attitudes* where Griselde is referred to as 'the masculine ideal of womanhood'. p.113, 114. Also see the critique of *Deborah, Woman-as-Mother-Earth* in Dimple Godiwala, '"The uncanny stranger on display": Arnold Wesker's monologues for women', forthcoming.

33.   Said to be Pope John VII (854–856), Pope Joan's hedonistic excesses presage those of Leo X (1513–21) and Alexander VI (1492–1503). The papacy was often used as an instrument for promoting the personal ambitions of the Pope's 'nephews', as the illegitimate sons of popes came to be called by the 15th century. See: *Hobbes to Hume*, W.T.Jones, Harcourt Brace Jovanovich College Publishers, second edition, 1980. pp.48–49.

34.   Lines kindly translated from the Latin by Dr. Peter Glare, St. Cross College.

35.   Judith Butler's synthesis of Irigaray in *Gender Trouble: Feminism and the Subversion of Identity*, Routledge, 1990. p. 9.

36.   Trevor R. Griffiths, 'Waving not Drowning: The mainstream, 1979–88', in *British and Irish Women Dramatists since 1958*, eds., Trevor R. Griffiths and Margaret Llewellyn-Jones, Oxford University Press, 1993.

37.   For a portrayal of this contemporary dilemma see Pam Gems' *Loving Women*, in the chapter on Pam Gems, later in this book.

38.   The quote, which represents the attitude of most Anglocritics to the figure of Marlene, is from Christopher Innes, *Modern British Drama: 1890–1990*, Cambridge University Press, 1992. p.460.

39.   Jane Thomas, 'The Plays of Caryl Churchill: Essays in Refusal', in *The Death of the Playwright?*, ed. Adrian Page, The Macmillan Press, 1992. p. 184.

40. In *The Order of Things* Foucault charts out three (western) epistemes: Renaissance knowledge, the classical episteme and the modern episteme. However, underlying all three epistemes of knowledge is *the patriarchal impulse* which—seen from the feminist point of view—unites the epistemic ruptures to form an unbroken episteme of patriarchy as demonstrated by the text of *Top Girls*.

41. Again, Innes' analysis is representative of the opinion of the Anglocritics. *Modern British Drama*, p.466.

42. ¹ 1928–1979. It had hardly been half a century since all women were given franchise that Margaret Thatcher became Prime Minister of Britain.

43. Janet Brown, 'Caryl Churchill's *Top Girls* Catches the Next Wave' in *Caryl Churchill: A Casebook,* ed. Phyllis R. Randall, Garland Publishing, 1989. pp.117–129.

44. The reference is to the 1991 BBC production of *Top Girls* directed for television by Max Stafford-Clark.

45. If I seem to be taking the subaltern waitress beyond a recognizable limit, this is because I can fully imagine a production of *Top Girls* where the waitress is played by a black woman. This performance-reading does not diverge from the *nebentext*.

46. See Dimple Godiwala, conclusion to 'Asian Theatre in Britain' in *Hard Times*, Issue 67/68, Autumn 1999. p.59.

47. *File On Churchill*.

48. This book does not take into account any drama written or produced after 1999.

49. Lois McNay notes that 'the process of epistemic transformation must be initiated by a force *external* to the *episteme*: a *non-discursive force*.' [*Foucault*, p.65. My emphases.] In the context of the patriarchal episteme, the 'external force' would be feminism, although to what extent can a transformative force be *non*-discursive? And, in view of the system and its rules, there is nothing outside the episteme! The discursive matrix entire *is* the episteme, at once permeable and viscous. ('each transformation may have its own particular index of temporal 'viscosity'. *Archaeology*, p.175) This is another problematic reading by McNay. See 'Change and Transformations', Chapter 5, *Archaeology of Knowledge*. Also see Ernesto Laclau and Chantal Mouffe, who support my view. Quoted by McNay, p.71. In this context refer back to footnote 1 where I define *post*-discursive. Practices, institutions, technologies come into being as a result of discourse, being formulated and constituted within the matrix. Thus Laclau and Mouffe are right in saying that there is nothing non-discursive. If it is seen as *outside* discourse, then it forms *another* discourse which does not (currently) share the boundaries with the first. *But all is within the episteme*, even if there are different demarcations of a particular episteme.

50. In an afterword to *Chiaroscuro* in *Lesbian Plays*, introduced by Jill Davis, Methuen, 1987. pp.82–83.

51. *Bloomsbury Theatre Guide*, Trevor R. Griffiths and Carole Woddis, Bloomsbury, 1988 and 1991. p.194.

52. Kay, *Lesbian Plays*, p.83.

53. I mean for there to be a difference between a *sign* and a *symbol*. Whilst almost everything from prop to actor is a signifier signifying a signified or signifying a signifier as the case might be, a symbol is something (in this case five props) explicitly and consciously used to signify a signified which has a strata of meanings, making the symbol

function on the level of the conscious, the sub-conscious and, as the case may be, the unconscious, all of which may be collective.

54. Kay, *Lesbian Plays*, p.83.

55. Kay, *Lesbian Plays*, p.83. Kay's obsession with naming reflects an African heritage, as pointed out by my anonymous reader at Peter Lang. Many Africans will know the day of the week on which they were born and their position in the family. This is because many African groups took their children's names from the day in the week on which they were born in combination with their birth order in the family. Indians are similarly named according to the '*rashi*' or astrological birthchart which takes into account the day and time of birth.

56. It took the Stephen Lawrence inquiry to get a culture to acknowledge that racism operated at the level of the unconscious: '*The Colour of Justice* [which was the 1999 dramatization of the inquiry] puts on stage […] a chilling acknowledgement that racial prejudice exists at conscious, subconscious and unconscious levels in the psyche of the dominant culture/s […] [I]t points to the need for the dominant grouping/s to acknowledge and come to terms with the fact that racial prejudice has infiltrated through the practice and institutions of British society.' 'Asian Theatre in Britain', p.59.

57. This is by no means to be read as the definitive form of lesbian attachment. See, *e.g.*, Jill Dolan, *Presence and Desire*, University of Michigan Press, 1993 or, for an overview, see Tamsin Spargo's introductory essay 'Foucault and Queer Theory', Icon books, 1999.

58. Kay is quoting Ntozake Shange's *Three Pieces*.

59. *Bloomsbury Theatre Guide*, p.194.

60. This is certainly *not* to claim that women have in any measure achieved a full equality, as gender discrimination does exist in institutionalized forms. It is merely to claim that, *e.g.*, Virginia Woolf's ideal of having a room of one's own and a sum to get by on, is easily achievable by many women today if, indeed, they see this as an ideal life. That certainly points to a difference in societal status and a kind of freedom unavailable to so many a century ago.

61. I am grateful to Barbara Alice Mann for pointing out that Engels was working from a close reading of Lewis Henry Morgan, *League of the Haudenosaunee* (1851) and more importantly (as far as Engels was concerned), Morgan's *Ancient Society* (1877). Both were considered leading anthropological studies in their day, and the League still is, largely because Morgan's ghost writer was Ely Parker a Seneca Chief. In both studies, Morgan largely detailed Iroquian society, which was, and still is, matriarchal.

62. Terry Eagleton, *The Illusions of Postmodernism*, Blackwell Publishers, 1995.

63. Cf. Robert Young, *Torn Halves: Political Conflict in Literary and Cultural Theory*, Manchester University Press, 1996. p.89. '[T]he pressure of feminism, and more recently Black Studies, has meant that today the political cannot be ignored by anyone and may be responsible for the white male retreat into Marxism. Marxism can compete with feminism and Black Studies in so far as it offers to return literary criticism to its traditional moral function, *but can, more covertly, also act as a defence against them.*' My emphasis.

64. *Archaeology*, p.167–175.

65. Cf. Michel Foucault, 'History, Discourse and Discontinuity'in *Foucault Live: Collected Interviews 1961–1984*, ed.Sylvère Lotringer, trans. Lysa Hochroth and John Johnston, Semiotext(e), 1989. p.37.

66. *Archaeology*, p.167–175.

67. *Archaeology*, p.177.

68. *Anti-Oedipus*.

69. I am thinking of the historian, Eric Hobsbawm. *The Short Twentieth Century* is an example of the discourse of history having, willy-nilly, to take up the strand of gender as *integral to* the history of a century, whilst his first three volumes make no attempt to be inclusive. See Eric Hobsbawm, *The Age of Revolution [Europe] 1789–1848*, Weidenfeld and Nicolson, 1962; *The Age of Capital 1848–1875*, Weidenfeld and Nicolson, 1975; *The Age of Empire 1875–1914*, Weidenfeld and Nicolson, 1987; *The Age of Extremes: The Short Twentieth Century 1914–1991*, Michael Joseph, 1994.

70. Paralogy: logically unjustified conclusions. See Jean-François Lyotard, *The Postmodern Condition: A Report on Knowledge*, trans. Geoff Bennington and Brian Massumi, University of Minnesota, 1984, Manchester University Press, 1986.

71. *The Postmodern Condition*, introduction, p. xxiv.

72. *A Stage of Their Own: Feminist Playwrights of the Suffrage Era*, ed. Sheila Stowell, Manchester University Press, 1992; *'How the Vote was Won' and other Suffragette Plays*, ed. Dale Spender, Methuen, 1985.

73. Cf. Lyotard, *The Postmodern Condition*, p. xxiv.

74. Lyotard, *The Postmodern Condition*, p.xxiv–xxv

75. Ferdinand de Saussure, *Course in General Linguistics*, trans. Wade Baskin, Fontana/Collins, 1974. p.120. Authorial emphases.

76. See: *Revolution in Poetic Language*, 1974, trans. Margaret Waller, Columbia University Press, 1984; *Desire in Language. A Semiotic Approach to Literature and Art*, trans. Thomas S. Gora, Alice Jardine, and Leon S. Roudiez, Basil Blackwell, Oxford, 1984; 'The System and the Speaking Subject', in *The Kristeva Reader*, ed. Toril Moi, Blackwell, 1986.

77. Kristeva, 'The System and the Speaking Subject'.

78. *Anti-Oedipus*, p.12. The authors are quoting from Samuel Beckett, 'Enough' in *First Love and other Shorts*.

PART TWO
Breaking the Bounds of the British Main/Male Stream:
Five Contemporary Dramatists and Their Transgressive Re-formations in the Predominantly Male Territory of British Mainstream Drama

1. Endist speculation gained currency in the decades closing the millennium as thinkers forecast the end of 'history, humanism, ideology, modernity, philosophy, Marxism, the author, 'man', and the world'. Stuart Sim paraphrasing Derrida, 'Derrida and the End of History', Icon books, 1999. p.12. Jacques Derrida refers to this 'apocalyptic tone in philosophy' as 'the classics of the end' in *Specters of Marx: The State of the Debt, the Work of Mourning & the New International*, trans. Peggy Kamuf, New York & London:

Routledge, 1994. See pp.14 and15 where he accuses Anglo-America for being (in this regard) late to the end of history.

2.   Cf. Reina Lewis, *Gendering Orientalism: Race, Femininity and Representation*, Routledge, 1996. Lewis comments on the 'gender-blindness' of the death of the author debate; it forecloses 'the possibility of a narrative authority to which women had never really acceded'. p.23–4.

CHAPTER TWO
Effecting a Rupture with Male Dramatic Discourse: Caryl Churchill

1.   Gilles Deleuze and Félix Guattari, *Kafka: Toward a Minor Literature* [1975], trans. Dana Polan, University of Minnesota Press, 1986. p.28.

2.   Catherine Itzin remarks on this shift in *Stages in the Revolution: Political Theatre in Britain since 1968*, Eyre Methuen, 1980. p.283. Churchill's socialist period begins with *Light Shining in Buckinghamshire* (Joint Stock) and her feminist period with *Vinegar Tom* (Monstrous Regiment), both in 1976, after the solo *Traps* written after a painful miscarriage. Itzin sees a shift 'from the expression of personal anger and pain to the expression of public political perspective'. p.285. Also see Helene Keyssar, *Feminist Theatre*, Macmillan, 1984. Keyssar notes that 1976 marks a break between the early Churchill and the later collaborative and more mature work. p. 91.

3.   For Monstrous Regiment see *Feminist Theatre Voices*, ed. Elaine Aston, Loughborough Theatre Texts, 1997. p.52–76.

4.   Joint Stock was founded in 1974 by Max Stafford-Clark, David Hare and William Gaskill. It was committed to socialist and political theatre and a collective process of writing and ensemble acting. See *The Joint Stock Book: The Making of a Theatre Collective*, ed. Rob Ritchie, Methuen, 1987.

5.   Michael Selmon, 'Reshuffling the Deck: Iconoclastic Dealings in Caryl Churchill's Early Plays' in *Caryl Churchill: A Casebook*, ed. Phyllis R. Randall, Garland Publishing, 1989. p.55.

6.   'Reshuffling the Deck', p.65.

7.   *Feminist Theatre*, p. 77.

8.   *Feminist Theatre*, p.79.

9.   Christopher Innes, *Modern British Drama: 1890–1990*, Cambridge University Press, 1992. pp. 460–1.

10.   *Owners* was written in the three days following a painful miscarriage.

11.   *Feminist Theatre*, p.85.

12.   Alex Renton in *The Independent*, 8 April 1987.

13.   *The Guardian*, 9 April 1987.

14.   *Feminist Theatre Voices*, p.18.

15.   See Victoria's husband, Martin, in *Cloud Nine*, below.

16.   As Alan Ayckbourn put it, '[S]he embodies what the majority of this country believe, and aim for, and strive for. She's there because they put her there. […] She was our representative […] what we all jointly created'. Duncan Wu, *Six Contemporary Dramatists*, St. Martin's Press, 1995.p.150.

17. This is why drama is so important. It is able to record living moments of society in an immediate way that film and television productions simply cannot do. See *Changing Stages*, narrated by Richard Eyre, episode telecast on 3 December 2000.

18. See Gilles Deleuze and Félix Guattari, *Anti-Oedipus:Capitalism and Schizophrenia* Vol. I [1972], trans. Robert Hurley, Mark Seem, and Helen R. Lane, Athlone Press, 1984.

19. Gilles Deleuze and Félix Guattari, *A Thousand Plateaux: Capitalism and Schizophrenia* Volume II [1980] trans. Brian Massumi, Athlone Press, 1988, reprt.1999. pp.9–10.

20. Anne McClintock, *Imperial Leather: Race, Gender and Sexuality in the Colonial Contest*, Routledge, 1995. p.8.

21. *Imperial Leather*, p.5.

22. *Imperial Leather*, p.17.

23. *Imperial Leather*, pp.44–5.

24. For a history of Joint Stock, see *The Joint Stock Book—The Making of a Theatre Collective*, ed. Rob Ritchie, Methuen, 1987. I am indebted to Nizwar Karanj for an insider's view on Joint Stock's working methods.

25. Michel Foucault, *The History of Sexuality, Volume I*, trans. Robert Hurley, Penguin, 1978, 1990. p.47.

26. *The History Of Sexuality*, p. 47.

27. *Imperial Leather*, p.45.

28. Churchill's preface to the play. Edition quoted from is listed in the bibliography.

29. In this context see Thomas Macaulay's speech, *Minute on Indian Education*, extract to be found in *The Post-colonial Studies Reader*, eds. Bill Ashcroft, Gareth Griffiths and Helen Tiffin, Routledge, 1995. p.428 ff. The British Imperial powers wanted to construct 'a class of persons [...] English in taste, in opinions, in morals, and in intellect'. p.430. The play has the black man (problematically conflated with the white woman) passively complicit with the colonizer's intention as he says, 'What white men want is what I want to be'. (I, i)

30. '[T]he cross-dressed actor reveals that gender is socially constructed [(...) C]ross-dressing in history as well as current theatre practice is essential to understanding the nature of theatre [and gender as theatrical and social construction]'. Lesley Ferris, 'Introduction' to 'Cross-dressing and women's theatre', in Lizbeth Goodman, *The Routledge Reader in Gender and Performance*, Routledge, 1998. p. 168–9.

    Feminist theory and gay/queer theory has increasingly focused on cross-dressing in contemporary theatre. This critical study tends to focus on what has heretofore been elided in feminist readings of theatre, such as colonialism in *Cloud Nine* and bisexuality (rather than cross-dressing) in *Queen Christina*, below. For theories of cross-dressing in theatre see, *e.g.*, Michelene Wandor, *Carry On, Understudies*, Routledge, 1986; Marjorie Garber, *Vested Interests: Cross-Dressing and Cultural Anxiety*, Routledge, 1992; Kate Davy, 'Fe/ Male Impersonation: The Discourse of Camp, in *Critical Theory and Performance*, eds. Janelle G. Reinelt and Joseph R. Roach, University of Michigan Press, 1992; Lesley Ferris, ed., *Crossing the Stage: Controversies on Cross-Dressing*, Routledge, 1993.

31. The multiple ironies of her name are possibly more profuse than a production/ performance might bear across. Instances such as these point to the need for an analysis of *dramatic* text, as set out in my General Introduction, above.

32. Cf. David Macey, *Lacan in Contexts*, Verso, 1988. pp.177–209.

33. The eyes, in psychoanalysis, stand for the penis and blinding is, as in Oedipus, a metaphor for castration. *Lacan in Contexts*.

34. The feminine is a realm of darkness for Lacan as well. Man is day and light as woman is the night and darkness. *Lacan in Contexts*.

35. Cf. Joseph Conrad, *Heart of Darkness*.

36. *Imperial Leather*, pp.5–6.

37. *Imperial Leather*, pp.9–10.

38. *Imperial Leather*, p.6.

39. *Imperial Leather*, p.6.

40. See my essay, 'Invention/ Hybridity/ Identity: British Asian Culture and its Postcolonial Stages', forthcoming in *Journal for the Study of British Cultures*, 2001/2; and my survey, 'Asian Theatre in Britain', in *Hard Times*, 67/68, 1999.

41. See Albert Memmi, *The Colonizer and the Colonized* [*Portrait du Colonisé, précédé du portrait du colonisateur* 1957], trans. Howard Greenfield, The Beacon Press, 1967.

42. *Imperial Leather*, p.24.

43. *Imperial Leather*, p. 24.

44. *Imperial Leather*, p.26.

45. *Imperial Leather*, p. 28 and 31.

46. John M. Clum, "The Work of Culture": *Cloud Nine* and Sex/ Gender Theory' in *Casebook*. p.98; *Imperial Leather*.

47. From Peter Gay, *The Bourgeoise Experience—Victoria to Freud: Volume II The Tender Passion*, Oxford University Press, 1986. p.205. Also in *Casebook*, pp.91–115.

48. Ann Laura Stoler, *Race and the Education of Desire: Foucault's History of Sexuality and the Colonial Order of Things*, Duke University Press, 1995. p. 141.

49. *Education of Desire*, p. 137. Cf. *Colonial Desire*.

50. *Education of Desire*, p. 138.

51. *The History of Sexuality: Volume I*, p. 42.

52. Women's glossy magazines like *Cosmopolitan* have made it their task, since western women's mid-century sexual liberation, to keep their readers regularly informed about their bodies as constituted within the discursive matrix of autoeroticism and masturbatory practices. This is evidence that distinguishes Foucault's discourse (which obviously centres around the male child), from that of the female child. For the former, surveillance leads to discovery, and the formulation and labelling of practices elicit what would otherwise perhaps have been regarded as a 'natural' discourse which constitutes the child's sexuality. Women's apparent 'lack' however, requires an information system which is rather more sophisticated than a mere technology of surveillance. It would be strange if men's magazines needed to disseminate information on the 'how to' of male masturbatory practice in almost every issue. This evidence, still found at your local newsagent every month, points to the male bias of Foucault's theory of child sexuality as documented in *The History of Sexuality: Volume I*. Support for the masculinism of Foucault is to be found in Kate Soper, 'Productive Contradictions' in *Up Against Foucault: Explorations of Some Tensions between Foucault and Feminism*, ed. Caroline Ramazanoglu, Routledge, 1993. Soper notes that Foucault 'might be said to

be somewhat implicitly reliant on a masculinist conception of the subject as the support for his polemic with humanism. There is also something markedly androcentric' in his examination of sexuality. p.39.

53. *The History of Sexuality: Volume I*, p. 42.

54. *Education of Desire*, pp. 143–5.

55. Cf. Gayle Rubin, 'The Traffic in Women: Notes on the "Political Economy" of Sex', in *Toward an Anthropology of Women*, ed. Rayna R. Reiter, Monthly Review Press, 1975 and Judith Butler, *Gender Trouble*, Routledge, 1990. pp.72–8.

56. The body-without-organs is an inert machine which awaits an energy-machine: see *Anti-Oedipus*, p.1.

57. As explicated by Philip Goodchild, in *Deleuze and Guattari*, Sage Publications, 1996. p.78.

58. The condition of the indigenous African woman comes to mind. For persons aware of these practices it seems almost unimaginable that Churchill ignores the comparative text, as the only colonized women in the play belong to the white family of man, and black women do not, for the authors of this play hailed by many a feminist critic as critical of the colonial regime, exist. See Mary Daly, *Gyn/Ecology: The Metaethics of Radical Feminism*, Beacon Press, 1978. Also see Audre Lorde's response: 'An Open Letter to Mary Daly', in *Sister Outsider*, The Crossing Press, 1984. pp.66–71. See the novel, *Possessing the Secret of Joy*, Alice Walker, Vintage, 1993.

59. Robert Young, *Torn Halves: Political Conflict in Literary and Cultural Theory*, Manchester University Press, 1996. p.81.

60. *Imperial Leather*, p.45.

61. Elizabeth Grosz, as quoted in Helen Gilbert and Joanne Tompkins, eds. *Post-colonial Drama: Theory, Practice, Politics*, Routledge, 1996. p.204.

62. *Post-colonial Drama*, p. 207.

63. 'Closing No Gaps: Aphra Behn, Caryl Churchill and Empire' in *Casebook*. pp. 168, 169, 172. Emphasis mine.

64. Clum in *Casebook*, p. 105.

65. 'Travesty and Transgression: Transvestism in Shakespeare, Brecht, and Churchill' in *Performing Feminisms: Feminist Critical Theory and Theatre*, ed. Sue-Ellen Case, Johns Hopkins University Press, 1990. p.308–9. Emphasis mine.

66. See, *e.g.*, Sartre's preface to *The Colonizer and the Colonized*, or any reliable history of the British Empire.

67. *Anti-Oedipus*, p.50.

68. The patriarchal impulse, the colonial impulse and the capitalist impulse.

69. Cf. Claude Levi-Strauss. See *Colonial Desire*. See 'Travesty and Transgression' for Herrmann's comment on 'the most transgressive moment' in the piece: the moment of incest as Edward defines himself as a lesbian. p.314.

70. Robert Young's analysis of 'capitalism's extraordinary adaptability and ability to metamorphosize itself into different forms, its inherent instability and constant mode of revolutionary change [...] its skill—[which is] the central dynamic of the system— in deferring indefinitely that lonely last instance when its contradictions would produce its own self-destruction' makes it part of the larger system which is also sub-

strated by the patriarchal impulse and the colonial impulse. *Torn Halves: Political Conflict in Literary and Cultural Theory*, Manchester University Press, 1996. pp. 8–9. Capitalism hastens the fracturing of the twin impulses which sustain patriarchy and colonization—the patriarchal impulse and the colonial impulse—as it produces consumers in women and third world markets.

71. *Feminist Theatre Voices*, p.63.

72. For feminist collectives see Lizbeth Goodman, *Contemporary Feminist Theatres: To Each Her Own*, Routledge, 1993, and *Feminist Theatre Voices*. Also see the collected volumes *Plays For Women*, Methuen.

73. Peter Hulton's interview with Gillian Hanna, in 'Theatre Papers', Second Series, No.8, Dartington College of Arts,1978. p.3.

74. 'Theatre Papers', p.3.

75. 'Theatre Papers', p.3.

76. Austin E. Quigley, 'Stereotype and Prototype: Character in the plays of Caryl Churchill' in *Feminine Focus: The New Women Playwrights*, ed. Enoch Brater, Oxford University Press, 1989. p.27.

77. 'Theatre Papers', p.9.

78. 'Theatre Papers', p.8.

79. Janelle Reinelt, 'Beyond Brecht: Britain's New Feminist Drama' in *Performing Feminisms: Feminist Critical Theory and Theatre*, ed. Sue-Ellen Case, Johns Hopkins University Press, Baltimore and London: 1990. p. 157.

80. 'Beyond Brecht', pp. 157–8.

81. Churchill, in an afterword to *Vinegar Tom* in *Plays by Women: Volume I*, ed. Michelene Wandor, Methuen, 1982.

82. 'Stereotype and Prototype', p.29.

83. 'Stereotype and Prototype', p.28.

84. 'Stereotype and Prototype', p.28.

85. Robert Cushman in *The Observer*, February 1983.

86. Churchill in her preface to *Plays: One*.

87. In *The Joint Stock Book*, Churchill relates how this materialized: 'Then Max and I had the idea, first a joke, then seriously, that perhaps there wasn't any need to write the missing scenes if it wasn't quite clear which character was which and different actors played the same character in different scenes. This [...] gave an effect we liked of many people having the same experience during the revolution'. p.120.

88. Geraldine Cousin, *Churchill: the Playwright*, Methuen, 1989. p.19. This book is a detailed appraisal of Churchill's early stageplays.

89. Abraham Maslow famously said hunger and thirst were basic needs, whilst every other need was classed as a 'want' thereby not essential for bare physical survival. Maslow placed human wants in a hierarchy which ranged from safety and security to love, finally leading the person to the highest want, self-actualization. One suspects that self-actualizing persons are not caught up in an infinite material desire but take recourse in much that is spiritually sustaining.

90. Dr. Max Lüscher, *The Lüscher Colour Test*, trans. Ian Scott, Jonathan Cape, 1970. pp.59–60.

91. *Anti-Oedipus*, p.4.

92. Giles Gordon in *The Spectator*, January 1984.

93. All references to Michel Foucault's *Discipline and Punish* are cited with the aid of extracts in *The Foucault Reader*, ed. Paul Rabinow, Penguin, 1984 and Barry Smart, *Michel Foucault*, Routledge, 1988.

94. Churchill in the preface to *Softcops*.

95. Interestingly, Sarah Daniels' *Masterpieces* played simultaneously at the Royal Court: a play which examines some of the causes of crime, see section on Daniels, below.

96. Janelle Reinelt, *After Brecht: British Epic Theatre*, University of Michigan Press, 1994. p.96.

97. See Deleuze and Foucault's discussion about power, 'Intellectuals and Power' in *Foucault Live Collected Interviews 1961–1984*, trans. Lysa Hochroth and John Johnston, ed. Sylvère Lotringer, Semiotext(e), 1989. Deleuze, p77.

98. Foucault, *Foucault Live* , p.79

99. The space of immanent social relations.

100. See Deleuze and Guattari's hypothesis in *Anti-Oedipus*.

101. Here, 'schizo' is the sick schizophrenic, incarcerated in the asylum.

102. *Anti-Oedipus*, p.245–6.

103. *Anti-Oedipus*, p.245–6.

104. Churchill in her preface to *Plays: Two*.

105. *After Brecht*, p.97.

106. *Anti-Oedipus*, p.250.

107. *Anti-Oedipus*, p.240–1.

108. Previously, she had used it to great success in the dinner scene in *Top Girls* as it united the disparate women in a bond of intimacy and shared moments and camaraderie.

109. Neil Collins in *The Daily Telegraph*, 30 March 1987.

110. Michael Coveney in *The Financial Times*, 30 March 1987.

111. *Anti-Oedipus*, pp.254–5.

112. *Anti-Oedipus*, p.231.

113. Victoria Radin in *The New Statesman*, 3 April 1987.

114. Michel Foucault, *Mental Illness and Psychology*, trans. Alan Sheridan, Harper and Row, 1986. pp.84–5.

115. *Anti-Oedipus*, pp.2,4.

116. From the Lancashire word *to skrike* meaning to grizzle or to complain.

117. Self-styled 'feminists' such as Lois McNay problematically conflate mental illness with the marginalization of gender. In *Foucault: A Critical Introduction*, [Polity Press, 1994] McNay begins with what is a very sympathetic reading of *Mental Illness and Psychology* and *Madness and Civilization* which are the texts, along with those of R.D.Laing and the later Deleuze and Guattari, to have brought madness out of the western closet to a large extent. McNay alarmingly leaps from the summary of Foucault's work on madness (pp.18–30) to 'a consideration of, for example, the way in which a notion of madness is deployed in dominant constructions of feminine identity [and] the perception of madness as a peculiar 'female malady. [That] femininity is inextricably linked

with [...] madness'. (p.30). In the context of her introduction to Foucault's painstaking and groundbreaking research from the ostracism of those abandoned on the ship of fools giving way to a period of confinement and surveillance which are but another kind of social and psychological ostracism, a status which, as Foucault points out was extended to the unemployed, criminals, the sick and the aged, is too extreme to be glibly linked to Elaine Showalter's work on madness being feminized and hystericized. Feminism is an issue, and a serious one; but works such as these perform a dis-service by linking the travails of gender to, what may be seen—socially and psychologically and indeed medically—as quite a separate issue, and perhaps more in need of funds and social support. Works such as these are fodder for the reactionary tendency which feminism continually struggles against by making what may be seen as 'hysterical' claims; hysterical used here nominally as the pejorative it has been for centuries. McNay is, as noted elsewhere, fairly dubious in several places, especially in her rather facile and naive 'definition of the episteme as *a hybrid formation of words and things*' (p.70, emphasis mine) which she seems to directly attribute to Michel Foucault.

118.   Benedict Nightingale in *The Times*, 29 January 1994.

119.   Michael Billington in *The Guardian*, 29 January 1994.

120.   'Children's language' was a definition offered by Nicholas Wright at the Cottesloe Platform 1994. This was an after-show interview with the playwright. His comment was negated by the author who clarified that the skriker's was intended to be 'a damaged language' closest to the schizophrenic breakdown in language.

121.   That Kelpie is a *centaur*, the Deleuzean *Homo natura*, is indicated only in the dramatic text and not realized in the production.

122.   It would not be surprising if the idea of toads and wishes occurred to Churchill via an acquaintance with Feng Shui's mystical toad which grants wishes. It is represented by a toad or frog with a detachable piece of money in its mouth. Splitting the eastern conceptual unity into western binaries, the toads in the play come across as negativity whilst the coins seem like a reward. An 80s critic suggested that Churchill is overtly influenced by Buddhist, Jainist, Taoist and Hindu philosophical tenets; that Churchill's 'dramatic devices [...] are more consistent with Eastern philosophy than with Western'. This is a naïve claim in terms of western philosophy's problematic of irreconcilable 'torn halves' that don't quite add up (Adorno; see Robert Young, who flags up this notion in *Torn Halves*, marginalized in Adorno), as well as the western feminist complaint of binarily opposed categories which derogate the female/ *feminine* (see Hélène Cixous, quoted elsewhere in this text). As a comparative text I would like to point out an example from one of the 'eastern' philosophies mentioned; that of yin and yang, which represent an opposition not of conflict but one of a harmonious simultaneity, best expressed conceptually as a oneness which is inscribed with its own alterity. The claim that links Churchill with eastern philosophy is dubious as she does the classical western thing with eastern unities: she prises them apart, specifically in *Traps* and *Owners*, two of the texts mentioned by the aforementioned critic, Mark Thacker Brown, 'Constantly Coming Back: Eastern Thought and the Plays of Caryl Churchill', in *Casebook*. pp. 25–45.

123.   *Anti-Oedipus*, p.5.

124.   Barbara Thorden in *The Times Literary Supplement*, 4 February 1994.

125. All quotes by Churchill at the Cottesloe platform, where she reiterated 'damage' as a keyword time and again.

126. In *The Guardian* of 29 January 1994, Michael Billington remarked that the skriker 'oscillates between evil spirit and fairy godmother'. It is this blend of the benign and the evil natures which makes the skriker both Oedipus and anti-Oedipus, transforming the figure into a ringing metaphor for the repressive materialistic society of twentieth century Britain.

127. Don Shiach, *From Page to Performance*, Cambridge University Press, 1987.

CHAPTER THREE
White Women's Mythologies: Pam Gems

1. *la femme n'existe pas*; by which he means that there is something about femininity which escapes and exceeds discourse. See David Macey, *Lacan in Contexts*, Verso, 1988.

2. S. Harding, 'Reinventing Ourselves as Other', in L. Kauffman, ed., *American Feminist Thought at Century's End—A Reader*, Blackwell, 1993. p.156

3. For an early critical appraisal and biography of Gems, see Michelene Wandor, *Carry On, Understudies*, Routledge and Kegan Paul, 1981, 1986. pp. 161–166.

4. Pam Gems, 'Imagination and Gender', in Michelene Wandor, ed., *On Gender and Writing*, Pandora Press, 1983. p.148.

5. Katherine H. Burkman, 'The Plays of Pam Gems: Personal/ Political/ Personal', in *British and Irish Drama since 1960*, ed., James Acheson, Macmillan, 1993. p.191.

6. The other RSC dramatist is Timberlake Wertenbaker, but her plays are adaptations and re-workings of Greek classics. Gems manages to bring feminism directly to the mainstream with subversive intent.

7. This early feminist consciousness which celebrated difference by including women of race, class and colour is reflected in the now defunct 70s feminist journal 'Spare Rib'.

8. 'Imagination and Gender', p.149.

9. Interview with Ann McFerran in *Time Out*, 21–27 October 1977, as quoted in *Carry On*, p. 162.

10. Pam Gems, in an afterword to *Dusa, Fish, Stas and Vi*, in *Plays by Women: Volume I*, ed., Michelene Wandor, Methuen, 1983. My emphasis.

11. 'Imagination and Gender', p.150.

12. 'Imagination and Gender', p.150. My emphasis.

13. Gems in *Plays by Women: Volume Five*, ed., Mary Remnant, Methuen, 1986. p.48.

14. The historical Queen Christina is reported to have said this. All historical references to Christina are from Betty Millan, *Monstrous Regiment: Women Rulers in Men's Worlds*, The Kensal Press, 1982. pp.168–181.

15. Simone de Beauvoir in 'Talking to Simone de Beauvoir', an interview with *Spare Rib*, Vol.56, 1977. p.8.

16. Marjorie Garber, *Vice Versa: Bisexuality and the Eroticism of Everyday Life*, Hamish Hamilton, 1995. p.70.

17. Hélène Cixous, 'The Laugh of the Medusa', in *New French Feminisms*, eds. Elaine Marks and Isabelle de Courtivron, Harvester, 1980.

18. Pam Gems in 'Spare Rib', September 1977. My emphasis.

19. See Roland Barthes, *Mythologies* [1957], trans. Jonathan Cape, 1972, Vintage, 1993. pp.109–159; and the later *Image—Music—Text*, Fontana Press, 1977. p.165.

20. Cf *Mythologies*, p.128.

21. *Mythologies*, p. 127.

22. *Mythologies*, p. 123.

23. Cf *Mythologies*, pp. 120–122.

24. There is a group of feminists who oppose the writing of Herstory. e.g., Christina Crosby, in *The Ends of History: Victorians and "The Woman Question"*, insists that revealing women where there had been only men is still to occupy the space of formation of the discourse of history; that such herstoricizing would reveal 'the truth' about women's lives just as history had purported to about man's identity (that women have always occupied the space of the Other); and thirdly, women would be conceptualized as a unified category of similar individuals with similar experiences, where differences would be neglected. Diane Elam counters by asserting that *'her-story is not just one story'* (authorial emphasis). As Cixous put it in *The Newly Born Woman*, there are always several [herstories] underway at once. The diversity and plurality of herstories must then be acknowledged and accounted for. Anti-herstorians must recognize that history can be an integrated whole only if the achievements—both personal and political—of both genders are recorded. Most importantly, feminists who work within a recognized canonical/ patriarchal discourse destabilize the bounds of that discourse by demanding ideological accommodation within it. Herstoricizing thus *breaks the bounds* of his-tory. Diane Elam, *Feminism and Deconstruction: Ms. en Abyme*, Routledge, 1994. p.37. Christina Crosby, *The Ends of History: Victorians and 'The Woman Question'*, Routledge, 1991. p. 153. Quoted in Elam, ibid.; Hélène Cixous, *The Newly Born Woman*, [*La Jeune Née* 1975], co-written with Catherine Clément, trans. Betsy Wing, University of Minnesota Press, 1986. p.160.

25. *e.g.*, The Women's Theatre Group and Elaine Feinstein's *Lear's Daughters* (1987).

26. *Feminism and Deconstruction*, p.67.

27. Quoted in 'The Plays of Pam Gems' in *British and Irish Drama*. p.192.

28. *Feminism and Deconstruction*, pp. 42–43.

29. Judith Butler, *Bodies That Matter: On the Discursive Limits of "Sex"*, Routledge, 1993.

30. *Bodies That Matter*. See also her earlier *Gender Trouble: Feminism and the Subversion of Identity*, Routledge, 1990. The heterosexual matrix might be defined as the discursive field of normativity which prescribes heterosexuality as a regulatory ideal. The heterosexual matrix would be imbricated within the patriarchal field of discursivity which activates the patriarchal perceptual screens through which subjects view the world.

31. *Bodies That Matter*.

32. *Gender Trouble*, pp.142–143.

33. This dialectical movement runs through everything Hegel wrote: that every condition of thought or of things leads irresistibly to its opposite, and then (ideally) unites with it to form a higher or more complex whole. It is an old thought, foreshadowed by Empedocles, and embodied in the 'golden mean' of Aristotle who wrote 'the knowle-

dege of opposites is one'. Will Durant, *The Story of Philosophy*, Washington Square Press, 1926. Reprt. 1953. pp.272, 292 ff.

34. *Feminism and Deconstruction*, p.75.

35. *Gender Trouble*, pp.144–145. My emphasis.

36. Just as Christina's identity was 'forced into materialization' by her patriarch's decision to rear her as a man, so was Garbo formulated by the Garbo experts: director, photographer, costume expert, script writer. The censors similarly played a role in demanding any 'tinge of lesbianism' be underplayed. See: *Queen Christina*, Marcia Landy and Amy Villarejo, British Film Institute, 1995. Cited as *Queen Christina*, BFI publication.

37. *Queen Christina*, BFI publication, p.22.

38. *Monstrous Regiment*.

39. *Carry On, Understudies*, p.164.

40. *Queen Christina*, BFI publication.

41. Adrienne Rich, *Of Woman Born: Motherhood as Experience and Institution*, first published, USA: 1976; UK Virago 1977. p.235.

42. *Carry On*, p. 149.

43. For usurping the feminine, see Butler's interpretation of Foucault's reading of Herculine Barbin. *Gender Trouble*, pp.99–101.

44. *Gender Trouble*, p.111.

45. Parker Tyler, quoted in *Gender Trouble*, p.128.

46. *The Newly Born Woman*, p.85.

47. *The Newly Born Woman*, p.85.

48. *The Newly Born Woman*, pp.84–85.

49. *Gender Trouble*, p.93.

50. *Gender Trouble*, p.93.

51. *Gender Trouble*, p.93.

52. *Gender Trouble*, p.96.

53. *The Newly Born Woman*, p.85.

54. *The Newly Born Woman*, p.88.

55. Simone de Beauvoir, *The Second Sex* [*Le Deuxième Sexe*, 1949], trans. and ed., H.M.Parshley, Jonathan Cape, 1953, reprt. Penguin 1983.

56. See Stella Sandford, 'Contingent Ontologies: Sex, gender and 'woman' in Simone de Beauvoir and Judith Butler', *Radical Philosophy*, No.97, September/October 1999, pp.18–29.

57. *The Second Sex*, p.580.

58. *The Second Sex*, p.585.

59. *Feminism and Deconstruction*, p.37.

60. *The Newly Born Woman*, p.160.

61. Nancy Cotton, *Woman Playwrights in England c.1363–1750*, New Jersey, London and Toronto: Associated University Presses, 1980. p.64.

62. Katherine Worth, 'Images of Women in Modern English Theatre', in Enoch Brater, ed. *Feminine Focus: The New Women Playwrights*, Oxford University Press, 1989. p.10.

63. George Bernard Shaw, Preface to *Mrs. Warren's Profession* in *Plays Unpleasant*.

64. *The Second Sex*, p.569.

65. *The Second Sex*, p.569.

66. Margaret Llewellyn-Jones, 'Claiming a Space: 1969–78' in *British and Irish Women Dramatists since 1958*, ed. Trevor R. Griffiths and Margaret Llewellyn-Jones, Oxford University Press, 1993. p.36.

67. *The Second Sex*, p.578.

68. Roland Barthes, 'The Lady of the Camellias' in *Mythologies*, pp.103–105.

69. *Mythologies*, pp.103–105.

70. *The Second Sex*, p.571–72.

71. *The Second Sex*, p.577.

72. *British and Irish Women Dramatists*, p.36.

73. *The Second Sex*, p.580.

74. *Mythologies*, p.104.

75. *The Second Sex*, p.585.

76. *Mythologies*, p.104.

77. *British and Irish Women Dramatists*, p.37.

78. *British and Irish Women Dramatists*, p.37.

79. *British and Irish Women Dramatists*, p.37.

80. James Redmond, '"If the salt has lost his savour": Some "useful" plays in and out of context on the London stage', in *The Play out of Context: Transferring Plays from Culture to Culture*, eds. Hanna Scolnicov and Peter Holland, Cambridge University Press, 1989. p.73.

81. *British and Irish Women Dramatists*, p.37.

82. Heidi Stephenson and Natasha Langridge, *Rage and Reason: Women Playwrights on Playwriting*, Methuen, 1997. p.91.

83. *Carry On*, p.162.

84. *Carry On*, p.163.

85. *The Second Sex*, p.578–79.

86. Jack Tinker, *The Daily Mail*, 14 December 1993.

87. *The Second Sex*, p.575.

88. *Legends of the Twentieth Century: Edith Piaf*, EMI CD

89. See Pam Gems' introduction to *Marlene*, Oberon Books, 1998.

90. However, the evocation of myth by the citation of an overused fragment takes time. Gems' *Piaf* is too young in audience memory and production history for this statement to be valid at this moment in time. To evoke Edith Piaf however, a few strains of 'Je ne regrette rien' would be enough.

91. Michael Billington in *The Guardian*, 15 December 1993.

92. Sheridan Morley in *The Spectator*, 1 January 1994.

93. Benedict Nightingale in *The Times*, 15 December 1993.

94. Louise Doughty in *The Mail on Sunday*, 19 December 1993.

95. Sheridan Morley in *The Spectator*, 1 January 1994

96. Clive Hirschhorn in *Sunday Express*, 19 December 1993.

97. Louise Doughty in *The Mail on Sunday*, 19 December 1993.

98. Irving Wardle in *The Independent*, 19 December 1993.

99. Jane Lapotaire, comments Pam Gems, was well cast as Piaf. 'The actress as famous as Gielgud for her tongue—when accosted by a friend as she came out of the Brompton Oratory [she said]: 'Fuck off, can't you see I'm in a state of fucking blues?' Letter to the author from Pam Gems, 8 November 2000.

100. Benedict Nightingale in *The Times*, 15 December 1993.

101. Irving Wardle in *The Independent*, 19 December 1993.

102. Charles Spencer in *The Daily Telegraph*, 15 December 1993.

103. *Feminist Theatre*.

104. John Barber in *The Daily Telegraph*, 2 February 1984.

105. Michael Ratcliffe in *The Observer*, 5 February 1984.

106. John Barber in *The Daily Telegraph*, 2 February 1984.

107. Adrienne Rich, *Of Woman Born: Motherhood as Experience and Institution*, first published USA, 1976; Britain: Virago, 1977. p.282.

108. In Lyn Gardner's phrase, quoted in 'The Plays of Pam Gems' in *British and Irish Drama*. p. 190.

CHAPTER FOUR
From Hetero-Normativity to the View from Lesbos:
Through the Looking Glass with Sarah Daniels

1. See, *e.g.*, Lynda Hart, 'Identity and Seduction: Lesbians in the Mainstream', in *Acting Out: Feminist Performances*, ed. Lynda Hart and Peggy Phelan, University of Michigan Press, 1993.

2. Jill Dolan's conclusion to *Presence and Desire*, in Chapter 10 'Practicing Cultural Disruptions'. p.201. University of Michigan Press, 1993. The essay is also included in the earlier anthology, *Critical Theory and Performance*, ed. Janelle G. Reinelt and Joseph R. Roach, University of Michigan Press, 1992.

3. Dolan citing bell hooks. 'Practicing Cultural Disruptions', p.192. Dolan's own preference is for '[e]xtending hook's analogy to "I practice lesbian sex" (in all its varieties) [which] would initiate a discourse that might […] break open the sanctimonious strictures of politically correct lesbian identifications […] as the choice of sex acts are what mark gay and lesbian bodies as different agents within history.' p.193–194.

4. 'Daniels in the Lion's Den: Sarah Daniels and the British Backlash', *Theatre Journal*, Vol.47, No.3, Oct. 1995, p.393, 394.

5. Sarah Daniels in an interview with Lizbeth Goodman. As quoted in Lizbeth Goodman, *Contemporary Feminist Theatres: To Each Her Own*, Routledge, 1993. p.130.

6. John Barber, *Daily Telegraph*, 11 October 1983.

7. Jack Tinker, *Daily Mail*, 11 October 1983.

8. Ann McFerran, *Time Out*, 11 October 1983.

9. Daniels and John Burgess in the introduction to *Daniels: Plays One*, Methuen, 1991. Newspaper critics are not only guilty of using the term as a pejorative (*e.g.*, Nicholas

De Jongh in The Guardian, 10 January 1994, where he describes *Masterpieces* as 'superficial, melodramatic and flawed') but responsible for its widespread dissemination as well.

10. R.B. Heilman, *Tragedy and Melodrama: Versions of Experience*, University of Washington Press, 1968. p.79.

11. Trevor R. Griffiths and Carole Woddis, *Bloomsbury Theatre Guide*, Bloomsbury, 1988.

12. *Tragedy and Melodrama*, p.79.

13. James L. Smith, *Melodrama*, Methuen, 1973. pp.7–10.

14. William Sharp, 'The Structure of Melodrama', in James Redmond, ed. *Themes in Drama 14: Melodrama*, Cambridge University Press, 1992. pp.270–271.

15. Heilman refers to the prevailing 'monopathic' tone of melodrama, where monopathy is a 'quasi-wholeness': *i.e.*, 'the sensation of wholeness that is created when one responds with a single impulse or potential which functions as if it were his [sic] whole personality'. *Tragedy and Melodrama*, pp.84–86.

16. *Melodrama*, pp.10–11. Emphasis mine.

17. cf. *Melodrama*, pp.72–77.

18. In wresting away camp from Susan Sontag and the regularizing dominant discourse, Meyer attempts a re-definition of camp based on Linda Hutcheon's definition of parody. See *A Theory of Parody: The Teachings of Twentieth-Century Art Forms*, Linda Hutcheon, Methuen, 1985.

19. Judith Butler's theories have been elaborated in the section on Pam Gems, above.

20. For an appraisal of the need for history by minor or alternative discourses and the need to get away from the doomsday Christian classics-of-the-end, see my essay 'Invention/ Hybridity/ Identity: British-Asian Culture and its Postcolonial Theatres' in *Journal for the Study of British Cultures*, Vol. 8, 1/2001.

21. All quotations from Meyer are from 'Reclaiming the Discourse of Camp' in *The Politics and Poetics of Camp*, Routledge, 1994.

22. cf. Sue-Ellen Case, 'Towards a Butch/Femme Aesthetic' in Lynda Hart, ed. *Making a Spectacle: Feminist Essays on Contemporary Women's Theatre*, University of Michigan Press, 1989. p.297; and Jill Dolan, '"Lesbian" Subjectivity in Realism: Dragging at the Margins of Structure and Ideology' in Sue-Ellen Case, ed. *Performing Feminisms: Feminist Critical Theory and Theatre*, Johns Hopkins University Press, 1990. p.41–43. These critics maintain that the use of realism is 'deadly' to feminist theatre; that realism is ideologically patriarchal and ought not to be used by feminist dramatists. See my argument which follows, below.

23. *Contemporary Feminist Theatres*, pp.114–119.

24. We have seen how this forms the central *gest* for Jackie Kay's *Chiaroscuro*.

25. *Contemporary Feminist Theatres*, pp.114–119.

26. 'The lack of legislation about the lesbian […] forms the base for a powerful, because covert, attack on […] all forms of lesbian representation.' Goodman quoting Jeffrey Weeks, *Contemporary Feminist Theatres*, p.120. This serves as a regulatory mechanism of the prevailing order, rendering silent, indeed, invisible, the majority of those who call themselves lesbian.

27. Jill Dolan's *Presence and Desire: Essays on Gender, Sexuality, Performance* ends with a

call for pornography on the stage. 'The most transgressive act at this historical moment would be representing [gay male or lesbian sex] in excess, in dominant and marginalized reception communities. The explicitness of pornography seems the most constructive choice for practicing cultural disruptions.' University of Michigan Press, 1993. p.201.

28. See *Contemporary Feminist Theatres*, pp.117–120.

29. See Tim Miller and David Román, 'Preaching to the Converted', *Theatre Journal*, Vol.47, No.2, May 1995.

30. See Hélène Cixous, 'The Laugh of the Medusa', in *Literature in the Modern World*, ed., Dennis Walder, Oxford University Press, 1991.

31. Catherine Itzin, 'Entertainment for Men' in Catherine Itzin, ed. *Pornography: Women Violence and Civil Liberties—A Radical New View*, Oxford University Press, 1992. p.42.

32. Catherine Itzin, Introduction to *Pornography* (Itzin), p.1.

33. See: Susanne Kappeler, 'Problem 2: Human Rights', in *The Pornography of Representation*, Minneapolis: University of Minnesota Press, 1986. Also see Catherine Itzin, 'Legislating Against Pornography without Censorship'; 'Pornography and Civil Liberties: Freedom, Harm and Human Rights'; Catherine McKinnon, 'Pornography, Civil Rights and Speech'; Andrea Dworkin, 'Against the Male Flood: Censorship, Pornography and Equality'. All essays in *Pornography* (Itzin).

34. It is interesting that so many broadsheet critics, including women, were amazed at Rowena's ignorance of pornographic materials, thus betraying the insidiousness of pornography in western culture: 'I can't believe that this 26-year-old social worker had never seen a porn mag', wrote Ann McFerran in *Time Out*, 11 October 1983. Michael Billington wrote dismissively in *The Guardian* that 'she has apparently never set eyes on a porno magazine until her late 20s'and that the play makes 'false', 'arbitrary connections'; *The Standard*'s Milton Shulman remarked that Rowena, in this 'blatantly polemical' play, is 'surprisingly sheltered from life'. Worst of all perhaps was Robert Cushman of *The Observer*, who proceeded to admire the female actors' legs in most of his write-up, after having dismissed the play as 'not worth much'.

35. Frantz Fanon, *Black Skins, White Masks*, Pluto Press Limited, 1986. p.85. Referring to M. Mannoni's *Prospero and Caliban: Psychology of Colonization*, Fanon critiques it on the basis that 'A given society is racist or it is not'; that some people being 'less racist' than others is a 'subjective experience' not available to the black man. 'Is there in truth any difference between one racism and another? Do not all of them show the same collapse, the same bankruptcy of man?'pp.85–86. In the context of our play, each woman comes to the realization of the distance between herself and her husband as each of them displays instances of misogynistic thought and/or behaviour albeit on a differing scale. The difference between some men being 'less' misogynistic than others is a subjective experience available only to the male: to a feminist a given man is misogynistic or is not.

36. Peter Baker, 'Maintaining Male Power: Why Heterosexual Men use Pornography' in *Pornography*, (Itzin), p. 138–141.

37. For research on 'the role of pornography in predisposing some males to want to rape', and its role in 'undermining some males' internal and social inhibitions against acting out their desire to rape', see Diana E. Russell, 'Pornography and Rape: A Causal Model', in *Pornography* (Itzin), pp.310–349.

38. Michael Betzold, 'How Pornography Shackles Men and Oppresses Women', in J. Snodgrass (ed.), *For Men Against Sexism. A Book of Readings*, as quoted by Peter Baker, in *Pornography* (Itzin), p. 139.

39. Floyd Winecoff, a psychologist working with men, in his evidence to the Minneapolis Hearings. See note 375 above. As quoted by Peter Baker in *Pornography* (Itzin), p.139.

40. For an account of the contents of pornographic materials, see Catherine Itzin, 'Entertainment For Men': What It Is and What It Means.' *Pornography* (Itzin).

41. Deborah Cameron and Elizabeth Frazer, 'On the Question of Pornography and Sexual Violence: Moving Beyond Cause and Effect', in *Pornography* (Itzin), pp. 359–383.

42. See *The Pornography of Representation*. In 'Problem 6: Why Look at Women?' Kappeler maintains that in western culture the male gaze has been directed toward animals and women in a similar fashion through the centuries. In a daring inversion of John Berger's *About Looking* (1980) she draws on his essay 'Why Look at Animals?', substituting 'women' for 'animals'. 'The essay reads entirely plausibly with the substitution of 'women' for 'animals' (p.63). 'Woman, in the [western] cultural perspective, is much closer to the animal Other'. (p.69).

43. Roland Barthes, 'Sade II: The Helmet' in *Sade, Fourier, Loyola*, [1971], trans. Richard Miller, Hill and Wang, 1976. p.143. (Authorial italics; emphasis in bold, mine).

44. Itzin, in *Pornography* (Itzin), pp.34–35.

45. Kappeler, 'Pornography: The Representation of Power', in *Pornography* (Itzin), p. 97.

46. Aminatta Forna, 'Pornography and Racism', in *Pornography* (Itzin), pp. 105–106. Emphasis mine.

47. Itzin, in *Pornography* (Itzin), pp.49–50.

48. Itzin, in *Pornography* (Itzin), pp.49–50.

49. Janice Raymond, 'Pornography and the Politics of Lesbianism', in *Pornography* (Itzin), p.97.

50. See, *e.g.*, *Contemporary Feminist Theatres*.

51. Gilles Deleuze and Félix Guattari, *Kafka: Toward a Minor Literature* [1975], trans. Dana Polan, University of Minnesota Press, 1986. p.17. Emphases mine.

52. Dr. Jill Lockwood, to Maureen Freely and Dr. Cecilia Pyper in an article on in-vitro fertilization (IVF) in 'Life, The Observer Magazine', 4 June 1995.

53. Foreword to *Byrthrite* by Jalna Hamner in Daniels, *Plays: One*.

54. Bonnie Zimmerman, 'What Has Never Been: An Overview of Lesbian Feminist Literary Criticism', in *New Feminist Criticism*, ed., Elaine Showalter, Virago, 1986. p. 201.

55. See, *e.g.*, Gillian Beer, 'Representing Women: Re-presenting the Past', in *The Feminist Reader: Essays in Gender and the Politics of Literary Criticism*, ed., Catherine Belsey and Jane Moore, Macmillan, 1989.

56. Virginia Woolf, as quoted by Zimmerman, 'What Has Never Been', p.79.

57. See above. *Queen Christina*.

58. 'What Has Never Been', p.208. Zimmerman also speaks of the lesbian critical retrieval of Emily Dickinson, whose lines 'Tell all the truth/ but tell it slant' have been interpreted as the coded creativity of a lesbian writer. p.207.

59. 'What Has Never Been', p.212.

60. Compare *Vinegar Tom*, above.

61. 'What Has Never Been', p.206.

62. 'What Has Never Been', p. 205.

63. See above. *Queen Christina*

64. In May 1995 China implemented the compulsory sterilization of the nation's mentally ill and handicapped, and India briefly implemented a similar policy in the 70s Emergency to control growing population figures.

65. Adrienne Rich, 'When We Dead Awaken: Writing as Re-Vision' in *On Lies, Secrets and Silence*, Virago, 1980.

66. See *Contemporary Feminist Theatres*, pp.114 ff. Lesbian (fringe) theatres are separatist by nature as they assume an all-woman or even, all-lesbian audiences.

CHAPTER FIVE
Soliloquizing Woman: Clare McIntyre and Anne Devlin's Subjects of Desire

1. See Jean Grimshaw, 'Practices of Freedom' in *Up Against Foucault: Explorations of Some Tensions between Foucault and Feminism*, ed. Caroline Ramazanoglu, Routledge, 1993. p.54.

2. Judith Butler, *Subjects of Desire: Hegelian Reflections in Twentieth-Century France*, Columbia University Press, 1987. p.x.

3. Michel Foucault, *Afterword* to 'The Subject and Power', in Hubert Dreyfus and Paul Rabinow, *Michel Foucault: Beyond Structuralism and Hermeneutics*, , University of Chicago Press, 1982. p.216. Emphases mine.

4. See *The Foucault Reader*, ed. Paul Rabinow, Penguin, 1984. p.22.

5. See his comments to Jana Sawicki, *Disciplining Foucault: Feminism, Power and the Body*, Routledge, 1991. p.15.

6. See *Up Against Foucault*.

7. Jana Sawicki, *Disciplining Foucault*, pp.103- 4. Emphases mine.

8. *Subjects of Desire*, p.ix.

9. By *soliloquy* I mean an aside by a character on the stage. *Monologue* indicates the character is alone on the stage. A *monodrama* is a monologue drama with scenes such as in Alan Bennett.

10. Lloyd A. Skiffington, *The History of English Soliloquy*, University Press of America, 1985. pp.71–6.

11. Deborah Cameron and Elizabeth Frazer, 'On the Question of Pornography and Sexual Violence: Moving Beyond Cause and Effect' in *Pornography: Women, Violence and Civil Liberties*, ed. Catherine Itzin, Oxford University Press, 1992. pp.368–369.

12. 'On the Question of Pornography and Sexual Violence', p.359.

13. Luce Irigaray, 'This Sex Which is Not One', trans. Claudia Reeder in *New French Feminisms*, eds. Elaine Marks and Isabelle de Courtivron, University of Massachusetts Press, 1980. pp.99–100.

14. Luce Irigaray, 'Women-Mothers, the Silent Substratum of the Social Order', in *The Irigaray Reader*, ed. Margaret Whitford, Blackwells, 1991. p.52.

15. 'Women-Mothers, the Silent Substratum of the Social Order', pp.35–6.

16. Michael Earley and Philippa Keil look at this speech as one of 'unembarrassed free-dom'. That this 'freedom' is the trapped space delimited for the feminine in patriar-chal society doesn't enter their analysis as they are too closely implicated within western society themselves. *The Contemporary Monologue (Women)*, Methuen, 1995. p.62.

17. Luce Irigaray, 'The Bodily Encounter with the Mother', in in *The Irigaray Reader*, p.45

18. Lorraine Gamman and Merja Makinen, *Female Fetishism: A New Look*, Lawrence and Wishart, 1994. p.61.

19. *Female Fetishism*, p.61.

20. 'The Bodily Encounter with the Mother', p.45. Emphasis mine.

21. *Female Fetishism*, p.216.

22. Trevor R. Griffiths, 'Waving not Drowning: The Mainstream 1979–88' in *British and Irish Women Dramatists since 1958*, eds. Trevor R. Griffiths and Margaret Llewellyn-Jones, Open University Press, 1993. p.68.

23. Jane Edwardes in *Contemporary Women Dramatists*, ed. K.A. Berney, St. James' Press, 1994. p.163.

24. Paula Webb in *Time Out*, 12 February 1992.

25. *The Observer*, 12 February 1992.

26. Andrew Rissik in *The Independent*, 17 February 1988.

27. Hélène Cixous, *Là* [1976], in *The Hélène Cixous Reader*, trans. and ed. Susan Sellers, Routledge, 1994 p.58.

28. Anna McCullan, 'Irish Women Playwrights since 1958' in *British and Irish Dramatists since 1958*, eds. Trevor R. Griffiths and Margaret Llewellyn Jones, Open University Press, 1993. p.111.

29. 'Irish Women Playwrights since 1958', p.111.

30. 'Irish Women Playwrights since 1958', p.111.

31. Jill Dolan, *The Feminist Spectator as Critic*, University of Michigan Press, 1991. p.7.

32. Adrienne Rich, 'The Anti-Feminist Woman' [1972], in *On Lies, Secrets and Silence*, Virago Press, 1980. p.72.

33. Anne Devlin, *Landmarks of Contemporary Drama*, ed. Emilie S. Kilgore, Methuen, 1992. p.231.

34. Anne Devlin, *Landmarks*. p.231.

35. 'Irish Women Playwrights since 1958', p.120.

36. *La*, p.58.

37. *Women's Literature A-Z*, ed. Claire Buck, Bloomsbury, 1992.

38. Anne McClintock, *Imperial Leather: Race, Gender and Sexuality in the Colonial Contest*, Routledge, 1995. p.52–3.

39. *Imperial Leather*, pp.55–6.

40. *Imperial Leather*, p.53.

41. Homi Bhabha, 'Of Mimicry and Man: The ambivalence of Colonial Discourse' in *The Location of Culture*, Routledge, 1994. p.86. Lacan quoted ibid., at p.85.

42. *Anti-Oedipus*, p.201–2.

43. See *Anti-Oedipus*, pp.139–141.

44. *Anti-Oedipus*, p.315.
45. *Anti-Oedipus*, p.293.
46. Cf. Judith Butler's variation in repetition which constitutes the agency of the gendered subject. *Gender Trouble*.
47. *Anti-Oedipus*, p.131.

—⚬⚮⚬—

BIBLIOGRAPHY

Primary Sources

Play-Texts
—Churchill, Caryl:
Churchill—Plays One. Methuen, 1985.
Icecream. Nick Hern Books, 1989.
Churchill—Plays Two. Methuen, 1990.
Mad Forest. Nick Hern Books, 1990.
Shorts. Nick Hern Books, 1990.
The Skriker. Nick Hern Books, 1994.
Blue Heart. Nick Hern Books, 1997.

—Daniels, Sarah:
Daniels—Plays One. Methuen, 1991.
Daniels—Plays Two. Methuen, 1994.

—Devlin, Anne:
Ourselves Alone. Faber and Faber, 1986.
After Easter. Faber and Faber, 1994.

—Gems, Pam:
Queen Christina. St. Luke's Press, 1982.
Dusa, Stas, Fish and Vi in *Plays by Women: Volume I*. Ed., Michelene Wandor, Methuen 1983.
Three Plays: Piaf/Camille/Loving Women. Penguin, 1985.
Stanley. Nick Hern Books, 1997.
Marlene. Oberon, 1998.

—Kay, Jackie:
Chiaroscuro in *Lesbian Plays*. Ed., Jill Davis, Methuen, 1987.

—McIntyre, Clare:
My Heart's a Suitcase and Low Level Panic. Nick Hern Books, 1994.

Primary Sources

Theoretical Texts

The first citation of a work in every chapter is in full. Subsequently abbreviated by reference to short title of the work.

Acheson, James, ed., *British and Irish Drama since 1960*, The Macmillan Press Limited, 1993.

Althusser, Louis, *Lenin and Philosophy and other essays*, trans. Ben Brewster, Monthly Review Press, 1977.

Anderson, Walter Truett, *The Fontana Postmodern Reader*, Fontana, 1995.

Ashcroft, Bill, Gareth Griffiths and Helen Tiffin, *The Post-Colonial Studies Reader*, Routledge, 1995.

Aston, Elaine, 'Daniels in the Lion's Den: Sarah Daniels and the British Backlash', in *Theatre Journal*, Vol.47, No.3, October 1995.

Aston, Elaine, ed., *Feminist Theatre Voices*, Loughborough Theatre Texts, 1997.

Austin, Gayle, *Feminist Theories for Dramatic Criticism*, University of Michigan Press, 1990.

Austin, J.L., *How to Do Things With Words: The William James Lectures 1955*, Cambridge University Press, 1975.

Barthes, Roland, *Mythologies*, [1957], trans. Annette Lavers, Jonathan Cape, 1972; Vintage, 1993.

Barthes, Roland, *Critical Essays* [1963], trans. R. Howard, Northwestern University Press, 1972.

Barthes, Roland, *Sade, Fourier, Loyola* [1971], trans. Richard Miller, Hill and Wang, 1976.

Barthes, Roland, *Image—Music—Text*, trans. Stephen Heath, Collins, 1977.

Beauvoir, Simone de, *The Second Sex* [*Le Deuxième Sexe*, 1949], trans. and ed., H.M. Parshley, Jonathan Cape, 1953, reprt., Penguin 1983.

Belsey, Catherine and Jane Moore, eds., *The Feminist Reader: Essays in Gender and the Politics of Literary Criticism*, Macmillan, 1989.

Berney, K.A., ed., *Contemporary Women Dramatists*, St. James Press, 1994.

Bhabha, Homi, *The Location of Culture*, Routledge, 1994.

Bhatt, Chetan, 'Primordial Being', *Radical Philosophy, No.100*, March/April 2000.

Brennan, Teresa, ed., *Between Feminism and Psychoanalysis*, Routledge, 1989.

Boyne, Roy, *Foucault and Derrida: The Other Side of Reason*, Routledge, 1994.

Brater, Enoch, ed., *Feminine Focus: The New Women Playwrights*, Oxford University Press, 1989.

Buck, Claire, ed., *Women's Literature A-Z*, Bloomsbury, 1992.

Butler, Judith, *Subjects of Desire: Hegelian Reflections in Twentieth Century France*, Columbia University Press, 1987.

Butler, Judith, *Gender Trouble: Feminism and the Subversion of Identity*, Routledge, 1990.

Butler, Judith, *Bodies That Matter: On the Discursive Limits of 'Sex'*, Routledge, 1993.

Case, Sue-Ellen, *Feminism and Theatre*, Macmillan, 1988.

Case, Sue-Ellen, *Performing Feminisms: Feminist Critical Theory and Theatre*, Johns Hopkins University Press, 1990.

Cixous, Hélène and Catherine Clément, *The Newly Born Woman* [*La Jeune Née* 1975], trans. Betsy Wing, University of Minnesota Press, 1986.

Cohn, Ruby, *Retreats From Realism in Recent English Drama*, Cambridge University Press, 1991.

Cohn, Ruby, *Anglo-American Interplay in Recent Drama*, Cambridge University Press, 1995.

Cotton, Nancy, *Women Playwrights in England c. 1363–1750*, Associated University Presses, 1980.

Counsell, Colin, *Signs of Performance*, Routledge, 1996.

Cousin, Geraldine, *Churchill—The Playwright*, Methuen, 1989.

Crosby, Christina, *The Ends of History: Victorians and "The Woman Question"*, Routledge, 1991.

Daly, Mary, *Gyn/Ecology: The Metaethics of Radical Feminism*, Beacon Press, 1978

Davis, Jill, ed., *Lesbian Plays*, Methuen, 1987.

De Beauvoir, Simone, *The Second Sex*, [*Le Deuxième Sexe*, 1949], trans. H.M. Parshley, Jonathan Cape, 1953, reprt. Penguin, 1983.

Deleuze, Gilles and Félix Guattari, *Anti-Oedipus: Capitalism and Schizophrenia Vol. I* [1972], trans. Robert Hurley, Mark Seem, and Helen R. Lane, Athlone Press, 1984.

Deleuze, Gilles and Félix Guattari, *Kafka: Toward a Minor Literature* [1975], trans. Dana Polan, University of Minnesota Press, 1986.

Deleuze, Gilles and Félix Guattari, *A Thousand Plateaus: Capitalism and Schizophrenia Vol. II* [1980], trans. Brian Massumi, Athlone Press, 1988.

Derrida, Jacques, *Margins of Philosophy* [1972], trans. Alan Bass, Harvester Wheatsheaf, 1982.

Derrida, Jacques, *Specters of Marx: The State of the Debt, the Work of Mourning, & the New International* [1993], trans. Peggy Kamuf, Routledge, 1994.

Diamond, Elin, ed., *Performance and Cultural Politics*, Routledge, 1996.

Diamond, Elin, *Unmaking Mimesis*, Routledge, 1997.

Dolan, Jill, *The Feminist Spectator as Critic*, University of Michigan Press, 1991.

Dolan, Jill, *Presence and Desire: Essays on Gender, Sexuality, Performance*, University of Michigan Press, 1993.

Dolan, Jill, 'Geographies of Learning: Theatre Studies, Performance, and the "Performative"', *Theatre Journal*, Vol. 45, No.4, December 1993.

Donovan, Josephine, *Feminist Theory: The Intellectual Traditions of American Feminism*, Frederick Ungar Publishing Company, 1985.

Donovan, Josephine, ed., *Feminist Literary Criticism: Explorations in Theory*, The University Press of Kentucky, 1975, reprt., 1989.

Dowling, W., *Jameson, Althusser, Marx*, Methuen, 1984.

Durant, Will, *The Story of Philosophy*, Washington Square Press, 1926, reprt., 1953.

Dworkin, Andrea, *Pornography: Men Possessing Women*, The Women's Press, 1981.

Eagleton, Mary, ed., *Feminist Literary Theory*, Basil Blackwell, 1986.

Eagleton, Terry, ed., *Ideology*, Addison Wesley Longman Limited, 1994.

Eagleton, Terry, *The Illusions of Postmodernism*, Blackwell Publishers, 1995.

Earley, Michael, and Philippa Keil, eds., *The Contemporary Monologue (Women)*, Methuen, 1995.

Elam, Diane, *Feminism and Deconstruction: Ms. en Abyme*, Routledge, 1994.

Elam, Keir, *The Semiotics of Theatre and Drama*, Methuen, 1980.

Engels, Friedrich, *The Origin of the Family, Private Property and the State*, [1884] Lawrence and Wishart, 1972.

Fanon, Frantz, *Black Skins, White Masks*, Pluto Press, 1986.

Fitzsimmons, Linda, *File on Churchill*, Methuen, 1989.

Foucault, Michel, *Mental Illness and Psychology*, [*Maladie Mentale et psychologie*, 1962], trans. Alan Sheridan, Harper and Row, 1976.

Foucault, Michel, *The Order of Things: An Archaeology of the Human Sciences*, [*Les Mots et les choses: une archéologie du regard médical*, 1966], trans. Alan Sheridan, Pantheon, 1970.

Foucault, Michel, *The Archaeology of Knowledge*, [*L' Archéologie du savoir*, 1969], trans. A.M. Sheridan Smith [1972], Routledge, 1997.

Foucault, Michel, *The History of Sexuality Volume I*, [*La Volonté de savoir*, 1976], trans. Robert Hurley [1972], Penguin, 1990.

Foucault, Michel, *Politics, Philosophy, Culture: Interviews and Other Writings 1977–1984*, ed. Lawrence D. Kritzman, Routledge, 1988.

Foucault, Michel, *Power/Knowledge: Selected interviews and other writings 1972–1977*, ed. Colin Gordon, The Harvester Press, 1980.

Foucault, Michel, 'Afterword' in *Beyond Structuralism and Hermeneutics*, Hubert Dreyfus and Paul Rabinow, University of Chicago Press, 1982.

Foucault, Michel, *Foucault Live: Collected Interviews 1961–1984*, ed.Sylvère Lotringer, trans. Lysa Hochroth and John Johnston, Semiotext(e), 1989.

Gallop, Jane, *Feminism and Psychoanalysis: The Daughter's Seduction*, Macmillan, 1982.

Gamman, Lorraine and Merja Makinen, *Female Fetishism: A New Look*, Lawrence and Wishart, 1994.

Garber, Marjorie, *Vested Interests: Cross-Dressing and Cultural Anxiety*, Routledge, 1992.

Garber, Marjorie, *Vice Versa: Bisexuality and the Eroticism of Everyday Life*, Hamish Hamilton, 1995.

Gay, Peter, *The Bourgeois Experience—Victoria to Freud: Volume II The Tender Passion*, Oxford University Press, 1986.

Gay, Peter, *The Bourgeois Experience—Victoria to Freud: Volume III The Cultivation of Hatred*, Fontana, 1995.

Gilbert, Helen and Joanne Tompkins, eds. *Post-colonial Drama: Theory, Practice, Politics*, Routledge, 1996.

Godiwala, Dimple, 'Asian Theatre in Britain', in *Hard Times*, Issue 67/68, Autumn 1999.

Godiwala, Dimple, 'Hybridity/Invention/Identity: British-Asian Culture and its Postcolonial Theatres', *Journal for the Study of British Cultures*, Vol. 8, 1/2001.

Godiwala, Dimple, '"The uncanny stranger on dis-play": Arnold Wesker's monologues for women', (forthcoming).

Goodchild, Philip, *Deleuze and Guattari*, Sage, 1996.

Goodman, Lizbeth, *Contemporary Feminist Theatres: To Each Her Own*, Routledge, 1993.

Goodman, Lizbeth with Jane de Gay, *The Routledge Reader in Gender and Performance*, Routledge, 1998.

Goodman, Lizbeth with Jane de Gay, *The Routledge Reader in Politics and Performance*, Routledge, 2000.

Green, Gayle and Coppélia Kahn, eds., *Making a Difference: Feminist Literary Criticism*, Methuen, 1985.

Griffiths, Trevor, R., and Margaret Llewellyn-Jones, eds., *British and Irish Women Dramatists since 1958*, Open University Press, 1993.

Griffiths, Trevor, R., and Carole Woddis, eds., *Bloomsbury Theatre Guide*, Bloomsbury, 1988.

Hart, Lynda and Peggy Phelan, eds., *Acting Out: Feminist Performances*, University of Michigan Press, 1993.

Heilman, R.B., *Tragedy and Melodrama: Versions of Experience*, University of Washington Press, 1968.

Hobsbawm, Eric, *The Age of Revolution [Europe] 1789–1848*, Weidenfeld and Nicolson, 1962.

Hobsbawm, Eric, *The Age of Capital 1848–1875*, Weidenfeld and Nicolson, 1975.

Hobsbawm, Eric, *The Age of Empire 1875–1914*, Weidenfeld and Nicolson, 1987.

Hobsbawm, Eric, *The Age of Extremes: The Short Twentieth Century 1914–1991*, Michael Joseph, 1994.

Hulton, Peter, 'Theatre Papers', Second Series, No. 8, Dartington College of Arts, 1978.

Hutcheon, Linda, *A Theory of Parody: The Teachings of Twentieth-Century Art Forms*, Methuen, 1985.

Innes, Christopher, *Modern British Drama: 1890–1990*, Cambridge University Press, 1992.

Itzin, Catherine, *Stages in the Revolution: Political Theatre in Britain since 1968*, Eyre Methuen, 1980.

Itzin, Catherine, ed., *Pornography: Women, Violence and Civil Liberties*, Oxford University Press, 1992.

Jameson, Frederic, *The Political Unconscious*, Methuen, 1981.

Jones, W.T., *Hobbes to Hume*, Harcourt Brace Jovanovich College Publishers, second edn, 1980.

Kaplan, E. Ann, *Women and Film: Both Sides of the Camera*, Methuen, 1983.

Kappeler, Susanne, *The Pornography of Representation*, University of Minnesota Press, 1986.

Kauffman, L., ed., *American Feminist Thought at Century's End—A Reader*, Blackwell, 1993.

Keyssar, Helen, *Feminist Theatre*, Macmillan, 1984.

Kilgore, Emilie S., ed., *Landmarks of Contemporary Drama*, Methuen, 1992.

Kristeva, Julia, *Revolution in Poetic Language*, trans. Margaret Waller, Columbia University Press, 1984.

Kristeva, Julia, *Desire in Language. A Semiotic Approach to Literature and Art*, trans. Thomas S. Gora, Alice Jardine, and Leon S. Roudiez, Basil Blackwell, 1984.

Kritzer, Amelia Howe, *The Plays of Caryl Churchill*, Macmillan, 1991.

Kruger, Loren, 'The Dis-Play's the Thing: Gender and Public Sphere in Contemporary British Theater', *Theatre Journal*, Vol. 42, No.1, March 1990.

Landy, Marcia and Amy Villarejo, *Queen Christina*, British Film Institute, 1995.

Lewis, Reina, *Gendering Orientalism: Race, Femininity and Representation*, Routledge, 1996.

Lorde, Audre, *Sister Outsider*, Crossing Press, 1984.

Lüscher, Max, *The Lüscher Colour Test*, trans. Ian Scott, Jonathan Cape, 1970.

Lyotard, Jean-François, *The Postmodern Condition: A Report on Knowledge* [1984], trans. Geoff Bennington and Brian Massumi, Manchester University Press, 1986.

Macey, David, *Lacan in Contexts*, Verso, 1988.

Marks, Elaine, and Isabelle de Courtivron, *New French Feminisms*, University of Massachusetts Press, 1980.

McClintock, Anne, *Imperial Leather: Race, Gender and Sexuality in the Colonial Contest*, Routledge, 1995.

McNay, Lois, *Foucault: an Introduction*, Polity Press, 1994.

Memmi, Albert, *The Colonizer and the Colonized* [*Portrait du Colonisé, précédé du portrait du colonisateur* 1957], trans. Howard Greenfield, The Beacon Press, 1967.

Meyer, Moe, *The Politics and Poetics of Camp*, Routledge, 1994.

Millan, Betty, *Monstrous Regiment: Women's Rulers in Men's Worlds*, Kensal Press, 1982.

Miller, Tim, and David Román, 'Preaching to the Converted', *Theatre Journal*, Vol.47, No.2, May 1995.

Millett, Kate, *Sexual Politics* [1969], Virago, 1977.

Moi, Toril, ed., *The Kristeva Reader*, Blackwell, 1986.

Page, Adrian, ed., *The Death of the Playwright?*, The Macmillan Press, 1992.

Parker, Andrew and Eve Kosofsky Sedgwick, eds., *Performativity and Performance*, Routledge, 1995.

Pavis, Patrice, *Theatre at the Crossroads of Culture*, Routledge, 1992.

Phelan, Peggy, *Unmarked: The Politics of Performance*, Routledge, 1993.

Prentki, Tim and Jan Selman, *Popular Theatre in Political Culture: Britain and Canada in Focus*, Intellect Books, 2000.

Rabinow, Paul, ed., *The Foucault Reader*, Penguin, 1984.

Ramazanoglu, Caroline, ed., *Up Against Foucault: Explorations of Some Tensions between Foucault and Feminism*, Routledge, 1993.

Randall, Phyllis R., *Caryl Churchill—A Casebook*, Garland Publishing, 1989.

Reich, Wilhelm, *The Mass Psychology of Fascism*, Farrar, Straus and Giroux, 1970.

Reinelt, Janelle G., and Joseph R. Roach, eds., *Critical Theory and Performance*, University of Michigan Press, 1992.

Reinelt, Janelle, *After Brecht: British Epic Theatre*, University of Michigan Press, 1994.

Rich, Adrienne, *Of Woman Born: Motherhood as Experience and Institution*, USA, 1976; Virago 1977.

Rich, Adrienne, *On Lies, Secrets and Silence*, Virago, 1980.

Ritchie, Rob, ed., *The Joint Stock Book: The Making of a Theatre Collective*, Methuen, 1987.

Rorty, Richard, 'Feminism, Ideology, and Deconstruction: a Pragmatist View', *Hypatia*, Vol. 8 No. 2, Spring 1993

Sandford, Stella, 'Contingent Ontologies: Sex, gender and 'woman' in Simone de Beauvoir and Judith Butler', *Radical Philosophy*, No. 97, September/October 1999.

Sarup, Madan, *Post-structuralism and Postmodernism*, Harvester Wheatsheaf, 1993.

Saussure, Ferdinand de, *Course in General Linguistics*, trans. Wade Baskin, Fontana/Collins, 1974.

Sawicki, Jana, *Disciplining Foucault: Feminism, Power and the Body*, Routledge, 1991.

Schechner, Richard, *Performance Theory* [1977], Routledge, 1988.

Scolnicov, Hanna, and Peter Holland, eds., *The Play Out of Context: Transferring Plays from Culture to Culture*, Cambridge University Press, 1989.

Sellers, Susan, trans. and ed., *The Hélène Cixous Reader*, Routledge, 1994.

Shakespeare, William, *Hamlet*, c.1600.

Shaw, George Bernard, Preface to *Mrs. Warren's Profession* [1902], in *Plays Unpleasant*, Penguin, 1946.

Shiach, Don, *From Page to Performance*, Cambridge University Press, 1987.

Showalter, Elaine, ed., *New Feminist Criticism*, Virago, 1986.

Sim, Stuart, 'Derrida and the End of History', Icon books, 1999.

Skiffington, Lloyd A., *The History of English Soliloquy*, University Press of America, 1985.

Smart, Barry, *Michel Foucault*, Routledge, 1988.

Smith, James L., *Melodrama*, Methuen, 1973.

Spargo, Tamsin, 'Foucault and Queer Theory', Icon books, 1999.

Spender, Dale, *Man Made Language*, [1981], Pandora, 1990.

Spender, Dale, ed., *'How the Vote was Won' and Other Suffragette Plays*, Methuen, 1985.

Stephenson, Heidi and Natasha Langbridge, *Rage and Reason: Women Playwrights on Playwriting*, Methuen, 1997.

Stoler, Ann Laura, *Race and the Education of Desire: Foucault's History of Sexuality and the Colonial Order of Things*, Duke University Press, 1995.

Stowell, Sheila, ed., *A Stage of their Own: Feminist Playwrights of the Suffrage Era*, Manchester University Press, 1992.

Walder, Dennis, ed., *Literature in the Modern World*, Open University Press, 1991.

Walker, Alice, *Possessing the Secret of Joy*, Vintage, 1993

Wandor, Michelene, *Carry On, Understudies: Theatre and Sexual Politics*, Routledge & Kegan Paul, 1981.

Wandor, Michelene, ed., *On Gender and Writing*, Pandora Press, 1983.

Whitford, Margaret, ed., *The Irigaray Reader*, Blackwells, 1991.

Willett, John, trans. and ed., *Brecht on Theatre: The Development of an Aesthetic*, Methuen, 1964. Reprt. 1978.

Wilson, Edmund, *The Wound and the Bow*, W.H.Allen, 1941.

Woolf, Virginia, *A Room of One's Own; and; Three Guineas*, Chatto and Windus, 1984.

Young, Robert, *Colonial Desire: Hybridity in Theory, Culture and Race*, Routledge, 1995.

Young, Robert, *Torn Halves: Political Conflict in Literary and Cultural Theory*, Manchester University Press, 1996.

Secondary Sources

Newspapers and Magazines

Spare Rib, Vol.17, 1972.

Spare Rib, Vol.23, 1972.

Spare Rib, Vol.39, 1975.

Spare Rib, Vol.44, 1976.

Spare Rib, Vol.45, 1976.

Spare Rib, Vol.47, 1976.

Spare Rib, Vol.48, 1976.

Spare Rib, Vol.50, 1976.

Spare Rib, Vol.52, 1976.

Spare Rib, Vol.53, 1976.

Spare Rib, Vol.56, 1977.

Spare Rib, Vol.58, 1977.

Spare Rib, Vol.64, 1977.

Spare Rib, Vol.65, 1977.

Theatre Record, Compiled and published by Ian Herbert. [This is a handy compilation of broadsheet reviews of drama performances in Britain. All newspaper reviews are to be found in this source; organized by title of play.]

Loving Women

John Barber, *The Daily Telegraph*, 2 February 1984.

Michael Ratcliffe, *The Observer*, 5 February 1984.

Low Level Panic

Paula Webb, *Time Out*, 12 February 1992.

Fen

Robert Cushman, *The Observer*, February 1983.

Owners

Alex Renton, *The Independent*, 8 April 1987.
John Vidal, *The Guardian*, 9 April 1987.

Piaf

Jack Tinker, *The Daily Mail*, 14 December 1993.
Michael Billington, *The Guardian*, 15 December 1993.
Benedict Nightingale, *The Times*, 15 December 1993.
Louise Doughty, *The Mail on Sunday*, 19 December 1993.
Sheridan Morley, *The Spectator*, 1 January 1994.
Clive Hirschhorn, *Sunday Express*, 19 December 1993.
Irving Wardle, *The Independent*, 19 December 1993.
Charles Spencer, *The Daily Telegraph*, 15 December 1993.

Serious Money

Neil Collins, *The Daily Telegraph*, 30 March 1987.
Michael Coveney, *The Financial Times*, 30 March 1987.
Victoria Radin, *The New Statesman*, 3 April 1987.
Softcops
Giles Gordon, *The Spectator*, January 1984.
The Skriker
Benedict Nightingale, *The Times*, 29 January 1984.
Barbara Thorden, *The Times Literary Supplement*, 4 February 1994.

Compact Discs

Legends of the Twentieth Century: Edith Piaf, EMI CD.

Television programmes

Changing Stages, narrated by Richard Eyre, 3 December 2000.

Video

Top Girls, directed by Max Stafford-Clark, Open University/BBC, 1991.

INDEX